Christ's Church

Christ's Church
Her Biblical Roots, Her Dramatic History,
Her Saving Presence, Her Glorious Future

BO GIERTZ

Introduction and Translation by Hans Andræ

RESOURCE *Publications* · Eugene

CHRIST'S CHURCH
Her Biblical Roots, Her Dramatic History, Her Saving Presence, Her Glorious Future

Copyright © 2010 Bo Giertz. All rights reserved. Except for brief quotations in critical publications or reviews, no part of this book may be reproduced in any manner without prior written permission from the publisher. Write: Permissions, Wipf and Stock Publishers, 199 W. 8th Ave., Suite 3, Eugene, OR 97401.

Wipf & Stock
An Imprint of Wipf and Stock Publishers
199 W. 8th Ave., Suite 3
Eugene, OR 97401
www.wipfandstock.com

ISBN 13: 978-1-60899-703-9

Manufactured in the U.S.A.

This is a translation of *Kristi Kyrka*, published 1939 in Swedish by Svenska Kyrkans Diakonistyrelses Bokförlag (SKDB), the official publishing house of the Church of Sweden.

Bible quotes are rendered by the translator in English, conflated from these Swedish versions: The Church Bible 1917; The New Testament in Contemporary Swedish by Dr. David Hedegård, 1964; The New Testament in Modern Swedish by Bo Giertz, 1977–1981 (consecutively published during that period); Bible 2000 (produced by a commission appointed and funded by the Swedish government).

The picture on the front cover shows the altar triptych in the Linköping Cathedral in Sweden. The picture is produced from a photo in the cathedral archives and used here with special permission by the Dean of the Cathedral, the Very Rev. J. Peter Lundborg. See Appendix 2 for information about the triptych.

I dedicate this translation to the memory of my father

Anders Andræ
(1902–1961)

who fostered in me the same kind of deep love for the Church that he shared with Bo Giertz (1905–1998), his fellow pastor in the Linköping Diocese of the Evangelical-Lutheran Church in Sweden.

Hans Andræ

Contents

Author's Preface ix

Translator's Introduction xi

PART ONE The Essence of the Church

    1   Who Is She? / 3

    2   The Biblical Foundation / 6

    3   Una Sancta / 37

    4   The Church in Sweden / 74

    5   The Parish Church / 92

PART TWO The Presence of the Holy One

    6   God Is In Our Midst / 101

    7   God's Word and Promise / 104

    8   The New Covenant / 111

    9   The Second Birth / 122

    10   A Neglected Means of Grace / 132

    11   The Ministry of Reconciliation / 150

Author's Postscript 177

Appendix 1 180

Appendix 2 182

Bibliography 183

Index of Proper Names 185

BO GIERTZ

Born 31 August 1905 - Died 12 July 1998

Permission from Tre Böcker Förlag, Göteborg

Author's Preface

This book is a thank-offering to our Mother the Church from one of the many, to whom she within her walls has given a new faith in Christ the Savior and a new joy of life.

The oldest portions of this work were written seven years ago. Since then, the author has unceasingly been driven to devote himself to the issue of the essence of the Church of Sweden and to the inexhaustible richness of the legacy that she lavishes upon her children, a richness that the author has experienced both as a layman and as a servant of the Word.

The author has attempted to make this presentation in such a way that it would be readable also for those who are neither theologians nor academics.

Some readers will be annoyed that the Church often is spelled with a capital C in this book. Others would have liked it to be done consistently. The indulgent reader may realize that there is a conscious purpose in this inconsistency.

No ranking or valuation is intended when the subjects of the Pastoral Office and the Absolution have each received three times the space devoted to the Word. The reason for this is that I felt the need for dealing more exhaustively with misunderstood and neglected aspects of life in our church.

The main purpose of this book is to do justice to the Church of Sweden, to see and appreciate her as a branch of Christ's Church - the one and holy Church catholic.

Torpa Parsonage, Palm Sunday 1939
Bo Giertz

Translator's Introduction

SINCE I IMMIGRATED TO the United States in 1979, I have made numerous visits to my native Sweden. At one of those visits, I was granted the privilege of interviewing Bo Giertz. It was on Monday in Holy Week 1997. I asked him then for permission to translate some of his works into English. He was happy to give me his permission but added, "Make sure you work with someone whose mother tongue is English." I gratefully acknowledge that my American wife, Sylvia, while proof-reading my entire translation also made improvements to make it a good idiomatic rendering in the American language. My son, Eric, President of the International Giertz Society (English Language Section) and campus pastor in Pittsburgh, whose S.T.M. thesis at Concordia Seminary in St. Louis was an analysis of Giertz's theology, provided valuable suggestions for appropriate theological terminology in English. I also thank my daughters Rebecka and Christina as well as my daughter-in-law Paola for computer advice and proofreading.

THIS BOOK

Christ's Church, originally published 1939 in Swedish, provides inspiring reading for thoughtful Christians and also challenging reading for honest sceptics. And through this version in English, it is finally available to both these kinds of readers throughout the world.

This book explains in a clear and understandable way what the One Holy Catholic and Apostolic Church is. It presents her roots in the Lord God's choosing Israel as a people of His own possession (Deut 7:6). It describes her coming into being in New Testament times as "the household of God, built upon the foundation of the apostles and the prophets, Christ Jesus Himself being the cornerstone" (Eph 2:19f.). And it tells the story of how she was extended through the centuries to all nations.

In this impressive discourse on the Church, Bo Giertz gives the massive biblical foundation of the Church by quoting hundreds of Bible passages, makes us acquainted with the teachings of the Church Fathers on this subject, and deepens our knowledge of the concept of the Church as expressed in the Augsburg Confession and the other Evangelical-Lutheran documents that make up the Book of Concord.

The fact that a small portion of this book is devoted to how the Church came to a particular country, namely Sweden, and how she has fared there through a thousand years, should add to the value of this monograph for readers from other countries. It's good for any Christian anywhere to learn about the lives of fellow Christians in another nation, how the Church there related to the government, to the national culture, to other denominations, and, most of all, to the people in that country.

BO GIERTZ

In December 1999, KYRKANS TIDNING, the official weekly newspaper of the Church of Sweden, asked its readers, *"Who was the most influential Swedish church leader during the 1900s?"* Bo Giertz received more votes than anyone else! It was both through his inspiring leadership as a pastor and a bishop and as an author of many bestsellers, that Giertz exerted such matchless influence in Sweden and beyond.

Bo Harald Giertz was born 31 August 1905 into a very prominent family. His father, Knut Harald Giertz, was head of the fourth largest hospital in the country, an acclaimed surgeon, and one of Queen Viktoria's physicians. Bo, his six brothers, and his sister usually spent the summers with their maternal grandparents. His lifelong interest in technology was first kindled by his grandfather, Lars Magnus Ericsson, a pioneering inventor in the field of telecommunications and the founder of the global industrial Ericsson enterprise.

In 1924, Giertz enrolled in the School of Medicine at the University of Uppsala. In the university environment, he encountered on the one hand a radical atheism displaying an uninhibited hedonism. On the other hand, he met students of theology who explained their Christian faith with intelligence and lived their faith with sincerity. Through this experience, he moved away from his father's atheism to the faith of the Church. I would argue that another factor was the summers with his maternal grandparents. It was the custom of the Ericssons to attend with their guests the Sunday services in the parish church. In due time, God's Word that young Bo had heard there bore the fruit of faith.

Now desiring to become a pastor, Giertz devoted the years 1928–1932 to the required theological studies. However, before seeking ordination, he began in May 1932 work as a traveling consultant for the Church's High School Student Association. He conveyed to thousands of teenagers his own enthusiasm for the Church and the continued relevance of the Christian faith for our time. As a frequent writer both in periodicals and newspapers, he became known to the general public as a bold and gifted expounder of the Church's teachings as anchored in Scripture, confessed in the Creeds, and explained in the Lutheran Confessions.

Following his ordination in the Linköping Cathedral on 28 December 1934, Bo Giertz still traveled to the high schools for another six months. He then served as a vacancy pastor in the rural Östra Husby parish and thereafter in Ekeby parish (including factory town Boxholm), before he was called in May 1937 by Bishop Tor Andræ to be his assistant for promotion of ministry and mission in the congregations. Once again, Pastor Giertz's work entailed a lot of traveling, often speaking at meetings for clergy, lay leaders, or youth at various locations in the diocese. Even so he found time to start writing his first book, *Kristi Kyrka* (*Christ's Church*), early in 1938, an undertaking he completed a year later.

As assistant to the bishop, Bo Giertz was in charge of a regional youth conference in Vimmerby July 9–12, 1938. In this snapshot, we see him (with glasses) surrounded by fellow pastors, including the host, Anders Andræ, front row, second from right.
—*Translator's photo collection*

Acknowledging the need to spend more time with his growing family (children: Lars born 1933, Birgitta 1935, and Ingrid 1937), he applied for the position as pastor of the small rural Torpa parish in the Ydre Deanery. He accepted the call beginning in October 1938. During his ten and half years there, his first eight books were published: four significant theological works, *Christ's Church* (1939), *Church Piety* (1939), *The Great Lie and the Great Truth* (1945), and *The Battle for Man* (1946); two engaging novels, *The Hammer of God* (1941; English editions 1960, 1973, and 2005), and *Faith Alone* (1943); a retelling of the gospel events, *With My Own Eyes* (1947); and a textbook for confirmands, *The Foundation* (1942), with no less than 225,000 copies printed by 1977, not counting translations in several other languages (even Tamil and Zulu!). Each of the works produced in Torpa was reprinted several times over the years, as was all of Giertz's later production. The 7th edition, the most recent one, of *Christ's Church* came out in 1991! In all likelihood, more than one million volumes of Giertz's thirty books have been sold in fifteen languages, and we're still counting ...

The Hammer of God is arguably Giertz's most popular book. This novel was the #3 bestseller in Sweden 1941! And it has been printed in new editions not only in the Nordic languages but also in English and German. Giertz said that the reason he authored this novel was that he wanted to tell in down-to-earth stories what he already had described in his first two books, *Christ's Church* and *Church Piety,* namely the very heart of what the Church stands for: the Good News of forgiveness of sin through faith in Christ. Actually, *the theme in all the writings of Bo Giertz is the Atonement,* which he so powerfully proclaims in the very last lines of *The Hammer of God,* "... *drawn to God, conquered by the suffering-filled glory of the cross and cleansed by that sacrifice, which is the atonement for the sins of the whole world."*

The story of Bo Giertz in Sweden bears some striking resemblances to that of Martin Luther, whose impact was of course on a larger scale. Luther was 33 when he nailed his theses in Wittenberg on 31 October 1517, the Eve of All Saints Festival; Giertz was 33 when he "nailed his theses" in his first book, *Christ's Church*, published in Stockholm on 23 June 1939, the Eve of the Festival of St. John the Baptist. Both had large families and hospitable homes: Luther and his Catherine constantly entertained many students and other visitors, and so did Giertz and his Ingrid ("Ninni"), e.g. hosting Danes and Norwegians who were hunted by Gestapo during World War II. Both Luther and Giertz had an unfathomably comprehensive literary production while at the same time lecturing (Luther at the Wittenberg university; Giertz touring Sweden and elsewhere) and being parish pastors (Giertz also bishop). And Luther was of course *the* Reformer, leader of the greatest reformation movement ever in Christ's Church; Giertz was the leader of the Church Coalition for Bible and Confession (*Kyrklig Samling kring Bibeln och Bekännelsen*, KSBB), which he formed in 1957 precisely with the purpose of preserving and promoting the legacy in Sweden of Luther's reformation.

In the summer of 1942, the young family in the Torpa parsonage was hit by unspeakable tragedy. Ingrid and Bo Giertz were expecting their fourth child. Martin was born on 26 June, and both mother and child were doing just fine. However, six days later mother Ninni (age 33) died suddenly from a blood clot in her lungs. "Sleepless nights followed for me," Bo Giertz reports. "I read in my Bible and marked several passages, one of them being Psalm 145:17, *The LORD is righteous in all his ways, and merciful in all his works*." He wrote to Bishop Andræ in Linköping that even "in the midst of this awful darkness," he continued to know God's love in his life. Martin Giertz and his family now reside in his childhood home, the Torpa parsonage, where they hosted part of the program when the centennial of Bo Giertz's birth was celebrated in 2005. Since Torpa, Asby, and Norra Vi parishes nowadays are joined in a pastorate served by only one pastor, stationed in Asby, the parsonage in Torpa is no longer needed as home for a pastor.

On 14 December 1948, Bo Giertz, Associate Pastor (*komminister*) in the Asby and Torpa Pastorate, was elected bishop by an overwhelming majority of the clergy in the Göteborg Diocese (it was not until 1965 that the laity were allowed to participate in the election of bishops). It was an amazingly unusual election in many ways. Never before had a *komminister* been elected bishop. And to top it all off, he would be coming from a small rural parish to lead the largest diocese, to be sure not population-wise (Lund and Stockholm had more people), but it had the largest worship attendance and offerings of all the dioceses. The norm was that a bishop from another diocese, a cathedral dean *(domprost)*, a theology professor, or a senior pastor *(kyrkoherde)* from a big city parish would be elected bishop. Giertz was also remarkably young, only 43. He was the youngest to be elected bishop, since Olof Bergqvist (41), *kyrkoherde* in the huge (17,000 sq.km, an area larger than either the Göteborg or the Lund Diocese) Gellivare Pastorate in Lapland, in 1904 became the first Bishop of the new Luleå Diocese. During the last 106 years, Giertz remains the youngest to have been elected bishop in Sweden!

Up to the year 2000, when the state church system ceased in Sweden, the cabinet upon recommendation of the Secretary for Church Business appointed bishops from among the three who had received most votes in the elections. In 1949, there was a Social Democrat cabinet, and for them it was a painful dilemma to have to appoint Giertz or either of the other two nominees, because all three were confessional in a genuine Evangelical-Lutheran way and therefore regarded as reactionary by the government. However, eventually the unavoidable had to be done: Giertz was appointed on 1 April. That was almost three months after the slate of nominees was official, the longest time ever. Usually the time lapse was less than a month, the record being just one day: in the Stockholm Diocese 1971. It should be noted that King Gustav V, after the customary consultation with the archbishop, had previously, in 1943, called Bo Giertz to be a Court Preacher, an honor granted only a small number of pastors. That time the cabinet had no say!

It was a very festive and special day for the Church of Sweden, when Bo Giertz and Anders Nygren (for the Lund Diocese) were consecrated bishops by Archbishop Erling Eidem in the Uppsala Cathedral, the national shrine, on Rogate Sunday, 22 May 1949. They were probably the best known Swedish church leaders internationally: Nygren as the first President of the Lutheran World Federation (founded in Lund 1947) and as author of his famed work *Eros and Agape*, Giertz for his many books already translated not only into the five Nordic languages but into German and Hungarian as well.

During his time as bishop (1949–1970), Giertz did not produce many books, only four as compared with eight in Torpa during half the time span. Those four books all related to his being bishop in Göteborg: Pastoral Letter to the Clergy (*Herdabrev,* 1949), and reports to the Diocesan Clergy Assembly held every sixth year, *Time of Transition* (1957), *Migration* (1963), and *In the Melting Pot* (1969). However, those books gained thousands of readers outside Giertz's diocese! And so did the many tracts (often 16 pages), in which he explained basic church teachings, with titles such as *Does God Exist?, Is the Bible True?, The Creation Account and Natural Science,* and *The Gospel of Love.* One year he wrote in *Our Church* (the weekly magazine for Church of Sweden members) an exegesis every week of the upcoming Sunday's Gospel lesson, made available in 1957 as a book, *What Does God's Word Say?* It was published in 1967 by Augsburg with the title *Preaching from the Whole Bible*, and again in 2007 by Lutheran Legacy Publishing.

Bo Giertz, Bishop in the Göteborg Diocese 1949–1970.   –*Copyright holder unknown*

During his episcopacy, Giertz traveled extensively, including visits to Tanzania and India for the consecration of bishops, and to Brazil and the United States as second vice president of the executive committee of the Lutheran World Federation. Committee president was Franklin Clark Fry, Presiding Bishop of the United Lutheran Church in America. Fry was a church leader to whom Giertz referred with much respect and appreciation. One trip I believe that he made with great delight was to Cambridge in England, where he lectured on 22 February 1963 at the dedication of Westfield House "as a Lutheran House of Studies," an institution supported by the Lutheran Church–Missouri Synod.

In 1958, the Churchwide Assembly (*Kyrkomötet*) of the Lutheran Church in Sweden accepted a proposal by the government to open the pastoral office (*prästämbetet*) to women, a proposal the assembly had turned down the previous year. Those opposed to this change rallied to form the Church Coalition for Bible and Confession, which had no formal membership roster. With Bishop Giertz acting as chair, a coordinating committee with representatives from various church groups and organizations hosted annually a nationwide gathering, some years attracting two thousand attendees. This movement thus generated considerable support from pastors and active church members. However, their biblical and confessional arguments were not accepted by the media, the political parties, and a great majority of the general public, who instead argued that opposition to women's ordination showed contempt for women. This mischaracterization of his stand on that issue was a heavy cross to carry for Giertz through the last forty years of his life.

As Bishop Emeritus, Bo Giertz continued to be in great demand as a guest speaker. Now he was able to accept more of the invitations, in fact hundreds over the years. My wife, Sylvia, and I had the privilege of attending a meeting for our deanery in my birth town Vimmerby in 1976 with Giertz as the speaker. It was exciting to listen to the bishop speak on *To Be Filled with the Spirit*. He also continued until 1989 to serve as chair of the coordinating committee for The Coalition for Bible and Confession. As the chair of the Coalition chapter in the Linköping Diocese, I had the honor of welcoming him to the annual nationwide meeting which we hosted in 1979 in Söderköping.

As emeritus Bo Giertz once again became a prolific writer. Commissioned by the Christian Education Association *(Kyrkliga Studieförbundet)*, he authored *The ABC's of Our Christian Faith* (1971). *The Knights of Rhodes* (1972) is a dramatic historical novel about the order of St. John, also known as the Knights Hospitalers. It tells the story of how they were unable to stop the military onslaught of Islam; in 1522 they had to give up their stronghold on Rhodes. It became another bestseller for Giertz in Sweden.

A special gift to God's people are the two volumes *To Believe in Christ* (1973) and *To Live with Christ* (1974), with devotions for each day of the church year. In 2008, they were published in English by Concordia Publishing House, combined in a handsome hardcover volume, *To Live with Christ*. Not only do the meditations give guidance for everyday living but altogether they are also a textbook on the basic teachings of the Church as well as a tool for effective Bible study. In fact, three of the Epistles (Ephesians, 1 Thessalonians, and 1 John) are completely covered, and another three (1 Corinthians, Philippians, and 1 Peter) almost completely.

For a thorough study of the New Testament, Giertz produced both his own translation from the Greek text and a commentary about three times longer than the Bible text itself, a well-balanced ratio appreciated by lay readers, whom the commentator had in mind when he did this work, *The New Testament in Modern Swedish with Brief Commentaries for Lay People*. It was printed consecutively in twelve volumes from 1977 to 1981. It was later published in three volumes with a total of no less than 1,220 pages. Some argue that this might be Giertz's most remarkable literary achievement! On 11 October 1981, the bishop was granted an audience with King Carl Gustaf, to whom he presented the first copy of his New Testament translation. What a proud event for Bishop Giertz! Remarkably: this was two weeks before the Bible Commission, appointed by the government in 1972, completed its translation of the New Testament to replace the official 1917 version!

At age 90, Giertz published his last book, *The Living God, A Guide to the Christian Faith* (1995), containing three essays published separately in 1984–85. That book title sums up the intention of all Bo Giertz's writings! His purpose was always to guide the common church member and sincere seeker both to know what the Christian faith stands for and also to embrace that faith. This was obviously his goal with writings like *The Foundation*, his *New Testament Commentaries*, and *The ABC's of Our Christian Faith*, but actually just as much with his novels, and of course with his first two works, *Christ's Church* and *Church Piety*.

Bo Giertz fell asleep in the Lord on 12 July 1998 at the age of 92. *Lutheran Forum* included in Vol. 32, No. 4 (Winter 1998) an article by Bo Giertz with the title *My Last Will and Testament*, first printed 1986 in *Svensk Pastoral Tidskrift*. He points out that "our Swedish Church may be counted among those that have been given most of the inheritance that the Church catholic has been given to care for." However, considering the escalating secularization of not only society in general but also of the church in Sweden, he adds, "My deepest worry is that the Swedish church, . . . who for a thousand years has stood fast, should now fail (perhaps even at the eleventh hour before the coming of her Lord) and so lose her crown."

As with any true Teacher of the Church, a *Doctor Ecclesiæ*, the influence of Bo Giertz continues unabated after his death, or rather it is growing continuously. Here are a few examples: The two-volume *Söndagsboken* ("The Sunday Book"), published in 2006 and 2007, contains sermons given by Giertz from the 1930's to the mid-1990's with one sermon for each Sunday of the Church Year. In 2007, the first of the three stories in *The Hammer of God* was produced as a feature film (105 min.) in Swedish. In 2010 it has also become available with English subtitles, marketed here by Lutheran Visuals.

The spread of the novel *The Hammer of God* with its three engaging stories is truly amazing! In the last ten years it has been translated into four more languages: Latvian (2002), Faroese (2002), Slovak (2008), and Russian (2009, and with a second printing already now, in 2010!). Also, a new complete edition in English of the *Hammer of God*, now including the ninth and final chapter, was published in 2005. Other works by Giertz have also been translated recently: *Christ's Church* in Latvian (2006), *To Believe in Christ* in German (2000), and in Finnish (2006), *To Live with Christ* in Finnish (2007) and in English (2008 as reported above), *The Great Lie and the Great Truth* in Latvian (2008) and in Russian (2010), and *The Living God* in German (2002). And his third and last novel, *The Knights of Rhodes*, translated by the Rev. Bror Erickson, was published in English by Wipf and Stock in February this year! Also, this year Lutheran Legacy will publish a *Giertz Anthology* with essays by and about him, including presentations at the 2005 symposia in St. Louis and Ft. Wayne observing the centennial of his birth.

CONCLUSION

As an apologist for and as an educator in the Christian faith, Bo Giertz may be compared with his famous contemporaries, C. S. Lewis (1898–1963) and Dietrich Bonhoeffer (1906–1945). The three had of course different writing styles and also somewhat different theological emphases, but each was and remains a brilliant communicator of the Church's message. Anyone guided by these mentors will get an authentic understanding of the Christian faith. However, while all the works of Lewis and Bonhoeffer are available in "the world language," and therefore have been read and will continue to be read by millions, so far only a few of Giertz's works have appeared in English: *The Hammer of God; With My Own Eyes* (MacMillan Co., N.Y., 1960); *Preaching From the Whole Bible; To Live with Christ;* and *The Knights of Rhodes*. Augustana Book Concern also published in English substantial portions of Giertz's production in *Liturgy and Spiritual Awakening* (1950) and in *The Message of the Church in a Time of Crisis* (1953). It is now therefore with great expectation that I here present his first book, *Christ's Church: Her Biblical Roots, Her Dramatic History, Her Saving Presence, Her Glorious Future*, in that language which is known in all nations.

In his vision of the One Holy Christian and Apostolic Church, Bo Giertz as parish pastor, bishop, and writer integrated a vibrant Evangelical-Lutheran orthodoxy, the Church's traditional Bible-based liturgy, and sincere church piety into a harmonious and powerful wholeness.

Hans Andræ
Pastor Emeritus
First Trinity Evangelical-Lutheran Church in the City of Pittsburgh
June 29, A+D 2010, the Feast of St. Peter and St. Paul, Apostles.

In the Torpa Churchyard, the gravemarker for Bo Giertz displays his coat of arms as Bishop of the Göteborg Diocese with these words from First Corinthians 1:18,

VERBUM CRUCIS DEI VIRTUS
The Word of the Cross is the Power of God

Part One

The Essence of the Church

Chapter 1

Who Is She?

She raises her steeple high over the jagged contour of the forest. With her foundation of walls a yard thick, she is massively planted on the ground. But her spire is at the same time elevated high above our everyday world. When the sun has set, a pale reflection of daylight still shines for a long time on the white steeple. When walking in the deep dusk under the trees in the church yard, one can see it shimmering through the dark leaves of the maples, high up there, as a reflection of the heavenly city, the walls of which always are shining with light. When a new day dawns, the golden cross on the spire is the first thing in the area that catches the sunlight. The old church, though firmly planted on the ground, is also closest to heaven.

She stands there as a silent question, surrounded by majestic trees. The spire persistently points toward the sky, and it is as if the white tower lifts an exhorting hand over the area. Maybe those who are sensitive to the silent language of creation would know the silent question of the church as well. Her question is addressed to the farmer who passes by with his noisy wagon, it descends to the visitor who is tending to the family grave in the church yard, with the sound of the church bells it follows the motorist who is speeding by the church.

Why is the church standing there, pointing toward heaven?

Was it just an illusion that once moved these enormous forces that created the greatest edifice in the area? Was it just a mirage they followed, all those generations that for centuries crowded the slope up to the church?

Now the church has a question for you: Is it rather *you* who pursues nothing but emptiness, instead of having your life's stronghold at God's altar that is raised within these white walls?

We cannot escape this question. After all, she is not alone, the church here on the ridge. Not far away, behind the dark edge of the forest, there is another church steeple, from which one can see yet a couple church spires, and then more and more forming a silent chain that reaches over plains and forests, over nations and continents, and all of them are pointing toward heaven just as persistently as the church here on the ridge. This is either a gigantic mania, or . . . Yes, what is she really, the church? The question remains.

She may present a problem even for the one who loves her and feels at home within her walls. We are visually introduced to this problem, as we look out over the area from the church. Down there in the valley as the homes cling together forming a small village , we can also see the pointed windows of the Pentecostal chapel. Further away one can vaguely see the yellow-white gable of the Mission Covenant chapel. Now how does the old stone church relate to her small siblings down there in the village?

There are other questions that cannot be ignored. It is a fact that we each Sunday profess our faith in the One Holy and Catholic Church. But how do our parish church and our Church of Sweden relate to the universal Christ's Church, the name of which we really are entitled to spell with a capital C?

There are indeed many questions. Sometimes we push them aside, sometimes they insist upon being answered. But for the common church member it is not always so easy to find any answers.

On the following pages we shall attempt to put together a few facts, opinions, and quotations, which we hope shall be helpful for the understanding of why the church stands there, why she is the way she is, and maybe also what she could and should be, if we took care of all the treasures she has preserved within her walls.

We have intentionally chosen our point of departure for this presentation right outside the church door, because this book is first of all for those who not too seldom have entered that door and who have some notion of the life that is present within the church walls and also have some desire to understand that life better and know more about it. On the other hand, to an outsider there is a lot on these pages that hardly is accessible or understandable. It can't be any other way. It is true about the life of the church as it is with all spiritual life. One cannot attain to it through arguing or discussing it. It will only slowly open up itself for the one who continuously lives in the church with love and appreciation. Just as we must enter into the life of art and music, and only in that way gradually appreciate the richness of them, in a similar way we must participate in the life of the church in order to receive its treasures. The reward for such participation is a never-ending stream of new discoveries and new amazement over the church's inexhaustible legacy. If thus the attempt that we now shall make - to lift up something of these riches - would take us far beyond the limit where some readers would be unable to follow, then it is the hope of the author that it will cause neither vexation or disappointment but instead would encourage a deeper penetration into the spiritual legacy that could make us all far richer than we are today.

It is thus fully intentional that we choose our point of departure outside the door of our own parish church, since she is the one who causes us to deal with the questions we have met in this introductory chapter. However, in order to seek the answers we have to make a leap of two millennia back in time. The church has her roots in the world of the Bible. Our first task is therefore to inquire into her biblical foundation.

Chapter 2

The Biblical Foundation

THE NAME

WHAT IS THE CHURCH? Let us begin with these questions: What was she from the beginning? What does the Bible say about her?

The word "church" in our English versions of the New Testament corresponds to "ekklesia" in the original Greek New Testament, a word that may refer either to a local congregation or to the whole church. The first meaning is the most common. We read for example about the church of God that is in Corinth, about the church of the Thessalonians, about the churches in Galatia, and so forth (1 Cor 1:2 etc.). But when Paul admonishes the Corinthians to "give no offense to Jews or to Greeks or to the church of God" (1 Cor 10:32), it is clear that the church is no longer a local phenomenon but a designation of all Christians, all Christendom on earth. And when the letters to the Colossians and to the Ephesians state that Christ is the head of His body, the church, or when we read (Eph 3:10) that God "through the church" has made known His manifold wisdom even in the heavenly places, then it is evident that the church cannot be understood only as the totality of all believers on earth.

From this we can see that one may not simply, as the common Bible reader often does, regard it a matter of course that the church is the same as a gathering of people. The word "ekklesia" contains much more. So when the early church translated this word into Latin, one did not choose any of the Latin words for the word congregation, but retained the Greek word with its unique meaning. Thus we got the Latin "ecclesia."

What does this word mean: "ekklesia"? What is the Church of the New Testament? Again, let us begin with another question: Why did the first Christians choose ekklesia to designate themselves? Whence did they get the very word?

Bible scholars give us a definite answer. The first Christians got this word from their Bible, our Old Testament. In the Greek translation of the Old Testament, the Septuagint from approximately 250 BC, which was then generally read among the Jews, the word ekklesia appears with a definite religious meaning. It is a translation of the Hebrew word "qahál" used in the Old Testament as designation for the "assembly" of Israel as the chosen people of God. It is especially at solemn occasions that Israel is called God's qahal: when she assembles for offering sacrifice and praise, for listening to God's message, and for giving Him their vows. The whole qahal of Israel shall slaughter the paschal lamb on the fourteenth day in the month of Nisan (Exod 12:6); God speaks to His qahal on Horeb out of the midst of the fire, and that day is "the day of the qahal" (Deut 9:10; 18:16). When Solomon's temple is consecrated, the qahal of Israel gathers to be blessed (1 Kgs 8:14), and when Ezra intervenes with drastic means to preserve the restored Israel, it is the qahal that acts before God (Ezra 10:12–14). The unclean has no place in Yahweh's qahal (Deut 23:2), and the criminal will be eradicated from it (Num 16:33).

These examples give us an idea of the solemnity that was associated with the very sound of this word. The qahal is the LORD's assembly, the Israel that is chosen by God and tied to God. To an even higher degree this is true about the word ekklesia. The Hebrew Bible could even talk about the qahal of the heathen or of the sinners, but in the Septuagint ekklesia is not used in such passages, because it was regarded as too holy. Another word was used, namely *synagogé,* which also means assembly (Gen 28:3; 35:11; 48:4; Jer 50:9; Ezek 26:7).

Towards the time of Jesus, this distinction is maintained rather consistently. Speaking about God's people, the Israel that idealistically is an entity, the religious totality, one says qahal (ekklesia). But if one speaks about one of the local congregations of the Jews, found in almost every city around the Mediterranean Sea, one says synagogue. We shall soon see why this distinction is so important.

Already the fact that the first Christians called themselves God's ekklesia or qahal, makes it immediately clear what the Christian church from the beginning claimed to be: God's genuine qahal, the true Israel.

With this we have arrived at the first firm point, where we will be able to get a grip of the early Christian concept of the church and thus get an answer to what the Church is according to the New Testament.

GOD'S ISRAEL

It would be a mistake to believe that the first Christians in Jerusalem would have perceived themselves as champions for a new religion or would have regarded Jesus as a "founder of a religion." When a Jew agreed to be baptized, he did not convert to a new faith. He just drew the conclusion of the faith that he always had embraced. Israel believed that God had chosen His particular people not only for her sake but also for the benefit all nations. All the great things that God had done with his people Israel was pointing forward to something even greater: In the fullness of time God would send his Messiah. From Beth-Lehem Ephrathah would come forth One who would be ruler in Israel (Mic 5:2), the shoot from the stump of Jesse (Isa 11:1), and who would raise up the booth of David (Amos 9:11), so that upon the throne of David and over his kingdom there would be no end of the increase of his government and of peace (Isa 9:7). At the coming of the Messiah, something great would happen with the world. The Son of Man would establish the kingdom of God, the realm of peace, where the iniquity of the people would be atoned for, and where the whole world would experience the peace and happiness under God's rule, to which it once was intended in creation.

Among the people in general these concepts were often associated with nationalistic dreams of an earthly kingdom of happiness, where every Israelite would sit under his grapevine and his fig tree. But those people in the land who were "quiet" knew that something altogether new would come, a new world which demanded clean hearts and pure conduct and to which one must prepare oneself through repentance and penance.

John the Baptist came. For the first time in centuries, there was again a prophet among the people speaking with the same power and authority as the prophets of old. His message was precisely this tremendous: Now it happens! The kingdom of God is near! A shock pierced the people. Multitudes flocked down the Jordan, and large crowds went into the grey water to receive John's baptism, a baptism of repentance as a seal that one was among those who under repentance and penance desired to wait for the Coming One, He who is greater than John and of whom he had said that he was not worthy to untie the thong of His sandal.

In this environment Jesus began His activity. His message was in the beginning the same as that of John: The Kingdom of God is near. But He never spoke about anyone who would come after Him. Nor did He preach about the wrath to come as John had done. He came with the great offer of grace, of participation in the Kingdom for both tax-collectors and prostitutes. There was around Him and all His actions something of the very joy of God's Kingdom. Those who followed Him took notice of it day after day. Could the wedding guests fast, when the bridegroom is with them? When the evil spirits retreated, when the blind saw, and the deaf heard, and when the Good News was preached for the poor, was not then the Kingdom of God at hand, had not the promised new era mysteriously made its way into the old world and grazed this fallen and soiled earth as with the tip of God's finger?

The unrest and the joy that Jesus arouse wherever He appeared were thus connected with the burning issues concerning the Messiah, the Kingdom of God, and the future of Israel. Some maintained that they understood who He was, so they wanted to make Him their king. From them He withdrew (John 6:15). Anything that could arouse such expectations, He tried to keep secret and to silence. And actually, He remained a riddle to most people. But to the innermost circle of disciples, He revealed gently and slowly the secrecy of God's Kingdom. The apostles began little by little to grasp this enigma that God's Messiah had come as the poor, the homeless and the despised. They slowly began to surmise that this was true about God's Kingdom as well. It was the mustard seed that was put into the ground to become a great tree, the insignificant leaven containing a mysterious power to make everything new. Thus God's Kingdom had now come, lowered into the world in the figure of the Son of Man. Despised, seemingly powerless and without resources, yet He was filled with God's own invincible power. The carpenter's son was the Son of Man. His gospel was the proclamation of God's great, decisive intervention in the history of His people.

That this decisive intervention would take the form of *a new covenant*, the prophets had already known. God had proclaimed that in the days to come, He would make a new covenant with the house of Israel, "not like the covenant which I made with their fathers when I took them by the hand to bring them out of the land of Egypt, My covenant which they broke, though I was their husband" (Jer 31:31f). Through this new covenant, the law would be written on the hearts of the people. Israel would live in a new relationship to her God, founded on the forgiveness of sins.

The thought of the new covenant is behind the entire activity of Jesus. One catches a glimpse of it when he chooses the twelve apostles. Clearly, the number twelve is symbolic. It represents the twelve tribes. The twelve would be the Messiah's, that is God's, messengers to all of Israel, now that God intervened anew in her history. They would be the judges in the new Israel, God's representatives who in the new kingdom would "sit on thrones judging the twelve tribes of Israel" (Luke 22:30). At the same time, they would represent Israel in the circle around the Messiah. Wherever He wandered with His disciples, they were the image of the new Israel that would gather around Him. Just by their presence, they proclaimed in a prophetic imagery that a new era had come, when the twelve tribes of Israel would again join together around Him for whom the forefathers had been waiting.

We encounter the same thing in the story of Peter's confession. Jesus calls his disciple blessed, because he has understood the great mystery that only God can reveal to a human being: that the carpenter's son is the Son of the living God, and that God's Kingdom has come in the form of a despised servant of God, one who goes about forgiving sins. Then Jesus adds some remarkable words: "And I tell you, you are *Peter* (= the rock), and on this rock I will build My church, and the gates of hell shall not prevail against it" (Matt 16:18).

Thus Jesus proclaims here that He shall establish His Church, the ekklesia, in the world. This concept, with which we have already dealt, was well known to the disciples from the Scriptures. It was the qahal, Israel, God's chosen holy people. But Jesus is here referring to *His* Israel. And He indicates what will be the border between the old and the new Israel. The foundation for His Church shall be the confession that Peter just had made: You are the Messiah, the Son of the living God. That is the way we must understand the meaning of Jesus' words. The rock foundation could not possibly be Peter as an individual human being. Briefly afterwards Jesus could say to the man Peter, " Get behind me, Satan . . . for you are not on the side of God, but of men" (Matt 16:23). As long as Peter had the thoughts of men, he was nothing else but a sinner, ruled by the prince of this world. But with his confession of the Messiah he was an instrument of God's. And as he now was the first one for whom God had opened the eyes to see the great mystery, and as he had been chosen by Christ to be the foremost of the apostles, he could on the strength of his confession and the apostolic office, which both had come from God, become the rock on which Christ would build His Church. And the Church would be mightier than the gates of hell, than the power of death. Within its walls people would find a refuge from both death and judgment.

Jesus proclaims the establishment of the new covenant most clearly, when He is together with his disciples for the last time. The institution of the Lord's Supper signifies the solemn establishment of a covenant that succeeds the old covenant of which the paschal lamb bore witness, the one that was established when God delivered His people out of the slavery in Egypt. This new covenant is now being established, Jesus says, not with the blood of sacrificial animals but *in My blood*. It is being founded not on the law but it is entered into *for the forgiveness of sins*. And it is not only for the old Israel but for *the many*, which in the language of that time meant the large despised multitude of sinners and heathen.

This was thus God's great intervention in the history of His people: a covenant of grace in stead of the old covenant of the law, forgiveness of sins instead of judgment and retribution, reconciliation instead of bondage, salvation for all nations instead of delivery for old Israel only. It was a new covenant, yet it was rooted in the old one, foretold by the prophets, prepared through the education and the chastisement of the law in Israel, and foreseen as God's ultimate goal for Israel's peculiar history. The fact that salvation would come from the Jews (John 4:22), that the Messiah would be given as a light to the nations, and that His "salvation would reach to the end of the earth" (Isa 49:6), every Jew knew long before Jesus appeared. The words that old Simeon said when he took the child Jesus in his arms express what every pious Jew expected the Messiah to be: "a light for revelation to the Gentiles, and for the glory to Thy people Israel" (Luke 2:32).

That all this actually had been fulfilled through Jesus Christ was not totally clear to the disciples until after the resurrection and Pentecost. Only then could they understand the full depth of God's mystery: that the Messiah had to suffer all these things and thus enter into His glory, and that this was indeed God's way to restore the world. In the light of the resurrection they began to grasp the meaning of the mystery of the atonement, and it became the core of their faith "that Christ died for our sins in accordance with the Scriptures, that He was buried, and that He was raised on the third day in accordance with the Scriptures" (1 Cor 15:3-4). The history of Israel reached its culmination in Christ's death and resurrection. God had in Christ accomplished atonement for the sins of His people, when He allowed His Anointed One to be the great sin offering, and God Himself had established a new kingdom, when He raised His Anointed One. The resurrection meant such an overwhelming victory over all the powers that brought Christ on the cross that none of the disciples could hesitate in the choice between the crucified Messiah and the powers of this world. They knew that something absolutely new had come. They themselves experienced this overwhelming and incomprehensible reality. A new era had broken in. Death was overcome and life revealed. God's kingdom was established. The Messiah had come, not with judgment, not with fire and wrath, but as Savior and Redeemer. Here God had established the longed-for covenant of peace. Here forgiveness and eternal life were now offered to everyone who believed in God's Messiah and allowed himself to be baptized and admitted into the covenant. The gates of salvation were opened anew, not only for Israel but for all nations. Only when the gospel had been preached to all and grace had been offered to all, would the last act in the drama occur: the Son of Man would come again and judge the world.

Thus God had not forgotten His people. On the contrary: it was only now that Israel had reached her destiny. Only now would the promised blessing come to Israel and through Israel reach out to the whole world. Israel would now gather around her Messiah, and all nations and tribes would gather around Israel to receive the blessing, that God had promised Abraham when He said: All peoples on earth will be blessed through you (Gen 12:3).

To the first Christians it was a matter of course that they were Israelites, since they had received the promised Messiah. When others rejected him, they had followed God's calling, believed the prophecy, and received the Lord's Anointed who would "reign over the house of Jacob forever" (Luke 1:33). They were thus the true continuation of the qahal of the old covenant, they were God's ekklesia, God's church.

The Church is thus from the beginning God's people, the true Israel, the fulfillment of all that the Old Testament had spoken of and that the faithful had been longing for. That is why it was altogether natural that the message first of all was directed to the Jews. Even the most apostate and the most despised were to be embraced by the divine mercy that was here revealed, "since he is also a son of Abraham" (Luke 19:9). And even if many of "the children of the kingdom," that is of the old Israel, hardened themselves and remained outside, and even if many strangers would come from east and west, it was firmly established according to Jesus' own words that they all would "sit at table with Abraham, Isaac and Jacob in the kingdom of heaven" (Matt 8:11). They would all be united with the old Israel, they would be her true members and heirs, they who had understood and received what God had desired to do through Abraham and the prophets.

The first Christians had not in any way assumed a new religion. The new that had come was not a new religion, but a new covenant, a new intervention by God. God had sent His Messiah. All those who in spirit and truth had understood and believed what Israel's God had done beforehand, they now entered the new covenant. Since they were true Israelites, they became true Christians. Since they belonged to God's people, God's qahal, they now called themselves by the old name: God's ekklesia, that is God's *church*. Thus the Church got that name that would remain hers through the ages.

One can trace the thought of the Church as the new Israel through the entire apostolic period. First of all one observes how a demarcation against the old Israel takes place, that is to say against those who remained under the law not acknowledging their own Messiah. They are now called "Israel according to the flesh" (1 Cor 10:18, cf. Rev 2:9). "For not all who are descended from Israel belong to Israel" (Rom. 9:6). "He is not a real Jew who is one outwardly, nor is true circumcision something external and physical. He is a Jew who is one inwardly and real circumcision is a matter of the heart, by the Spirit" (Rom 2:28–29).

God is now building up a new people for His own possession, "the Israel of God" (Gal 6:16), to which He also has chosen many who before were excluded. With monumental weight and power, the 2nd chapter of the Letter to the Ephesians describes the revolution that has taken place through Christ's atoning death: the dividing wall is broken down, the two halves of the human race are now united in one body, into one new man, and they who before were excluded from citizenship in Israel and aliens to the covenant of the promise, are now fellow citizens with the saints and members of the household of God. One must enter into the realism of the concept of the Old Testament covenant perceiving something of the boundless security in being chosen by God Himself, one must enter into what it was like then to be a heathen, "having no hope and without God in the world" (Eph 2:12), a proselyte, a religious "dependent" of a more favored people, in order to fully comprehend the full depth and power of this joyous message: *You are the household of God!* In the 11th chapter of the Letter to the Romans, Paul has carried out the same thought in the graphic image of the cultivated olive tree, where some branches have been broken off and into which others from a wild olive tree have been grafted.

Now this is not just an image. The early church knew herself to be the Israel that had not fallen away, the Israel that had received the Messiah and become the heir of the kingdom. Therefore she also knew herself to be the heir of old Israel's all privileges and obligations pertaining to the covenant. As a matter of course, of which any discussion never was needed, the followers of Jesus Christ took over Israel's holy Scriptures. Or rather: they retained their old holy Scriptures. That is how we must express the matter, when we see it from the point of view of the first Christians. Of course, there was much that they saw in a new light, both in the law and in the prophets, but that was only because they lived not in the time of the promises but in the time of the fulfillment. Only now was it that the holy writings of Israel could be fully grasped. Only when they were read with the life of Jesus as background, could it be discovered how everything is pointing forward to Christ, with sometimes hidden and sometimes obvious references to him. The first Christians realized that they too had been blind before. A veil had covered their hearts, when Moses was read, "because only through Christ is it taken away" (2 Cor 3:14). To them it became completely clear what all Christianity would encompass and confess till the end of the ages: that the Old Testament is about Christ, written to serve His congregation. It was unshakably firm that "it was written for our sake" (1 Cor 9:10). After all, Christ Himself had declared that it was written about Him "in all the Scriptures" (Luke 24:27).

Therefore the first Christians consistently held on to the temple and worshiped in the synagogue all the time until they were expelled or were prevented due to other external causes. They were the rightful heirs to all this, God's right qahal, the true Israel.

That is why they understood their relationship to God with exactly the same words with which Israel's status as a people of God's possession had been marked. Addressing his fellow Christians, Peter in his First

Letter (2:5) says, "You are a chosen race, a royal priesthood, a holy nation, a people for God's own possession," a direct quote from the Book of Exodus (19:5–6). The people of the covenant still exists but now in the forms of the new covenant.

* * *

This is the basic view. We can now draw a number of important conclusions regarding the proper concept of the Church.

If the Church is the true Israel, then she is from the beginning designed as a totality, an indivisible unit, which came about through an election and an act of creation by God Himself. Any individualism and sectarianism are excluded. One cannot be an Israelite on one's own. Nor can one become one through one's own resolve. The qahal of the Lord cannot possibly be formed through human resolutions and efforts. In the same way, it is just as impossible to form an ekklesia. It is there beforehand, indivisible and whole, complete in itself, created by God: one can only be received into it. It would have been an absurd thought to all biblical piety that some Jews (or even worse some Greeks!) in some corner of the world would have united themselves and then "formed" a people for God's own possession. Just as absurd was the thought that people would unite and form a Christian congregation, an ekklesia. One became a right member of the people for God's own possession through birth, through the circumcision, and through faithfulness toward the covenant of the law. In the same way one must be born into God's Israel through baptism and live there by faith in the gospel. The Church is obviously first there. The starting-point is totally with God. God's deeds, begun already with Abraham, Isaac and Jacob, continued through the prophets, and completed in Christ and his apostles, created the objective fact, the covenant established by God, into which one can be received but which one can never create. This fact of reality is the Church.

If the Church exists before the individual Christian, she also exists before the individual local congregation. It is inconceivable that a number of individual congregations, each named ekklesia, first came into being, which then gradually joined together into a alliance that was named after the parts. The very name ekklesia is sufficient proof of the matter. If a number of independent congregations first came into being, they would have called themselves by the usual name for such a union: *synagogé*. But *ekklesia*, God's *qahal*, is according to its very essence *one*. It is created by God and does not come into being through a union of several smaller units.

Further: Since the Church is the true Israel, the form of her life is a covenant, and this covenant has its *signs*. While "the circumcision of the heart" and the internal life of faith are greatly emphasized, the external signs were important as well. Both are necessary. There is no competition between them. The objective and the subjective belong inextricably together. One did not know any "purely inner" Christianity and would hardly have acknowledged it as Christianity. Faith was not just abstract thinking or inner experience: it was foremost a concrete external life in the new covenant, God's Israel, the Church.

Just as the old Israel had her covenant signs, her promises, the temple service, without which she would not have been God's qahal, the new Israel has her promises in the gospel, her "circumcision in Christ" (Col 2:11) in baptism, her covenant meal in the Lord's Supper, and so forth. Just as Paul can enumerate all the privileges of the Jewish people, the inner privileges and the external ones, in an inextricable combination: "the sonship, the glory, the covenants, the giving of the law, the temple worship, and the promises" (Rom 9:4), the Letter to the Hebrews can likewise capture all the privileges of the new covenant in a number of objective spiritual realities (Heb 12:22-24). Just as old Israel had its spiritual center in Jerusalem with its temple, likewise the Church has her stronghold, which is also a Jerusalem. "You have come to Mount Zion and to the city of the living God, the heavenly Jerusalem." Here God's Israel has Jesus, "the mediator of a new covenant," and a new "sprinkled blood." Here one enters into "the assembly of the first-born who are enrolled in heaven," God's elected assembly on earth, where one at the same time is united with "innumerable angels . . . and . . . the spirits of just men made perfect," the whole festal gathering in heaven. This has been expressed in the deeply edifying concept of the fellowship between the Church involved in spiritual warfare on earth, Ecclesia Militans, and the Church of triumph and victory in heaven, Ecclesia Triumphans.

Finally: If the Church is the true Israel, then the modern issue concerning the relevance of the Old Testament becomes as meaningless as it possibly could. For the early Church, and for the Church ever since, the Old Testament is not at all the annals of another people, but it is our own spiritual original history. When we Swedes were christianized, we were grafted into the holy root (Rom 11:16); we have a double family tree. Speaking with the language of the Bible: we have ancestors *kata sarka* (according to the flesh), our Nordic ancestors. But we have also our ancestors *kata pnevma* (according to the Spirit). We are in our full rights to count *Abraham*, *Isaac* and *Jacob* as our ancestors, to count their whole history interwoven with promises and purpose as our own. We are their rightful children and the people of the prophetic promises. Just as the first Christians did, we too can speak with warmth and joy about our father Abraham (Luke 1:73; cf Rom 4:16–17; Gal. 3:29). From a Christian point of view, trying to cut off the patriarchs and the prophets from our history is to rob it of its vital artery, its divine meaning. Our ancestors acted with fine Christian instinct and with a sense for living realities, when they named their children after our great spiritual forefathers, so that to this very day Abrahamsson, Isaksson and Jakobsson are firmly rooted Swedish family names, surely a great vexation to all anti-Semites. During the period when Sweden was a Great Power, our ancestors lived in their Old Testament. They loved it, were nurtured by it, and knew what it meant to be a people belonging to God. But today there are many who would rather amputate the name Israel from our history. That would be like amputating one of the auricles from a human heart! Without the Psalms, Isaiah, Proverbs, and Sirach (one of the apocryphal scriptures), the 1600s in our Swedish history would be incomprehensible. A Swede who would alienate himself from the Old Testament would have deprived himself of any possibility to understand his forefathers and his own history. Worse yet: He would miss the purpose of life losing the red thread which signifies God's intention and goal for our nation.

We do not want to lose that purpose. Therefore, as Christians we continue to treasure with pride and gratitude our wonderful history with its double roots in our Nordic soil and in the sacred events of Holy Bible. *We too belong to God's Israel.*

Of course, what I have said here is equally true not only for all those nations that through centuries or even millennia have been impacted by Christ's Church but also for those many peoples that in recent times have been reached with the Good News. They are all the children of Abraham through faith in Jesus Christ (Gal 3:7).

THE BODY OF CHRIST

We have seen that the Church from the beginning is God's Israel, the people of the new covenant, gathered around her risen Messiah and the signs of the covenant. But we have not exhausted what the Bible tells us about the essence of the Church. So far we have only dealt with the starting-point. To the extent that the early Christians lived their life with Christ in this covenant that He had established, it was increasingly filled with richer content which in its turn was expressed in new ways. The most profound that early Christianity would say about the essence of the Church was this: she is the *the Body of Christ*.

This expression occurs first in Paul's First Letter to the Corinthians and in his Letter to the Colossians. The concept is perfected in the Letter to the Ephesians. The expression itself is pauline, but its content comes from Jesus Himself. Already the parable of the vine and the branches as well as many other thoughts that the Gospel of John has preserved for us, say exactly the same about the essence of the Christian life.

That the Church is the Body of Christ (Eph 1:22–23; 5:23–30; Col. 1:18, 24) means first of all that the Church, and thereby the individual Christian, exists in a real life-giving connection with the risen Lord. In the same way as each member gets its strength, its warmth, its nourishment from the body, with which it is grown together, in the same way there is a real connection between the glorified, heavenly and immortal life of Christ and all the members of His church. They can confidently say, "We have been united with Him" (Rom 6:5). The Church is "His own flesh," we are "members of His body," and the phrase "the two shall become one flesh" is also used about the relationship between Christ and His church (Eph 5:29ff). This union is so intimate that Christ and the Church in certain circumstances become the same, so that one can say Christ, when one actually means the Church. We read in 1 Cor 12:12, "For just as the body is one and has many members, and all the members of the body, though many, are one body, so it is with *Christ.*" Here we would have expected *ekklesia*, but Paul is so absorbed by the thought of the congregation as a part of Christ Himself, that he here as a matter of fact says "Christ" instead of "the Church." One can hardly express more strikingly how tremendously real the New Testament envisions the fellowship between Christ and His body, the Church.

From this intimate fellowship follows not only that the Church/the body is totally subject (Eph 5:24) to Christ/the head (that is obvious) but also that she for her whole life and her growth is depending on Him, "from whom the whole body grows with a growth that is from God" (Col 2:19; cf Eph 4:16). She is also the object of His special love (Eph 5:25), as He "nourishes and cherishes" her.

In this fellowship the Church also becomes a participant in the whole fullness of the deity, since in Christ "the whole fullness of deity dwells bodily" (Col 2:9). Therefore it consistently can be said that the Church *is* the fullness (pléroma) of Christ (Eph 1:23)! One can hardly express the biblical faith in the Church more clearly. From this everything else follows: her unlimited possibilities, her imperishableness, her necessity for our salvation.

Furthermore, when this view of the Church is applied to each one of us, its deeply edifying character is best shown. It has consequences that fill the whole Christian life with meaning and purpose.

Through baptism the individual becomes a member of the Body of Christ: "By one Spirit we were all baptized into one body" (1 Cor 12:13). Thereby the individual has entered into this real, "pneumatic" life connection with Christ. The fullness of Christ begins to flow through the person. The holy forces have begun their work. The Lord's Supper is one of them: "The cup of blessing which we bless, is it not a participation in the blood of Christ? The bread which we break, is it not a participation in the body of Christ? Because there is one loaf, we who are many are one body, for we all partake of the same loaf" (1 Cor. 10:16). This participation in the Body of Christ is of course not a participation of flesh and blood, but a communion with the Lord's heavenly, transfigured body and a participation in its resurrection life. Also on earth is the Body of Christ, that is the Church, built up through this communion.

The pastoral office is also one of these holy forces. Apostles, prophets, evangelists, and teachers have been given to the church in order to equip the saints for ministry, "for building up the body of Christ" (Eph 4:11–12). The Word belongs here by which "the man of God may be complete, equipped for every good work" (2 Tim 3:17).

Life in the Body of Christ is thus *a process of growth*. In the beginning, one is a child in the faith. Right after the passage in Ephesians 4 that we just quoted, in verse 13, we learn that "we all reach unity in the faith and in the knowledge of the Son of God and become mature, attaining to the whole measure of the fullness of Christ." Thus the fullness (pléroma) that the Church has, the baptized does not have from the beginning. He has only connected with it. It is a force that shapes his life, a goal toward which he is pressing on.

The same conviction of a real union with Christ and participation in His heavenly life is characteristic of a considerable number of assertions in our New Testament. It is because of this real fellowship that our bodies are called "members of Christ" (1 Cor 6:15), and that "the head of every man is Christ" (1 Cor 11:3). Through the same fellowship "our inner nature is being renewed every day" (2 Cor 4:16), and we "are being changed into His likeness" (2 Cor 3:18). For the same reason it is said that Jesus Christ is in us (2 Cor 13:15; Col 1:27), and on the other hand that we shall be "rooted and built up in him" (Col 2:7) and so "may escape from the corruption that is in this world because of passion, and become partakers of the divine nature" (2 Pet 1:4).

Becoming a member of the Body of Christ thus means a possibility and a calling to attain to the fullness of Christ. "Let the peace of Christ rule in your hearts, to which indeed you were called *as members in the one body*" (Col 3:15). This admonition is instructive: since the baptized is a member of the Body of Christ, he is also called to be a participant in His fullness, also including His peace. But this admonition includes a requirement as well, since I live in the one and same body as my fellow Christians. I am called *and obliged* to keep the peace with them. Here we have arrived at that point where the truth about the Body of Christ becomes one of the most powerful and compelling moral forces known in early Christianity.

As a heading one can choose Romans 12:5, "We, though many, are one body in Christ, and individually *we are members one of another.*"

The consequences of this may then be carried out in different directions.

First of all: The fellowship in the Body of Christ means to the Church the strongest possible obligation for unswerving *unity*. In His Body, the Church, Christ Himself has through his atoning death joined together those who previously were separated by the wall of hostility (Eph 2:14,16; 3:6). There is no longer Jew or Greek, slave or free, male or female, all are now one in Christ (Gal 3:28), in the same body (Eph 3:6). Thus the Christians are obliged by the strongest ties not to break asunder the unity that the Lord Himself has created. Even very deep-going differences must therefore be viewed as insignificant. The gifts may vary, talents, rank and position may be unevenly distributed. Typically, the early church experienced all that as richness: the body has many different members that need one another for mutual service (1 Cor 12:14–25).

Here is the second consequence of the great thought that the Church is the Body of Christ. It means *mutual responsibility and duty to serve.*

Yet another consequence remains to be considered. The imprisoned Paul writes, "I fill up in my flesh what is still lacking in regard to Christ's afflictions, for the sake of His body, which is the Church" (Col. 1:24). This thought, which to so many Christians today seems strange, is as a matter of fact prompted by the believer's deepest experience of life together in the Body of Christ. It is organically connected with the basic view we previously have seen and with that deep life in Christ, which this basic view reflects. Since we are a body with Christ and participants in His life, we must also participate in His afflictions, His scorn and His wounds. Paul writes that no one should "be moved by these afflictions. You yourselves know that this is to be our lot" (1 Thess 3:3; cf Acts 14:22). But since these afflictions are a fellowship in suffering with Christ, they cannot deter. The apostle gives a strong testimony, "I want to know the fellowship of sharing in His sufferings, becoming like Him in His death, and so, somehow, to attain to the resurrection from the dead" (Phil. 3:10f). The fellowship in suffering is after all only one side of that fellowship which also becomes a fellowship in the resurrection. The fellowship in the cross is also a fellowship in the glory. "We always carry around in our body the death of Jesus, so that the life of Jesus may also be revealed in our body" (2 Cor 4:10). Thus Paul knows that he must carry his measure of these "sufferings of Christ" (2 Cor 1:5), but he also knows that thereby the life of Christ shall be victorious both in his mortal body and in the church. And precisely here comes the other important aspect of the same matter: he is not only one body with Christ but also with all his fellow baptized. And now it is a fact: "If one part suffers, every part suffers with it; if one part is honored, every part rejoices with it" (1 Cor 12:26). Here is an indissoluble mutuality. But carrying one's portion of "Christ-sufferings" meant, as we have learned, to be like Christ and show something of His life. Where a Christian in suffering more deeply becomes connected with His Lord, there has *one* member been filled with a greater measure of "Christ-life," and that will benefit all the members. "If we are afflicted, it is for your comfort and salvation" (2 Cor 1:16). There is thus in the mysterious fellowship of the Body of Christ a dimension of a substitutionary suffering. That's why Paul says that he fills his measure of "Christ-sufferings" for the benefit of the Body of Christ which is the Church.

No doubt that contemporary Christendom ought to take these thoughts to heart which give martyrdom a completely new meaning, filling the catacombs with light.

Once again it is time to draw the consequences. The reader has already noticed, I am sure, how closely that view of the Church, which is summed up in the words *the Body of Christ*, coincides with the view of the Church as *the true Israel*, which I explored in the previous section.

1. The Church, too, appears as a totality, not as a sum of individuals. She is *one* body, and Christ is the head, the will, the source of life, and the power of all growth. *Any definition of the Church would be false, if it not first of all includes Christ and His spiritual riches*, his pleroma. Becoming a Christian means to be received into this life-fellowship through baptism. Being a Christian means living there through the Word and the Sacraments, in faith. A Christian by oneself is no Christian. One cannot live as a disconnected member.

2. Now we shall consider the significance of the sacraments. This whole pneumatic (by the Spirit, in the Body of Christ effectuated) life-fellowship with the risen Lord is perceived sacramentally. One can never understand this life-giving relationship only in terms of obedience or discipleship. The gospel actually means that there exists a real association with the glorified Christ and His resurrection life. It is mediated both by the Word and the Sacraments, when they are received in faith. Then Christ's heavenly life flows into us, fills us, and transforms in secret our mortal bodies and our corrupt existence into likeness with His immortal, glorious body. One should not be horrified and recoil at this faith. It is truly filled with life abundant and with mysterious intimacy. The more one surrenders oneself to it, the more it shows its depth and its inexhaustible ability to regenerate and transform one's everyday life and sufferings.

3. Here is also confirmed that which we learned when viewing the church as the true Israel. She has her heavenly foundation. She exists not only on earth but encompasses also a heavenly Jerusalem. Just as the Letter to the Hebrews refers (12:22, 23) to the fellowship of the Christians with "innumerable angels" and "the spirits of righteous men made perfect," so the Letter to the Ephesians says (2:6) that "God raised us up and seated us with Him in the heavenly realms in Christ Jesus." The church reaches into

the heavenly realms, since she is the Body of Christ. Whoever is received into the church has fellowship with the heavenly Jerusalem.

4. To this must be added a thought that takes us further than the teaching on the true Israel. The Body of Christ is a living organism, richly differentiated, continually growing and yet permeated by the same blood and controlled by the same will. One of the Church's most important features is made manifest here: *she lives*. In spite of her being an institution, established on a divine foundation and on truths which once for all have been revealed, she even so owns her great adaptiveness, her richly pulsating life, her power to grow, and yet keep her essence unchanged.

* * *

The same basic thoughts appear once again, if one considers a third sphere of images by which the Bible presents the Church's essence: the image of a building (Matt 16:18; 1 Cor 3:9,16,17; Eph 2:20; 1 Pet 2:5). One would be inclined to think that here would appear a more individualistic way of looking at the matter. After all, a house is built of separate stones, and an assembly could likewise be formed through the union of individuals. However, such thoughts are totally foreign to the gospel. The building we are reflecting on is in reality not like other buildings, where the material comes from the outside. That the Church is a uniform and living organism is clear here, too. This fact is so strong that it shapes the whole image. Yes, it is said (Eph 2:20–21) that Jesus Christ is the cornerstone, but then the text continues, "In him the whole building is joined together and rises to become a holy temple in the Lord." Thus the cornerstone is not actually a stone; it is a living heart, from which there flows a power that causes the building to grow; it is as if it comes alive before our eyes. In reality it is the image of the Body of Christ, or rather: the consciousness that the Church is a living and uniform organism, that has shaped also this thought.

THE CHURCH AND THE CONGREGATIONS

It is obvious that the word *ekklesia* is used also about the local congregations even in plural. Does this not belie our statement that the Church in the New Testament always is thought of as a uniform organism, created by God and impossible to disjoint?

Not at all. The explanation is that the congregation in each place was regarded as the visible representation of God's one and uniform ekklesia. Development can be detected in our New Testament. At the beginning, only the small flock of Messiah believers in Jerusalem, God's chosen qahal, was the visible church on earth. As the number of disciples grew and small groups came into being in Samaria and Damascus, God's church ceased to be a confined entity but was still called *the* church. Thus we are told in Acts 8:3 that "Saul laid waste the church," and in 9:31, "So the church throughout all Judea and Galilee and Samaria had peace." But as the branches of the church spread and the local congregations began to live their own life, the word ekklesia began to denote the church such as she appeared in each place: what we call congregation. Thus Paul, using the word ekklesia, wrote to "the church of the Thessalonians" (1 Thess 1:1), "the church of God which is at Corinth" (1 Cor 1:2; 2 Cor 1:1), and "the churches of Galatia" (Gal 1:2). Note here: it never happens that there are two organized congregations in the same town. That would have been incongruous. The church was *one* and could in one and the same place only be represented by *one* uniform and united assembly, which simultaneously would be the church and the congregation. That she really was perceived as representing the *whole* Church, one can see from such passages as 1 Tim 3:5, where it is said about the bishop: "if a man does not know how to manage his own household, how can he care for God's church?" This is obviously referring to *one* congregation. And yet Paul says "God's church," since each local congregation represents the whole Church (cf. Acts 20:28).

The word ekklesia thus denotes both the whole Church and each local congregation. "The ekklesia of the living God" is in 1 Tim 3:15 called "the pillar and foundation of the truth," namely of the divine truth of salvation wrought for all people through Christ's atoning sacrifice (see 1 John 2:2). Only when a local congregation is faithful to that truth is it a true expression of the one ekklesia, the one Church.

If one's eyes have been opened to see the Church, the Body of Christ, in her earthly and heavenly greatness, then one realizes why this ekklesia must be the pillar and foundation of the truth, the only point where we obtain certainty and rest in this earthly life. We know that she has Christ's own life, filled with heavenly forces and thoroughly illumined with heavenly light. God's ekklesia in this world, whether we think of the whole Church or a local congregation, has above itself the heavenly church and

Christ, the head. Only in faithfulness to His commands and institutions, His word and sacrament, only in connection with Christ, in full and vital fellowship with all Christendom and with God's revelation in the past, can the church present the full and unshakeable truth.

THE NEW ERA

The New Testament concept of the Church is inextricably connected with the Bible's doctrine on the kingdom of God. One cannot rightly understand what the early church meant with the Church, if one does not understand what Jesus and His apostles meant with the kingdom of God. Here the truth about the Church emerges most clearly and deeply. But it is exactly this truth that is so hard to comprehend for those who are caught up in modern ways of thinking.

The Old Testament declared that when the Messiah came, then the Kingdom of God would also come. The Messiah would be the Prince of Peace who would establish and uphold His kingdom with justice and righteousness.

It was thus a given that Jesus proclaimed the kingdom of God (or the kingdom of heaven as it is called in Matthew). The Good News is, from the beginning, the gospel of the kingdom (Matt 24:14). And this kingdom is like other kingdoms: one can enter it, and one can stay outside it. We are told about the way that leads to it and about the gate to it. But at the same time, we learn that it is not of this world. It cannot be defended through military means. It is not yet established, but it will in due time come in great power and glory. It is called the era to come (Mark 10:30). It shall succeed the current era. Since God's creation had fallen into sin and had become distorted, no longer corresponding to the intentions of the Creator, God shall bring about a new creation with "new heavens and a new earth in which righteousness dwells" (2 Pet 3:13). The arrival of God's kingdom thus means the collapse of the old era. God only knows when this will take place. The gospel only proclaims that it will happen when Christ returns in glory at the resurrection of the dead.

God's kingdom is thus something yet to come. As we just pointed out, it is therefore called the era to come (Mark 10:30; see also Matt 12:32 and Eph 1:21). It is something that totally shatters the frame for our current existence. It renews and transforms everything: "Behold, I make all things new" (Rev 10:6). Time will cease, that which formerly was will then be gone for ever; no place will be found for the old earth and the old heaven (Rev 20:11; 21:1–5a).

It was this kingdom to come that Jesus proclaimed. But He did not only proclaim it. He also represented it. The great secret with His person was precisely that *the Kingdom of God and the eon to come already, in a hidden way, were present in Him.* The kingdom of heaven with all its resources had come to the earth and found a way into our existence.

Therefore, all the signs and miracles of the messianic age occurred where Jesus appeared. That is why even death must yield to His word. When He in God's name conquers the powers of darkness, it is candidly said: the kingdom of God has come upon you (Luke 11:20). All this is now a secret, an enigma, a mystery. That is so because the kingdom of God has not taken on its new form. It has not come in its power, it still conceals its glory. It can only be seen through the eyes of faith, by those who are "the children of wisdom" and to whom "it has been given to know the secrets of the kingdom of heaven." They are those who are longing for God and are awaiting His salvation. They acknowledge the secret that belongs to Christ, they perceive the new power in His words, they realize that they have the bridegroom in their midst, the one who is greater than both Solomon and Jonah.

Externally, the secret of the kingdom of God was preserved during the entire life of Jesus. He Himself did everything He could to subdue the waves of messianic sensation which at times arose around Him. It was easy for His enemies to defeat Him. There was nothing in His external appearance that proved to the people that He had power over both heaven and earth. They could at last triumph: He saved others; let Him save Himself, if He is God's Anointed!

And yet: precisely here in the deepest humiliation, the kingdom of God reveals its hidden glory. Here is the only point in the history of the world, where the new eon has appeared in its full power, unveiling its essence in the midst of this old world. Otherwise it was always hidden under the forms of the old existence. Here they were broken through and something completely new came about, something that never before had been seen in this world and which in reality meant the beginning of a new creation.

This is the significance of the resurrection. The entire earthly existence of Jesus was transformed. He appeared in a totally new form of existence. Although He was fully real and the same Jesus as before, although He could approach the disciples and be recognized by them, and although He was still their Master and Lord, He was different. He was no longer of this world. He had assumed the guise that is of the age to come. He had passed through the transformation that once will happen to all of existence at the end times, when God will create everything anew, when death will be swallowed up by life and this mortal will put on immortality.

Thus the kingdom of God had at one point appeared in its power. Quite consequently, the disciples asked the Risen One: Lord, will you at this time restore the kingdom to Israel? The answer was repudiating: It is not for you to know times or seasons which the Father has fixed by his own authority. But you shall receive power when the Holy Spirit has come upon you; and you shall be my witnesses in Jerusalem and in all Judea and Samaria and to the end of the earth (Acts 1:6–8).

That answer illuminates the entire existence of the Church. The kingdom of God shall not yet come in its power and glory. There will first be a time of waiting, during which the gospel shall be proclaimed in the whole world. For that purpose shall Christ give the Holy Spirit to his witnesses. That which occurred on Calvary shall be told to all nations. The atonement shall be presented to all of fallen humanity. Only then shall the Kingdom come.

The Church thus lives between two eras. She is built up in the old era, but she proclaims the new era and already lives the life of the new era, although in a hidden way and in the guise of humiliation. The situation of the Church in the world can thus be likened to that which one experiences early in the morning at the foot of a mountain range, where the peaks already glitter from the rays of the rising sun, although you yourself cannot yet see the sun over the horizon. Thus we can still say: The kingdom of God is near. At one point it has already revealed itself, because in Christ it has entered this world, and in His resurrection it has revealed its glory. The Risen One is the firstborn from the dead, a new Adam, who already in this existence is the head of a new generation, chosen to partake in the life of the new era.

Thus the new era is still hidden. It is in waiting to be revealed. It exists only in Christ: everywhere he works, there the powers of the new era are also at work. But they work as a mystery that the world cannot see. Just as the whole fullness of the Deity once dwelt bodily in the carpenter's son from Nazareth, so the powers of God's kingdom still dwell in the old era, where they are clothed in earthly guise. *And this precisely is the Church.* She is the sum of all that whereby God's kingdom appears in the world. She has that likeness with Jesus, that she too has an external earthly guise. Externally she resembles a human organization, an association, a "movement," or maybe a life-view. She has her "ideology," her officials and her adherents. The blind world cannot detect much more of her, just as it saw Jesus as nothing else but a bizarre prophet or political fanatic. But the kingdom of God exists in this external guise with all its saving and life-giving powers. In the Church, the new era is already at work.

Thus the Church is *the kingdom of God such as it appears in this world of sin and death.* She is the beginning of a new era. Her innermost essence is still hidden. She still is in the state of humiliation just as Jesus before the resurrection. But just as Jesus was exalted and glorified through His resurrection, so the Church shall once partake in the same transformation, when the world shall be born anew, and God "will change our lowly body to be like Christ's glorious body" (Phil 3:21).

One would almost dare to present this biblical thought as a painting. We are surrounded by the present world. It is God's creation, and therefore full of His glory. At the same time it is fallen in sin, and therefore full of suffering and death, soiled and distorted and liable to a just judgment. Above this world of sin and death, far beyond sun and moon, another world is hovering, yet still resting in God as a great possibility, a new creation design and a new existence. Christ descends from this new world. With Him He takes it along into the old world. He carries it in His hands, it is imbedded in His words, it radiates from His face and sounds from His lips. Everywhere where people believe in Him, they become mysteriously partakers of the new era. They become the children of the kingdom, marked with the mark of the new life. But in all this, the Kingdom is still hidden.

Then Christ rises. The death mask of the old era bursts open at one single spot and a glimpse of the light from the heavenly kingdom comes rushing in. Where the Risen One is present in this world, there the new era has already overcome the old. Death has been swallowed up and victory is won. When the Risen One sends out His apostles, when He institutes baptism and makes arrangements for His Church's future, then He puts in motion powers that are not of this world and do not belong to the old era. Yet these powers are still hidden in the guise of the old world. The apostles, who are sent out, and all that which comes with them: the gospel, baptism, the Lord's Supper, it is all clothed in the guise of the old world. The Christians are mortal human beings, who are still waiting for adoption as sons, the redemption of their bodies (Rom 8:23). All of Christ's Church goes in under the forms of the old world and wears its guise. But in the midst of all the mundane and strange that the Church carries out in the world, the kingdom of God lives and is at work, moving people to come in touch with the Risen One and making them partakers of that life which shall never die.

Now, this view is the foundation for everything that the New Testament says about the Church.

The Church being *the new Israel* does not in any way mean, as we already have seen, that she is a political entity or a human organization. It means that she is God's chosen people. Here it is not a matter of membership in some kind of association or participation in some human relationship. The Christian has become a participant in Christ, he has been received into a totally new life and has become an heir of God's kingdom. Therefore, the Church can on the one hand, just as Israel, be called *a people*. She has everything that belongs to a people and keeps it together: the vast legacy of laws, ceremonies, and customs. But at the same time, life in the Church is something totally new. Between the old and the new Israel stands Christ. With Him the new era has emerged in Israel's history. His resurrection is the great milestone in world history. Everything that happened before is only "a shadow of the good things to come" (Heb 10:1) and "an illustration for the present time" (Heb 9:9). It is true both for the prophecy, the law, and the temple sacrifices. Their time has now come to an end, and something new has come. Instead of the prophecy with its promises, the fulfillment has now come in Christ and His kingdom. Instead of the law with its salvation through deeds, the gospel with righteousness through faith now emerges. Instead of the sacrifices and the high priest's service in the Jerusalem temple, Christ has now "appeared as a high priest of the good things that have come" (Heb 9:11), who offers Himself and approaches God in our behalf.

In the new Israel, everything is thus truly new. Its spiritual center is not the Jerusalem temple but the heavenly Jerusalem, that is to say the kingdom that is to be revealed. The members of this new Israel have their citizenship in heaven. From there they await Jesus the Messiah as the Savior, who at His coming will change the lowly body of His people to be like Himself in the glory that is His after the resurrection. Already now, the powers that belong to the new kingdom of God are at work in God's Israel. Those are the powers that give the new birth to a person and makes her a partaker of eternal life.

The new Israel is thus simultaneously the continuation of the old Israel and the forerunner of the new era. It is simultaneously an heir and a people of the future. It is simultaneously anchored in the past, where it has its spiritual ancestors and from where it has inherited its holy scriptures, and in the future, where it has its goal in the city which is to come, over which Christ reigns, He who is the first fruits from the dead and who will make His people partakers of His own resurrection.

The new Israel, that is the Church, thus lives between two worlds. Behind it is the old era, that which leads to judgment and collapse. God's people still live in this era sharing its external forms. But it has heard the call from God and has broken up. It has left the spiritual Egypt and is now traveling through the desert to the promised land. On its forehead it has the mark of baptism, reaching toward the new era with the new life of faith in its heart. Therefore it must experience itself as a guest and stranger in this world, because the present era is heading toward its conclusion. It stands under judgment with all its kingdoms and powers, all its intelligence and its beauty. The future belongs to the kingdom of God, and blessed are those who will eat at the feast in the kingdom of God.

That which carries God's Israel and makes it God's people is therefore God's own actions, over which none of us can rule, nor be entitled to. That a human being can be a member in God's Israel is entirely a result of God's merciful dealing with her, receiving her into that immense chain of events, which encompasses all time from the beginning of the world to the end of the world. The first Christians clearly understood that it was not they who had "become Christians" or "formed" a church. Everything had come to them, prepared from eternity, carried out by God according to a plan covering thousands of years. The Christians have been taken up by God into that huge drama of salvation, that began at the fall, was prepared through *Abraham*, *Moses* and the prophets, culminated on Calvary, and finally will be completed, when the kingdom of God comes in its power. They were chosen in Christ. And Christ existed before the creation of the world. Everything in heaven and on earth has been created through Him and to Him. He was present in everything which happened in the Old Testament. He accompanied Israel during its desert journey. He spoke through the prophets. He was prefigured by *Melchizedek*. He was sung of in the Psalms. All the scriptures bore witness to Him. He was the goal and purpose of world history.

The Church emerges now in the world as a stage in God's vast plan of salvation, a stage in the "plan for the fullness of time." Her members are therefore those "who beforehand hoped in Christ." They were chosen before the foundation of the world. Their salvation is God's work "according to His good pleasure which He has purposed in Himself" and which is now carried out by Him, "who works out everything in conformity with the purpose of His will" (Eph 1:5–12). That a human being has become a member of the new Israel is just as great a miracle as her having been created. Here the Almighty has intervened in her life in a way, that she neither has earned nor could have earned. God Himself has stretched out His hand and saved her, not because of deeds done by her in righteousness, but in virtue of His own mercy through the new birth in the waters of baptism (Titus 3:4–7). Thereby she has been lifted into a new existence. She has become a child of a new era, and an entirely new way has been opened for her.

These thoughts become even clearer, if we proceed to the image of the Church as *the Body of Christ*, realizing how they connect to the idea of the new era.

Ephesians 1:23, where the Church is spoken of as the Body of Christ, is immediately preceded by the proclamation of Christ's resurrection as the beginning of a new era. God raised Christ from the dead and seated Him on His right hand in the heavenly realm and made Him Lord over everything not only in the present age but also in the one to come. "And God placed all things under His feet and appointed Him to be head over everything for the Church" (Eph 1:22).

The connection between these two thoughts is very clear: the same power which exalted Christ has also founded the Church. The same resurrection which resulted in Christ's victory over all the powers of evil and the establishment of His royal throne also resulted in the establishment of the Church. The same new epoch, which has begun with the raising of Jesus from the dead and His lordship, now emerges on earth through the Church. She is the body of the Risen One; she is his visible presence in this world. The Church is "the fullness of Him who fills all in all" (Eph 1:23). In her are those powers at work, which belong to the new era of Christ. It is precisely those hidden powers which make Christians the members of Christ.

Again we see, that the Church has a peculiar position between two worlds. She is the kingdom of God, such as it appears in this world. She is a divine kingdom, yet still living in the guise of humiliation. She is not of this world but she is still in this world. She belongs to the new era but in a hidden way, invisible to the world. She lives by faith, in hope.

The Church's position between two worlds is marked by two borders: the resurrection of Christ and the return of Christ. Before the resurrection of Christ, the Church existed only as a preparation and as a promise. Her era begins with the resurrection of Christ, with His going from humiliation to exaltation, assuming His power and authority. He equips His Church with the sacraments and the Spirit. He sends His apostles out into the world. He leads His Church from His heavenly royal throne. The Church herself remains in the world, where she represents Christ's kingdom. Not until Christ returns will the time come for her to take off the guise of her humiliation. Then she has completed her work in the world; this world perishes and the Church will be consummated in Christ's eternal kingdom.

These two borders are for the individual Christian marked by his *baptism* and his *death*. Baptism is the border between the old world and the Church. Through baptism God makes us, independent of any merits, participants in the new era that has come with Christ. Baptism means to be buried with Christ in order to rise to His new life. It means that the old man, all that in man that belongs to the old era, receives its sentence of death. It further means that precisely that man with his old connection with sin and guilt in the world is pardoned by virtue of the work of atonement that Christ for his sake accomplished on Golgotha. It means finally that man becomes participant in a new life in Christ. This life is still hidden with Christ in God. None the less, man is raised with Christ in order to live with Him. He has been placed in the heavenly world. Already here and now He shares in the inheritance that will be fully His in the world to come with all its glory.

This is the border of baptism, drawn between the Church and the old era. Anyone who has been transferred across that border has been marked thereof for all future. He has been called by God Himself to walk in the life of the new era, to put off the old man, to die away from the whole old context of selfishness, envy, greed and hatred, and instead to live for God in love, joy, peace and patience. The total ethics of the early church is a variation of this theme: "If then you have been raised with Christ, seek the things that are above" (Col 3:1).

The other border is marked by the Christian's death and the Day of Judgment. It is the border between the Church in this world and the world to come. It is the passage to glory. In death, the Christian's old sinful nature is destroyed with all that tied him to the old era, to sin and suffering. Then comes the resurrection when all the members of the Body of Christ are made a new creation unto likeness with Him who is the first fruits of the dead. Having been faithful to the calling of their baptism, they become partakers in all that has already happened to the glorified Christ. What will happen to the dead members, Christ has indicated in His words about the dry branches which are bound together and thrown in the fire.

This position between two eras, between resurrection and return, between baptism and death, characterizes all of a Christian's life. It means both suffering and joy of a kind that the world does not know. "For just as the sufferings of Christ flow over into our lives, so also through Christ our comfort overflows" (2 Cor 1:5). New waves of persecution come continually upon the Church from the surrounding world, but from Christ's kingdom-to-come flow just as unceasingly streams of that joy, which fills the eternal songs of praise before the throne of God. Thus the Church boasts of her sufferings, too. In hope she rejoices in unspeakable and glorious joy. Already here in their poverty, the disciples own what many prophets and righteous men desired to see and yet never got to see. The Lord of the Church gives that peace which the world cannot give and that joy which no one can take from her. Already on earth in the midst of persecutions, the disciples receive a hundredfold more than they have given up, "having nothing and yet possessing everything" (2 Cor 6:10). They live in the world of sin, death and suffering, and at the same time in the world of the resurrection and of joy.

Therefore the Church must remain an enigma in the world, eliciting questioning or hatred from the world. Obviously, the Church stands in the midst of the world. But the world sees only as much of her as can be robed in the guise of the old era. It sees a crowd of people with many faults and failings. It sees some old church edifices, to which it might credit some value in the history of the arts. It sees some strange sacraments, the insignificant external forms of which in no way seem to motivate the Church's reverence for them. Finally it sees the holy scriptures and hears the proclamation without understanding why *this* book is supposed to be the Book of books and *this* speech is supposed to be heard anew every Sunday. Precisely that which makes the church the Church, the risen Lord, who here admits people into His kingdom, is and remains hidden to unbelief. The Church is thus both visible and invisible. One may perceive her with both eyes and ears, and yet one can with seeing eyes see nothing and with hearing ears hear nothing. It must be this way, since the Church belongs both to this era and the era to come.

This double position also explains why there always has been and always will be a tension between the Church and the world, that is to say between church and state, between church and politics, between church and science. Although there is really no need for antagonism here, because the Church is no competitor or enemy either to the state, politics, or science. They each have their clearly defined tasks, given to them by God. The conflict arises, because this world so often neither is nor desires to be subject to God. The world which does not know God cannot acknowledge His Church. However, there is a definite distinction between different kind of people. God is active everywhere, also among those who do not believe. In nature and in his conscience, in art and society, again and again man encounters God, who is active in a thousand hidden ways in nature and in history. He creates and builds up, He grants power and reason and concepts of justice, even where people do not know the gospel or do not believe in it. All this occurs within the frame of the old era. It occurs in the homes and in society, through parental responsibility and patriotism, through organizational ability and social reforms, through respect for justice, and the search for truth. Since all human beings are created by God and no one ever can make himself independent of Him, this work of God occurs everywhere on earth, both among the heathen and the Christians, both among atheists and believers. But since Evil too is a real spiritual power, which everywhere and at all times fights against God, there is also a demonic element in all cultures and during all epochs that distorts and destroys God's work.

Therefore, every human being faces even in his civic life the two powers that ultimately define our existence: God and Satan. Already in his home and at work, in his studies and in his love life, in his business activities and his social duties, each human being must take a position for or against God. There are therefore two different kinds of people among those who do not believe. There are those of whom Jesus says they "are of the truth" or "do the truth." But there are also those who "suppress the truth by their wickedness," who "do not stand in the truth" but "do what is evil." About the former kind of people Jesus has said that they come to the light. But the latter belong to those who hate the light and who do not come to the light lest their deeds should be exposed. The former kind of people usually meets the church with respect. Even if they do not understand her message, they let the gospel stand for what it does, and sooner or later many of them will have their eyes opened for what the Church proclaims. On the other hand people of the latter kind are instinctive and hateful enemies of the church. They experience her mere existence as a challenge and accusation. They are the armor-bearers of the old era. Their thinking and will are totally ruled by the spiritual powers of this world. Their hatred for the church is therefore not defined by logical reason or rational deliberation. Again and again it has happened in history that political leaders have wasted their strength in a struggle against the church, which in no way was motivated by realistic politics. Ever since emperor Nero's persecution of the Christians and to the struggle against the church that is now going on in many countries, this attack has been based on the most fantastic lies and distortions. This fact is one of the many strange phenomena in the history of the church, which show that we here are dealing with irrational factors, or better expressed: with eternal spiritual powers that enlist people forcing them to use means, which they themselves could not have come up with.

In the final account, all these enigmas are to be understood in the realization that the Church is a stranger in the world, both revealing God's judgment upon everything in which the fallen world prides itself, and also offering to everyone God's gift of salvation through a Messiah, who to the world is foolishness and a stumbling block. The old era cannot accept judgment upon itself. The Church will therefore always remain a badly-tolerated stranger in the world.

It is obvious that the biblical thoughts concerning the new era are hard to comprehend for a modern human being. Maybe it is even more correct to state that they are totally incomprehensible not only for a modern human being but just as much for any human being in any previous epoch, *unless she is in touch with the realities concerning the Church.* This is because the "incomprehensible" in these thoughts are not on the intellectual plane. It is in the real nature of things. They are inaccessible in the same way as music is inaccessible to the tone-deaf or poetry to the hopeless prosaic. The common secular reason with all its worldly experience, limited to the old era, can never grasp the realities concerning the Church. The Bible describes a person who remains within the frame of this era in this way, "The natural man does not receive the gifts of the Spirit of God, for they are folly to him, and he is not able to understand them" (1 Cor 2:14). It is only the contact with the Spirit of God that enables man to understand the Church. In other words: only that person who himself is open to the new era and its saving powers can understand this new reality. The Church is therefore "a sign that will be spoken against," just as Jesus Himself was. They are both bearers of the same secret: the presence of the kingdom of God in the midst of a fallen world. The Church proclaims the same message as her Lord: The time is fulfilled, and the kingdom of God is at hand; repent, and believe in the gospel. Just as her Lord, she is a rock, causing men either to fall or to rise.

* * *

We have now examined the biblical foundation. Maybe it has surprised us that Scripture has so much to say about the Church. Maybe we have come to realize that so far we have only known some remains of the biblical concept of the Church. Maybe we now are in a state of wondering inquiry contemplating this whole world that has opened up for us.

In any case, we need to immerse ourselves daily in the world of the Word. We need to enter into the biblical conceptions. We need to meditate on them, pray about them, attempting to personally absorb them as people seeking salvation. We need to do this without worrying about how these biblical realities may be accepted or not accepted by others in church and society. We need more devotedly to live in the Holy Communion of the Lord's Supper. We need to be more sincerely aware of our baptism. We need courageously to fulfill the social consequences of the truth concerning the great fellowship between all the baptized in the body of Christ. To the extent that we live in the Church and of the Church, to the same extent the biblical concept of the Church will become clear to us in all its depth and overwhelming richness.

Chapter 3

Una Sancta

> We believe in the Holy Spirit,
> the holy, catholic church . . .

At every Swedish high mass, the same creed is repeated, as it has sounded across the earth ever since the days when the cæsars still ruled on the Palatine and small groups of Christians wandered through Porto Appia on their way to mass in the catacombs.

At the great festivals the Nicene Creed is often used, which since the 300s has been a banner for Christendom and which today is universally the most accepted of all confessional documents. In this creed, the church is called One, Holy, Catholic, and Apostolic.

These words are the summary of all that the Christian church has experienced of her own essence. They make up the completed building, raised on the biblical foundation. First it took about a century before the church gave indications even to the outsiders about her style and rising, which in due time would make her a global venture of unique magnificence. Then it took another two centuries before this building of the church's creed could be said to be completed. Each new generation has ever since expanded it and worked on the details. Each epoch has contributed with something from its own experience towards the shaping of the creed and even more towards the shaping of other means by which the church expresses herself in liturgy, through the arts, and in study and teaching. Some of these contributions did not survive the test of time. Other things were forgotten but were discovered anew centuries later, lending much blessing once again. Each epoch and each people have had their favorite places under the church's wide arches. However, in the midst of this confusing diversity and this overwhelming richness, the church preserves her essence: One, Holy, Catholic, and Apostolic.

This confession stands firm even in times of division and decay. The very words Una Sancta, the One and Holy, have become a rallying sign for all those forces which in our time try to lift the church out of division and unholiness. These words signify what she *has* been, what she *ought* to be, and what she *could* be. The more reality seems to contradict them, the more necessary it is that we recognize their original meaning, letting them impact us with the full power of their content. We shall therefore now devote a chapter to these words, attempting to interpret something of that which is embodied in the confession of the early church about her own essence.

COMPLETELY UNITED INTO ONE

"He might reconcile both of them to God in one body." Thus the Letter to the Ephesians (2:16) describes the two parts of the human race, the Jews and the Gentiles, once divided in enmity and separated by an insurmountable wall. This wall was broken down, when Christ offered himself on Golgotha. Jews and Gentiles are now under the same judgment. And both are included in the same reconciliation. Both are called to be members in the same body, Christ's holy Church.

This is the foundation for the church's unity: the connection with the same Savior in the same mystic fellowship, participation in the same reconciling sacrifice, which is received in *one* faith, conveyed through *one* baptism (Eph 4:5), and comprehended in *one* bread (1 Cor 10:17). This mystic fellowship of all Christ's followers is something far more than any human community of common interests. It emanates from God himself: it is He who does the binding together, when He, in inconceivable love, with the inexhaustible gifts of His grace, lowers Himself to everyone who believes, making them all into one. The unity is a great fellowship in the same forgiveness. All the threads in that variegated web of the church through the centuries come from the same mystery of the reconciliation. The life-giving warmth in the Church's fellowship comes from the source of existence, from the invisible heart of the universe, which is Christ himself, the Redeemer who takes away the sins of the world.

The unity of the Church is thus primarily a life-fellowship of the Spirit in the Body of Christ, something that cannot be measured and weighed but which belongs in the invisible world of those born anew. However, it was just as evident in the mind of the early church that this fellowship was visible as well. It must appear and take the form of a community in the world. The church of the New Testament is not invisible. She has of course her invisible parts: the heavenly King and the spirits of the departed, all that Jerusalem which is above. But on earth, she is always visible, appearing clearly and palpably with her apostles, prophets and teachers, her bishops, her presbyters and deacons in addition to the whole multitude of the baptized, gathered around the Word and the sacraments.

This visible church is by necessity *one*. Her unity follows from all that the Bible has to say about her.

The church is the true Israel. If a people split up in enmity, rallying under separate banners and beginning to speak different languages, it is no longer a people. This holds true also about the people of God.

The body is *one*. Severed members die. A mutilated body will bleed to death. This applies also to the church.

The kingdom of God is *one*. The new era is not divided and does not contain any conflicting wills. The same goes for the church, the fore-court on earth of the new era.

Jesus has therefore given an explicit admonition concerning His church's unity: Have salt in yourselves, and be at peace with one another (Mark 9:50)! He prayed for that unity even in the night when He was betrayed. He thought of all those who would become the church's children, and He prayed that they may "be brought to complete unity *to let the world know that You sent Me*" (John 17:23).

This unity was for the early church a holy duty. It was not easy to carry into effect. The differences in ways of thinking, traditions, and natural interests were so great that it no doubt would have blasted apart any human organization. The distance during the first century AD between a Jewish Christian in Jerusalem and a Greek slave in Corinth, who was a new convert to Christianity, was certainly greater than the distance today between a Pentecostal Christian and a Roman Catholic. But in spite of these significant differences, unity was maintained. It rested on a holy obligation.

The split within contemporary Christendom seems therefore all the more severe. It is nothing less than a sin, and a sin of the most fateful kind, a breach of the very own body of Christ. If the apostles were among us today, they would be shocked to see this split manifested in a typical

Swedish town. They would accuse us of having cut asunder Christ's holy body.

They themselves had been dealing with the same danger. When Paul wrote his first letter to the Corinthians, splitting up in sects was already well advanced. But he only had to ask them *"Is Christ divided?"* (1 Cor 1:13) to make obvious the total absurdity and culpability of such division. Is Christ divided? Facing that question was enough for the splitting forces to unite again. Either unity in Christ or no Christianity at all. That was the alternative.

The terrible conclusion today is that a divided church is not a true church any longer, at any rate not a sound and vigorous church. Acknowledging the Bible's view of the church, all of Christendom is today called to confess this sin of division. No one should justify the current situation saying that even the Bible speaks about "churches" (Gr. ekklesiai), because, as we have seen, they are just congregations representing the one indivisible church each in its own location. For the first generation of Christians it is absolutely unthinkable that we could have several "churches" in the same place. They might have been able to conceive of "the Church in Sweden," "the Church in Denmark," "the Church in England," and so forth, provided that there would be true concord between them, expressed in altar fellowship and as need be in joint appearances, e. g. through their bishops meeting together. In fact, such a situation would be acceptably close to the apostolic church in the New Testament. But that there are a number of Christian communities in the same town, each with their administration of the sacraments, with teachings opposing one another, and with mutual condemnation competing for the souls, that stands in irreconcilable contrast to everything that the New Testament has to say about unity in the body of Christ.

Once the biblical vision has taken hold of us, the full reunification of Christianity must stand forth for us as a demand from God and as a Christian duty. As long as we are divided, the body of Christ is bleeding, and we do not know when it will bleed to death. We must ask God to forgive our egoism on part of our own "church." We must pray that at least we should not be guilty of causing more division, so that the body of Christ would not be more broken than it already is. We must also pray God to overcome our weak faith and make us obedient toward any possibility for promoting the unity of the church.

* * *

How could we have become so divided? It is a tale full of painful humiliation, but it has to be recapitulated. Once again we shall look to the past.

The genesis of the Christian church is a miracle, constantly filling you with new amazement. When the apostles were about to begin their mission, they owned no resources whatsoever, humanly speaking. They owned only their office, that is the commission to convert a world of die-hard Jews, to whom Jesus was a convicted deceiver, of arrogant and superior Greeks, to whom the message of the cross and the resurrection was the height of foolishness, and of anti-Semitic Romans, who spat at everything that came from the despised Judea. The fact that the apostles at all took on this preposterous enterprise proves, more clearly than anything else, that they had faced in the resurrection of Jesus a miracle so obvious and so overwhelmingly great that it would have been an even greater mania to try to deny it and thus defy God Himself. Their being successful in building the church is the strongest proof that they were driven, not by hallucinations and imaginations, but by the living God, who Himself had intervened in history through Jesus Christ.

The difficulties did not diminish as the work of the apostles went on. For one thing, there was no defined doctrine. Through preaching and teaching, it was up to the apostles to define the significance of Jesus' death on the cross and of His resurrection. The relationship of Christians to the temple and to the law, to paganism and government authority, had to be regulated. Orders for worship and for the sacraments of Holy Baptism and Holy Communion must be formed. The offices of the church, church discipline, celebration of festivals, and indeed the whole area of caring for the needs of the church members, especially widows and orphans, must be organized. All this had to be done in an immense territory, throughout which the apostles were dispersed, and where Christians soon were to be found in all of the Near East, even beyond the borders of the Roman Empire, on the highlands of Asia Minor, and in the cities of Greece and Italy. In spite of persecutions and martyrdom, and of differences in language and national character in this diversified crowd of Syrians and Egyptians, of Greeks and Romans, a unified church came into being during a span of approximately one hundred years. However, there was no firmly-established order within the congregations: for various cases, one had to fall back on the provisions of the apostles, as long as they were still with them. Thereafter, one followed their authorized successors and other leaders, such as "prophets" and "teachers." To begin with, there was no defined creed, and except for the Old Testament no holy scriptures. What they did have was the orally received teaching of the apostles and also a few writings from apostles. There was no firm liturgy. Elements from the synagogue were used, such as lessons from the prophetic writings of the Old Testament and prayers from the Psalms, to which these first Christians added their own hymns and prayers.

This situation was not ideal. Rather, it was a distress with which one had to struggle as well as one could and which one was striving at overcoming. It was not a given that one would succeed in that struggle. After all, the church lived in the midst of pagan syncretism and gnosticism and had to deal with the threat of gnosticism within her own ranks. Time and again the small Christian congregations were almost drowned in the deluge of popular pagan religion that flooded the Roman Empire those days. Already in his Letter to the Colossians we see how Paul musters all his convincing eloquence and passion to battle false teachers. The latter were most dangerous when they appeared in Christian disguise, referring to Jesus or to the guidance of the Spirit.

The church was able to ride out the tempest. She did it because she lived in the Spirit. Under the guidance of the Spirit, a great consolidation of the church took place. She adopted the basic features that she would always keep. The teaching of the apostles was codified by their faithful successors into the canonical scriptures: *the church got her Bible*. The apostolic faith was defined in short phrases: *the church got her creed*. The church workers, endorsed in the congregations by the apostles, were consolidated with defined duties: *the church got her vocations*. Already toward the middle of the second century, the result of this development was quite obvious. What the apostles had begun in doctrine, in church order and in ritual ripened and bore fruit. All the many impulses, which had come from men as different as Peter, Paul, John and James, and which had been realized in different cultural and ethnic environments, had been melted together by the Spirit into a richly modulated and yet harmonious creation: the one and holy Church throughout the world.

The bishops meeting together soon became a visible proof of the unity of the church. They came from ever larger regions, until finally, following the end of the persecutions, the first general (ecumenical) meeting could convene in Nicæa in 325 AD. It was a great triumphant event of the One Church in the world. Totally lacking other means of power than those provided by the Spirit, she had emerged strong and unified under the leadership of her bishops.

It is not easy for us fully to appreciate the significance of this unity. One could travel from Spain along all the coast of the Mediterranean Sea and deeply into Arabia or up on the mountains of Armenia, and wherever one came or wherever one landed, one could enter churches, partake of the Lord's Supper and experience as a wonderful truth the words in the "ambrosian doxology," included in our Te Deum: *"Throughout the world the holy Church acclaims you."*

The blessing of this great fellowship reached to the outposts of civilization. It created an enriching interaction and a continuous exchange between the most remote provinces in the Roman Empire. As late as in the seventh century, the archbishop residing in Canterbury was a Greek, a native of Tarsus (Paul's hometown!) and educated in Athens - a man who made Greek culture a living influence in England's flourishing church life during the first centuries of the Middle Ages. The blessing of the church's wide-embracing fellowship can hardly be illustrated more beautifully.

And yet: there was already in Nicæa a subject of contention that later on would render the church apart. To be sure, there had been controversial matters right from the outset, which were not always settled in the Spirit of Christ. More than once, one did not live up to the unity which for the apostles had been a holy obligation. Every so often divisions occurred. Some of those disappeared by themselves. Others remained as insignificant minorities. Yet others developed into independent national churches, often in remote areas far beyond the border of the Roman Empire. Even so the great mother church steadily continued to grow. She lasted for more than eight centuries. Therefore, the final split, first time revealed in 867 and hopelessly completed in 1054, seems all the more tragic and harrowing . How it came to that point is a long story, which is not easy to judge impartially.

The large congregation in Rome had come to play a leading role in the church already toward the end of the second century. For one thing: Rome was the ruler of the world. Already its name had a ring of power and glory, which never since has been due any city on earth. Here was the largest Christian congregation in the empire, the only one in the western part of the church founded by an apostle. Here both Peter and Paul were buried, here several of the most prominent of the early church leaders, among them Ignatius and Justin, had died as martyrs. Rome had been the firm bulwark in the struggle against false doctrine. The first creed had originated here, and here the holy scriptures had been brought together. And from here, aid was given to fellow Christians elsewhere in times of persecutions and other calamities.

The authority that originally belonged to the *city* of Rome and the congregation there, the *bishop* of Rome began to claim for his office toward the end of the second century.

These claims were at first rejected almost unanimously, because they had no support in the church's old traditions. One was willing to acknowledge that the Bishop of Rome was *primus inter pares*, the foremost among equals, but not that he had jurisdiction and teaching authority over the church. Leading churchmen, provincial synods, and general synods have spoken clearly enough on this matter. It was generally acknowledged that the apostles had received their authority from Christ and that the bishops were their legitimate successors. But unknown in the early church were the ideas that Peter had authority as the church's absolute leader or that the Roman bishops would have been his successors with the same authority. Just as easy as it was for the bishops to be acknowledged as the church's leaders, just as difficult was it for the pope to enforce his claims. In the eastern part of the church, there was never any talk of accepting them. These claims were indeed gradually accepted in the western part of the church due to some very able popes, to special political circumstances, and even due to some falsified documents, which during the Middle Ages played a fateful role in the development of the papacy. Especially the pseudo-isidorian decretals (produced in the nineth century) have dominated the understanding in the West up to the Reformation, giving the papacy an appearance of being anchored in the church's early history, just as the Roman-Catholic Church even today is dominated by the basic beliefs that these decretals created.

When pope *Nikolaus I* (858–867) showed that he was fully determined to apply these claims also on the church in the East, a schism was unavoidable. Besides the matter of the primacy, a number of smaller issues had arisen. The most important was the one concerning the noted addition of *filioque* ("and of the Son"), which the church in the West had made in the Nicene Creed. As to the facts, Rome was in the right, but not formally, since no part of the church can make additions on its own to an Ecumenical Creed. Loyalty to the brethren in the East would have demanded that this issue should have been decided at an Ecumenical Synod. As late as in the beginning of the ninth century, the pope acknowledged this without reservations, displaying silver plaques with the unchanged version in his own church. This issue, which during centuries has taken on senseless proportions, would never have led to such fateful consequences, if it had not been coupled up with the power struggle between the pope in Rome and the patriarch of Constantinople. Both parties must be blamed. Neither of them displayed a determined will to keep the unity of the church. Thus the definitive division of the church became a fact in 1054.

Attempts have been made ever since to bring about reconciliation. However, they have resulted only in occasional progress The issue of *filioque* has diminished in importance. The difference between the two positions could be settled already on the basis of Greek theology in the eighth century. Thus it shows that it is more a matter of different expressions and terms than a real difference of faith. The pope's claims for primacy remain to this day the real dividing wall.

For all of Christendom the great schism has caused immeasurable harm. With deep pain, we have experienced that no isolated part of the church will ever be able to benefit from the whole richness of the Church's life.

In the East the consequences soon became obvious. Its theology soon lost all contact with the West, all fruitful cooperation was excluded. Orthodox piety cultivated more and more its unique features, the mystic intimacy and the joyful liturgy. It has yet much to teach us in the West. Simultaneously though, the church of the East stagnated and in many regions even glided into rigidity and death.

Externally, the schism was a disaster. Constantinople stood alone against the onslaught of Islam. When the crusaders came, they did not come as brethren in the faith but as conquerors, robber-knights and oppressors. The brief decades when the crusaders ruled in Greece was enough to sow the seeds there for a deep-rooted hatred against everything Latin, and this hatred rendered futile all later attempts for unity. The result of this hatred for the West caused the fall of Constantinople. Half of Christendom was laid under the rule of Islam, either liable to extinction or martyrdom for centuries. It is perhaps the most severe judgment that the God of history has imposed upon us.

To the West the schism was hardly less fateful. Severed from the Christian metropolises of the East, there was no power in the West that could compete with Rome. Thus one church province after the other was laid under the jurisdiction of the Bishop of Rome. Consequently, all such initiatives were stifled that marked the first centuries of the church, when there was freedom to adjust to new peoples and new languages. The Latin language and the Roman liturgy were to be used everywhere. The papal church's many peculiarities were introduced during the course of the centuries: the chalice was withheld from the laity at communion, and clergy marriages were forbidden, both novelties in obvious conflict with the orders of the Bible and of the church thus far. In the conviction about its right to create new doctrines, Rome has continued to do exactly that and therefore distanced itself more and more from the state of affairs in the undivided church. Some of Rome's new doctrines, adopted in the past one hundred years, may be the greatest obstacles toward a reunification of the divided church. Without any desire to judge in this matter, where no one is without fault, one cannot easily avoid the reflection, that the pope's claim for absolute supremacy over Christ's church is the foremost cause to the distress, from which we all suffer today.

There is streak of tragedy in the history of the papacy during the Middle Ages. Yet it must be acknowledged that the Roman Church in a world of barbarism promoted righteousness, mercy, peace and education. The medieval church was full of brilliant personalities, and she was able to create a homogeneous basis for the whole culture, a harmonious total view of life, which we today bitterly lack. But the tragedy was that the papacy in the final account was forced to view everything as a matter of politics and to make everything economically profitable in order to be successful in the struggle for power. Thus the falsifications, the inquisition, the persecutions of heretics, the sale of indulgences, and the anti-popes forced themselves upon the church.

The end was a disaster. The church fell into decay. The attempts from the bishops to reform her through the great reform councils were not endorsed by the popes, who in their turn lacked the ability to restore the spiritual life in the church, whose chief shepherds they claimed to be.

So it came to the point where *the Reformation* became a necessity, which emerged from the ranks of the clergy but also from the laity. We cannot sufficiently regret that the majority of the bishops did not understand what was happening. The church had thus to be restored in opposition to those who held the positions of leadership in the church. That would prove to be fateful.

The reformers themselves had no intentions whatsoever to break away from the old church. On the contrary: they were her children, they felt total loyalty to her, they only desired that the Church would restore the central place in her life to the gospel message of unmerited grace. Luther always maintained that he had never violated "the pure and catholic faith." He said that "it is dangerous and terrible to hear or believe anything contrary to the whole united testimony of the holy Christian church . . . which from the beginning, now during more than 1500 years, has been proclaimed in the whole world" (Elert, Werner. *Morphologie des Luthertums*. München, 1931, page 241). It was precisely the power of this faith and the respect for that Word which the church had put in his hands that forced him to oppose the abuses. It was love for the Church that necessitated a reform of the church at that time. When the pope reacted by pronouncing the ban of the church upon Luther, the split became a bitter necessity. But Luther maintained that "we stayed with the right old Church, indeed, *we are the right old Church*" (Elert, page 250).

The Augsburg Confession says the same in the conclusion of the first section, immediately following Article XXI, "This is about the sum of our teaching. As can be seen, there is nothing here that departs from the Scriptures or the catholic church or the church of Rome, in so far as the ancient church is known to us from its writers (the Fathers). . . . The whole dissension is concerned with a certain few abuses which have crept into the churches . . . Because these could not be approved with a good conscience, they have to some extent been corrected." This is again underscored in the introduction to the second section of this confession, "Our churches dissent from the catholic church in no article of faith but only omit a few abuses which are new and contrary to the canons."

What the Augsburg Confession so strongly points out is something very characteristic for the Lutheran Reformation, something to take notice of at the reading of its confessional documents. The given foundation is the old church, her teachings and her orders. *The abuses* were to be eliminated, not the church herself. The essential, righteousness through faith, should be upheld in its rightful place. Everything that obscured it should be removed. But all this could and should take place within the life and framework of the old church.

Luther chose here a different way from Zwingli and Calvin. He accepted the legacy of the church. He did not break with the past unless the Word of God prompted him to do so. Much of the spiritual richness that the church had stored up during the centuries was thus preserved. We were privileged in that we got to keep the ancient worship forms, the church year, the sacred music, and the sanctuaries with their altars and time-honored pieces of art. It was kept to serve the proclamation of the Word, to the extent that it was in harmony with the spirit of the gospel.

The Reformed adopted instead a very exclusive strategy. From the legacy of the church, they accepted only the Bible. According to its prescriptions, the church was to be rebuilt from the foundation. However, since the New Testament does not have any uniform order for the organization of congregations, one could not avoid a number of arbitrary and free constructions. Thus the break with the past became deeper than in the Lutheran Reformation. The result was an emancipation not only from Rome but from the ancient church as well.

Thus the Reformation did not lead to the restoration of a unified Church. There were only sporadic connections with the church in the East. Tentative attempts toward a rapprochement were not successful. Subsequent centuries were a time of division and sectarianism without precedent in church history.

Only in our time have we begun to see the dawn of a new day for Christ's divided church. The means of worldwide communication now available have pulled nations and churches out of their isolation. The division is therefore all the more humbling and painful. Especially those churches of the reformation, which are closest to the ancient church and which have preserved most of her legacy and spirit, are bound to experience the division as an accusation. If the gist of the Reformation was to arouse the church to eliminate the errors of the papacy, it ought to have been a simple consequence and a natural continuation thereof to seek reconciliation and re-unification with the church in the East, which a thousand years ago was severed from the fellowship with the Western church. The great sin that tore the body of Christ must be remedied. It is a promising sign that the situation is becoming a burning issue in the hearts of more and more Christians. Not at least the churches in Sweden and England have become instrumental toward the goal of reconciliation between the eastern and western branches of the Church.

Yet, the ecumenical idea needs to be a matter of conscience for the deep majority of church members everywhere in Christendom, not only for some church leaders. Church unity is something so essential for her essence and for her sound life, that no Christian may be indifferent to the division. It is and remains a sin which must be remedied and overcome by all of us, even if it would require centuries of struggle to accomplish.

Especially the suffering and persecutions of Christians during the past twenty years have caused a new and burning longing for unity in evermore widening circles. Even where confessional disagreements raise insurmountable walls between Christian brethren in the same country, thousands and again thousands invisible hands join before God's throne, lifted in one and the same prayer: the prayer for the re-unification of all Christians in one holy catholic Church. A cry of anguish emerges from many hearts: Why is it that the body of Christ must bleed because of us?

We shall conclude with such a cry for repentance. It comes out of the Evangelical Church in Germany. It has forced itself upon this church under the pressure of the events during the past few years, which to so many have revealed the absurd and contradictory in a situation where the church wants to be *true* and yet is *divided*:

> All confessions without exception have laid upon themselves a horrible guilt by embodying such an untruth in the name of the truth! After all, Christ has bound the truth to unity! There is no truth outside unity, at least no truth with authority and power! Not a truth that has the power to glorify and grant likeness with God. Everything depends on that matter alone. Read once again the verses at the conclusion of chapter 17 in John. They contain no less than the testament of Christ. Here two things are tied together: the concord between the disciples and their confidence in Jesus' own mission, and this with absolute validity. I am convinced that the situation will become even worse for us, if there will not be a complete turn-around regarding these two things: a conversion of all Christendom. Now the call must be issued: back to Oneness, back to Wholeness! Beyond the confessions: back to the undivided Christ... We must begin to learn once again to regard small things as small and great things as great. Let us consider all of church history. It then becomes obvious that each split in the history of the Church in spite of its seeming necessity in the final account bears the mark of a curse. A curse is hovering over the free church that loosed itself from the national church. A curse is hovering over the protestant churches, which loosed themselves from the Catholic

> Church. And a curse is hovering over the Roman church, which loosed itself from the Greek church. The end of it all can only be nihilism and anarchy. We cannot continue even one step further on that road. Now there is only one way that we must choose: a radical change of direction, a total change of heart! (Schütz, Paul. *Warum ich noch ein Christ bin*. Berlin, 1937. Pages 122–123.)

As an echo emanating from the same pain but from another side of the dividing wall, we may add some thoughts from a Russian author:

> A division is always a division, and it would never come about unless love has been driven out and hatred and indifference have taken its place. We Christians must everywhere at last acknowledge the fact that the One Holy Catholic and Apostolic Church has been divided through the sin of her earthly members and that just as God once allowed sinful people to crucify the Lord of glory, his only begotten Son, he has also allowed the Church's members to divide and torture Christ's living body in this world ... Acknowledging this means a radical realization of the necessity for repentance. What is needed is a conversion of the heart leading to a readiness and a willingness to begin a new life. (Nicolas Zernow in *The Church of God*, ed. E. L. Mascall. Oxford, 1934. Page 223.)

HE WHO SANCTIFIES AND THOSE WHO ARE SANCTIFIED

A serious issue is embodied in the words: a *holy* church. We have already been reminded of it. This church which is supposed to be *one* but due to our sin is divided, where opinion stands against opinion, and party against party, can she really be *holy*? Was she even holy when she still was united? If so, how could she ever have been divided?

This is an issue already in the church of the New Testament. The first Christians did call themselves *"the saints (the holy ones)."* And yet sin was a grim reality among them.

When Paul writes to the congregation in Corinth, he begins by calling them "those sanctified in Christ Jesus, called to be holy" (1 Cor 1:2). Yet in the same letter the apostle says about the Corinthians that there are divisions among them, they live in jealousy and strife, brother goes to court against brother, they indulge in immorality, they "wrong and defraud ... even /their/ own brethren" (1 Cor 6:8), their worship gatherings are disorderly, and the Lord's Supper is celebrated in an unworthy manner. Indeed, Corinth seems to have been one of Paul's most problematic congregations. Nevertheless, although these children of his are causing him so much sorrow, he calls them *"the saints (the holy ones)"* and includes them without any hesitation whatsoever in the *holy* church, with one exception to which we soon shall return.

How is this possible?

Already from this one letter we can get the explanation and thus a rather clear picture of what early Christianity meant with the holiness of the church. To begin with: the Corinthians are baptized, thus made members of the body of Christ (1 Cor 12:13). But one who is just baptized is still "a babe in Christ" (1 Cor. 3:1). Only gradually he will grow and become a "spiritual human being" (3:1). Catechization must be adapted accordingly. "I gave you milk, not solid food, for you were not yet ready for it" (3:2). Thus a process of spiritual growth remained. However, the decisive thing had occurred: in baptism the Corinthians had been connected with Christ, in His church they would be nourished by the spiritual life forces. The problem in Corinth was that there was no spiritual growth in many of the newly baptized. They were "still of the flesh" (3:3) and they were full of bad habits. But even so, the covenant of baptism remains. He who once became a member of the body of Christ will not so easily be severed from it. Even if he goes to a prostitute, it is the members of Christ that he dishonors by making them the members of a prostitute (1 Cor 6:15). His body is not his own, it belongs to God (6:19). "You were bought with a price. So glorify God in your body "(6:20).

The holiness of the Church rests on this fact: *You were bought with a price.* You are God's own, consecrated for God. *The Church's holiness is God's holiness,* not the people's. It is given from heaven. It cannot be gained on earth.

No one is holy but God alone. Nobody but God can sanctify anything, that is, grant it participation in His holiness. That was so already in the Old Testament. Those things were called holy which according to God's command had been set apart for His service: the temple, the altar, the priest.

But all this was only "a copy and shadow" (Heb 8:5), an expression of man's infinite need for atonement, a tangible preparation of that redemption which God in due time would accomplish when He sanctified His Son and sent Him into the world (John 10:36). Then God's holiness descended to the earth. The holy one was born in human form (Luke

1:35). A few noticed it and confessed, "We believe and know that you are the Holy One of God" (John 6:69). But most rejected him. They shied away from God's holiness.

Jesus knew that it would be so. That's why He says the night before His suffering, "For their sake I *sanctify* myself, that they also may be *sanctified* in truth" (John 17:19). And so, "at the right time Christ died for the ungodly" (Rom. 5:6). Jesus suffered "in order to sanctify the people through His own blood" (Heb 13:12). "By a single offering He has perfected for all time those who are sanctified" (Heb 10:14).

These are some of the words, with which Scripture interprets God's greatest miracle, the victory for His holiness and His love. In the great sacrifice of the atonement, God found a way for his holiness to come to us unholy human beings.

Holiness is, ever since, a possibility, that can be a reality in the midst of sinners. After God had raised His "holy servant Jesus" (Acts 4:27), the same holy Spirit that was in Him is now given by virtue of his resurrection life, in fellowship with Him, on the basis of His atonement. Since the resurrection, the holy Church is on earth where the Holy Spirit comes to people bestowing participation of Christ's holy and heavenly life. Old Israel had its well of holiness in the temple and the altar therein. The new Israel is itself a temple, built around the Golgotha offering altar, of which is said, "We have an altar" (Heb 13:10), "Christ, our Passover lamb, has been sacrificed" (1 Cor 5:7), and Christ "gave Himself up for us as a fragrant offering and sacrifice to God" (Eph 5:2). Just as a reflection of the Lord's holiness shone above the Jerusalem temple, so His holiness fills the Church, who herself is "a holy temple in the Lord" (Eph 2:21). Anyone who enters this church will partake of its holiness, indeed himself become "a temple of the Holy Spirit" (1 Cor 6:19).

In the Church's great temple, Paul experiences himself as priest, himself covered with God's holiness, "in the priestly service of the gospel of God" (Rom 15:16). In gratitude he presents his congregations before the altar of God as "an offering acceptable to God, sanctified by the Holy Spirit" (Rom 15:16). Before the same altar he also presents himself. Facing his martyrdom he writes, "I am already on the point of being sacrificed" (2 Tim 4:6). "Even if I am being poured out like a drink offering on the sacrifice and service coming from your faith, I am glad and rejoice with all of you" (Phil 2:17).

All these expressions from the old temple service mirror the overwhelming sense of God's holy presence that filled the early church. Just as the pious Jew in trembling reverence approached the altar, the Christian lived in the blessed and overpowering certainty of always being surrounded by God's holiness, transferred into his holy life sphere by partaking of the Church's life.

All this holiness descends on the Church as a *gift* from God. It is given to the Church, because "Christ loved the Church and gave Himself up for her to make her holy, cleansing her by the washing with water (baptism) through the word, and to present her to Himself as a radiant Church, without stain or wrinkle or any other blemish, but holy and blameless" (Eph 5:25–27). By God's "doing you are in Christ Jesus, who became to us . . . sanctification" (1 Cor 1:30). To have been thus sanctified is the same as having been "justified in the name of the Lord Jesus Christ and in the Spirit of our God" (1 Cor 6:11), as having been lifted out of the realm of death and from the terrible connection with guilt and instead having been placed "in the heavenly realms in Christ Jesus" (Eph 2:6).

The church's holiness comes thus altogether from God. And this means that it is the same for all Christians. They are called "holy," because they are baptized and thus "share in a heavenly call" (Heb 3:1) as members of Christ's body. The whole truth about the holy Church is captured in the words we have chosen as heading for this chapter: "*He* who *sanctifies* and those who *are sanctified*" (Heb 2:11).

The church's holiness is thus not based on our lifestyle, nor can it be measured according to our moral standard. It rests on God's holy sacrifice in Christ. Since God always is present and acts in the gospel and the holy actions of the sacraments, the church is and remains holy in spite of the failings of her members. Thus the Augsburg Confession states (Article VII) that the church is "the assembly of saints in which *the gospel is taught purely and the sacraments are administered rightly.*" That is the criterion of her holiness. Therefore, Luther did not hesitate to acknowledge that the Roman church in the midst of her deep decay yet was a holy church: "Thus we, too, call the Roman church holy and all the offices of bishop holy, although both the bishops and their ungodly servants are misguided . . . Albeit she is worse than Sodom and Gomorrah, in the Roman church still remain *baptism, the Lord's Supper, the words and text of the gospel, the Holy Scripture, the offices, Christ's name, God's name.* The treasure is there. Therefore the Roman church is called holy." (Luther's *Great Commentary* on *Galatians* as quoted in Bishop Bengt Jonzon's *Herdabrev [Pastoral Letter]*, page 80, 1938.)

It is not correct to say that the church is Church only as long as she does the will of God, if one therewith maintains that the blameless life of the laity or the clergy would be thought of as a condition precedent for the Church's ability to act in behalf of God. Fortunately, that is not way it is. The Church is a covenant of grace, not a law treaty. God can go on giving, even when nobody cares to receive. Therefore, the church is Church as long as she has the means of *grace*, as long as her voice in the Word, be it only in the Scripture readings in the Divine Service, offers forgiveness in behalf of God, and as long as baptism and the Lord's Supper are administered according to God's institution. Even during the darkest centuries of the Middle Ages, God again and again nurtured living faith, which victoriously manifested itself in powerful movements of renewal within the church. Even in his monastery cell, buried under heaps of requirements as a monk, entangled in bad theology and perverted practice, Luther could encounter God's grace. He knew whom he should give credit for that: the Church which had baptized him in the name of the Triune God and subsequently put the Word in his hands. Also, let us never forget that Henric Schartau had his decisive encounter with God's judgment and grace when he participated in a celebration of Holy Communion that was preceded by a less than well conducted confession by an unworthy pastor. Thus the Holy Spirit is present and able to sanctify in the midst of human shortcomings and in a church being in a state of decay. This is no excuse for the sinner or for anyone who must share the guilt of the church's decay. But it is a consolation for him who sincerely desire to find God. He can be assured that the Lord is in His holy temple, coming to us in his word and sacraments. It is a deeply evangelical and comforting truth that our Augsburg Confession (Article VIII) points out with these words, "The sacraments and the word are effective, since they are based on the ordinance and command of Christ, even if they are administered by evil men."

We shall now be able to comprehend these words in the Apostles' Creed: *the communion of saints* (communio sanctorum). The words may be understood in different ways and were also expounded differently in the early church. One may take them to mean "the communion of all saints" in heaven and on earth, as many as have been granted participation in God's holiness: patriarchs and prophets, apostles and martyrs, revered saints and other faithful departed together with the whole heavenly host. We enter into this exalted communion when we are received into the Church, because she is both Church Militant and Church Triumphant. But the words can also mean the *fellowship* of the saints. Then the emphasis is on fellowship in the body of Christ, on the intimate state of belonging together which is shared by all Christians, known and unknown, living or dead. Finally the words can be rendered *partaking in the holy things*, that is the sacraments. In that meaning, too, they have been understood and expounded in the early church. They would then indicate from where the Christians receive their holiness, pointing to the greatest of the privileges that the Church offers.

All three renderings are possible and harmonize well with the basic view that we have summed up in the words: He sanctifies and we are sanctified. We may therefore think of any of these three nuances of meaning when we profess our faith with the words of Apostolicum.

We have thus seen why Paul without hesitation can call the Corinthians "holy" and at the same time passionately reprimand them for their terrible sins. Likewise he can still include the Galatians in the Church (Gal 1:2), and yet he tells them, "You are severed from Christ . . . You have fallen away from grace" (Gal 5:4). After all, they are baptized. They had been "running a good race" (Gal 5:7). So Paul is not giving up on them. The Church is the mother who continues to fight for the life of her children, be they degenerated and defiant. Yet, they are *her* children, and she cannot let them go. That passion and that struggle vibrate throughout Paul's letters.

* * *

What does this all mean to the Christian as an individual?

Through baptism he has been transferred into the realm of this holiness, *made holy* by the God, who "called us with a holy calling, not in virtue of our works but in virtue of His own purpose and the grace which he gave us in Christ Jesus" (2 Tim 1:9, cf. Titus 3:5). God has Himself stretched out His hand, touched me and made me his own.

This holy calling is the beginning and the foundation. Therefore Paul addresses the Christians as "beloved of God, called to be saints" (Rom 1:7) or "sanctified in Christ Jesus, called to be saints" (1 Cor 1:2), rather than "the converted and holy" or "the righteous and holy" or some other designation that would point to what man is or has accomplished. Our holiness is not our achievement, but is given to us by God who calls us through his gospel of unmerited forgiveness. One becomes holy in Christ Jesus, never outside of him (Phil 1:1).

In this new reality, God has made open to me infinite possibilities, which are my responsibility. Do I live worthily according to my calling "as is fitting among saints" (Eph 5:3). The obligations are obvious. "As God's chosen people" we must clothe ourselves with "compassion, kindness, humility, gentleness and patience" (Col 3:12).

In this new realm, where everything depends on Christ's atoning sacrifice, my own life must also be a living sacrifice (Rom 12:1). It is my own life, the indivisible wholeness of my own self and my will, which shall be the sacrifice that I day by day surrender as a gift to God.

First of all, it is a matter of not yielding our members to sin (Rom 6:13) but "to keep oneself unstained from the world" (Jas 1:27). This is the first and most evident consequence of belonging to the holy Church. "If anyone destroys God's temple, God will destroy him. For God's temple is holy, and that temple you are" (1 Cor 3:17).

But still something else follows from the Church's holiness. It is not difficult to compile a good many Bible passages which, in connection with the holy, speak about *love and service*, about "aid" and "needs" and "offering" and "work of ministry" (see Rom 12:13; 15:25; 1 Cor 16:15; 2 Cor 8:4; 9:1,12; Eph 1:15; 4:12; Col 1:4; Phlm 5; Hebr 6:10). This is no coincidence. Holy means set apart for God. Each Christian belongs to God through baptism and is a member of Christ's body. Therefore these words of Jesus are true in the most literal sense, "Whatever you did for one of the least of these brothers of mine, you did for me" (Matt 25:40). One cannot be connected with Christ and at the same not be indissolubly bound to one's fellow Christians in mutual responsibility. Bearing one another's burdens is thus fulfilling the law of Christ (Gal 6:2) and carrying into effect the solidarity between the members of the body. All the baptized make up a family created by God. The visible sign of this in the early church was the "holy kiss" that was exchanged in the liturgy (1 Cor 16:20), or the common cup in the Lord's Supper.

What happens if a church member does not lead a life worthy of his holy calling? If he ignores the needs of others and without remorse lives in obvious sin?

Paul had to deal with that situation in Corinth. He handles the matter bluntly and does not mince his words, "Do you not know that the wicked will not inherit the kingdom of God? Do not be deceived: Neither the immoral nor idolaters nor adulterers nor sexual perverts nor thieves nor the greedy nor drunkards nor slanderers nor swindlers will inherit the kingdom of God" (1 Cor 6:9–10). And yet, he won't regard the sinners as excommunicated. To be sure, they are in a crisis, an extremely severe crisis. God and Satan are battling for lordship, and indeed it seems as if evil would prevail. Paul makes it abundantly clear that if there will be no turn-around, the end will be disaster. But the crisis can still change direction for the spiritual health of the sinners and the well-being of the church in Corinth. The apostle warns and threatens, but he excommunicates no one from the church which alone can give cure and healing.

Paul uses tougher measures in only one case. It is concerning a man who has committed "immorality . . . of a kind that is not found even among the pagans" (1 Cor 5:1). Here Paul gives inexorable orders: he is to be removed from the church fellowship (5:2) and delivered "to Satan for the destruction of the flesh." Note the reason for this: "that his spirit may be saved in the day of our Lord Jesus" (5:5). Even for this man Paul is not excluding salvation in the final account. After all, he has been baptized. So in spite of everything, Paul thinks that God by punishing this sinful man in this life shall find a way to save him on the day of judgment.

Regarding other incidents with sinful behavior, Paul recommends that the church members for some time would avoid associating with the offenders (1 Cor 5:11; cf. Rom 16:17 and Eph 5:5). At least in some cases, they seem to have been excluded from the Lord's Supper. For all of them, one was hoping for repentance and reconciliation soon to take place (2 Cor 2:5–8; 2 Tim 2:25–26; cf. 2 Thess 3:14–15). However, there were some cases where there seemed to be no hope and where the offenders were regarded as definitely lost (Heb 6:4–6; 10:26, 1 John 5:16).

Later on, during the second century, a tendency toward understanding the whole gospel as a new law caused the church to deal more harshly with apostates, even to the point where they were denied the possibility of forgiveness. Finally though, following lengthy discussions and difficult antagonisms, the more evangelical approach was victorious, but not until early in the fourth century. It was then once for all determined that there is always forgiveness for a repenting Christian. The outcome of these first centuries of the church was that she got *the ban* and *the penance.* Through the ban (excommunication) the unworthy and the non-repenting can be excluded from the Church's fellowship, through the penance the repenting can be restored to the fellowship. Both remain to this very day.

The penance has many forms, maybe most often as an element of private confession. Even if this is the way that someone who was excommunicated is restored into church membership, it is by far more often the way any church member who is burdened by his sin will receive forgiveness and be restored to peace with God.

The ban is still used by the Roman church, the Orthodox church, and by some churches that are branches of the Reformed church. Other churches, such as the Anglican church and the Church of Sweden, retain it as a possibility but almost never use it. The major ban, which imposes total excommunication from the church, has not for centuries been used in our church. The minor ban may be used by any parish pastor, meaning that he can warn obviously un-repenting persons from partaking in the Lord's Supper and, if they yet approach the altar, to pass them by at the communion. However, even in that way it is probably never used except in special cases in the pastor's "care-of-souls" and then unnoticeably to others. There is hardly any use for the old church discipline in our time when Christians who desert the Christian faith in reality have "excommunicated themselves" (Brilioth, Yngve. *Svensk Kyrkokunskap [The Church in Sweden]*. Stockholm, 1933. Page 286) by staying away both from the Lord's Supper and indeed from all worship services. If they later on would return, it is an advantage in the "care-of-souls" and as a sign of love that the church door is welcomingly open. Acknowledging how much deep-rooted bitterness and unnecessary hardness of heart came about, when the ban all too often was issued in unwise zeal, one shall hardly regret the abrogation of it in our church. On the other hand, the church should not totally disregard the possibility of excluding a sinner who deliberately abuses his membership in the church to harm and prevent the proclamation of the gospel. Such a situation could happen (God forbid!), where the church must act because what is at stake is nothing less than the eternal well-being of her children.

* * *

Now it is time to conclude our considerations concerning the holiness of the Church. We have seen that one can love her with one's whole heart and yet have a watchful and keen eye for her faults. There is no inconsistency in praising her with a jubilant voice and yet criticizing the laxity and decadence in her actual appearance. What one thereby is praising is God's glory, which has descended on earth in the Church's message and holy acts. And God's glory remains here as long as the gospel is proclaimed and the sacraments are distributed. There is no sin in these means of God's grace; the sin is in us, in our deficient faith, in our immense ingratitude and in our selfish hearts.

One can be seized by deep despair when considering the state of many parishes in our church. One could be tempted to clean the membership rolls, brand at least the worst ingratitude, cut off the dry branches and cleanse God's church from all the obvious sinners, all the coarse despisers of God's grace and all the silent saboteurs, thus keeping only those who loyally participate in the church's life. However, such thoughts are revealed as human thoughts in the light of the great vision of the church as the body of Christ. After all, God has made us all mutually unified members of that body. Even the dead members must be dragged along. Love cannot give up on them as lost. Even the perfectly indifferent or haughty, even the consciously rebellious, they shall all be encircled by the warmth and the life that Christ's body gives to all members. And maybe for some of them, their breastplate of hardness and unbelief will then melt down. On judgment day, God will sift the wheat from the chaff. The church must wait until then. If she already here and now would be cleansed from the "hopeless" sinners, she would no longer be "the holy mother who embraces *the nations* in her bosom in order to *nurture* them for God's kingdom and no longer be the bride of Christ, under whose banner she battles the prince of this world for the souls of her children" (Bring, Ebbe Gustaf.*Kyrkans Uppgift [The Church's Mission]*, an article in Swensk Kyrkotidning 1856, page 61).

CHRISTIANUS MIHI NOMEN EST, CATHOLICUS COGNOMEN

The Christian church is catholic according to her essence, and she has always claimed to be that. The word appears at the beginning of the second century, but the concept is already in the New Testament writings. In the Apostles' Creed, the Nicene Creed, and the Athanasian Creed, the three creeds, which we have inherited from the early church, the Church is designated as catholic. The word *"allmännelig"* in our Swedish versions of the Creeds is an attempt to render the Greek "catholic." (Translator's remark: The reader can probably see that the Swedish word "all-männ-elig" literally means "all-men-ly," that is having all things for all men.) We want to hold on to the substance and the meaning of the word "catholic." Also the Church of Sweden asserts, as we shall see in the next chapter, her will to be catholic. It is quite natural that she makes that assertion. Otherwise she would have departed from the faith which is expressed in that creed which, of old, all Christians everywhere in the world unanimously have professed.

As we now proceed to take a closer look at the proper meaning of the word catholic, I ask the reader to remember that the word throughout this book is used in its original sense and never in the erroneous usage as Roman-Catholic. It is thus a total obstruction of the meaning to equate catholic and Roman. We shall now dare to expose anew the genuinely Christian and infinitely rich concept of the Church being catholic.

* * *

Around the year 100 of our Christian chronology, the church in Antioch was blessed with the leadership of Bishop Ignatius. As so many of the heroes and martyrs of the early church, he would also have fallen into oblivion, had not his tormentors brought him to Rome in order to have him thrown to the beasts in the arena for the enjoyment of the big city mob. Transporting the prisoner proved to be very time-consuming, which gave Ignatius the opportunity to meet with representatives of the congregations in Asia Minor. He gave counsel, encouragement and admonitions everywhere. From this activity of his, we have seven letters preserved, full of fatherly love, of glowing longing for martyrdom, and of the never ceasing zeal of a true pastor. These seven letters, written around the year 110, are something of the most vivid and captivating that has been preserved from the generation immediately succeeding the apostles.

It is in Ignatius's Letter to Smyrna (Chapter 8) that the words the *catholic church* emerge for the first time, abruptly and without explanations. It shows that this expression already was accepted, and that it signified something which was known to everybody. Ignatius deals here as he often does with the meaning of the offices in the church. He writes,

> "Be always obedient to your bishop, as Jesus Christ was obedient to the Father, and to the presbyters as to the apostles . . . No one should take action in church matters without the bishop's consent. Only that celebration of the Lord's Supper is right that takes place with the bishop presiding or the one he ordains. The authentic church fellowship for the laity is where the bishop is, just as *the catholic church is everywhere where Christ Jesus is.*"

At first sight this statement is surprising. But it expresses a unified and well thought-out view. The Church is where Christ is. Just as the bishop represents the congregation with all its functions and people, Christ includes in himself all that the Church has of various gifts. Therefore, the whole richness of the Church's essence is everywhere where Christ establishes a congregation, because He Himself is there. *The Church's catholic essence flows out of her fellowship with Christ.*

Catholic means "allmännelig," all-inclusive, spanning the whole, or maybe rather embracing the entirety. Which entirety?

Scripture gives the answer: God was pleased to have all His fullness dwell in Christ (Col 1:19). And He gave Christ to be head over all things, to the Church, which is His body, filled with His fullness (Eph 1:22–23), and in Him we have become partakers of that fullness (Col 2:10).

Since the Church is Christ's body, she possesses the richness of His fullness. This is the "entirety," the fullness that she embraces. Therefore she is catholic in her essence.

It was God's eternal counsel that in the fullness of time He would "bring all things in heaven and on earth together under one head, even Christ" (Eph 1:10). Being the vehicle for this all embracing salvation, the Church must reach out to all people everywhere and in all times to be what she truly is. And that is catholic.

One of the greatest teachers in the early church, Cyril of Jerusalem, explains in his Catechism (XVIII:23) what catholic means with these words:

> The Church is called catholic, because she is spread out *over the whole world*, to every corner of the earth; because she unceasingly proclaims *all doctrines* that people need to know; because she nurtures *all kinds of people* into a right fear of God, be they in powerful positions or ordinary citizens, be they learned or uneducated; because she has *healing and remedy for all kinds of sins of soul and*

body; and because she possesses *all kinds of virtues* in deeds and in words as well as *all kinds of spiritual gifts*.

Cyril's definition is thus summed up in five points.

1. Catholic means world-encompassing. The church encompasses all oceans and continents, she moves the cross to the uttermost islands in Oceania and up to highest plateaus in the heart of Asia. Unremittingly she expands her boundaries, driven by her Lord's commission (Matt 28:19; Acts 1:8). It is contrary to the catholic spirit to be lukewarm for the cause of the church's global mission. God desires *all* people to be saved and to come to the knowledge of the truth (1 Tim 2:4). The church has not fulfilled her mission and realized her catholic essence until that day when all knees bow at the name of Jesus (Phil 2:10).

2. Catholic also means: owner of the whole saving truth. It is part of the fullness of our Savior that He is *the truth* (John 14:6; cf. 1:14), the saving and powerful Truth that alone is able to give purpose to life, lifting us out of illusions and lies and connecting us with God's eternal reality. This truth is imparted to the church. We have already pointed out that she is called "the pillar and bulwark of the truth" (1 Tim 3:15). She owns this truth in the Word (John 17:17), the living, oral or written message about the Savior. It is given to her once for all (Jude 3), unchangeable and steadfast, and at the same time so inexhaustibly rich, that no man and no epoch could ever be finished with this "inexpressible gift" from God (2 Cor 9:15). Each generation will anew draw from its abundant well and so "have power to comprehend with all the saints what is the breadth and length and height and depth, and to know the love of Christ which surpasses knowledge, that you may be filled with all the fullness of God" (Eph 3:18–19).

Even when a Christian focuses with all his love and all his understanding on one single point in order at least there to drink the whole cup of salvation, yet he finally must say as Luther said about the article of justification through faith, "This one article reigns in my heart: faith in Christ. From it, all my spiritual thoughts emerge and return day and night. And even so, I found myself to have grasped only a few powerless and meager crumbs from this high, deep and wide wisdom." (Luther's *Great Commentary on Galations* as quoted by Bishop Bengt Jonzon in *Pastoral Letter* 1938, page 67.)

Out of this overflowing wisdom, the church can in each generation derive new treasures and for every people emphasize new aspects, and yet always and everywhere proclaim precisely what everyone needs to know for his salvation. This richness also guards against all exaggerations and constrictions. If one epoch focused on one main aspect, the next will find in the excitement of an explorer that the Word contains yet more and that the life of the Church extends over larger expanses. As long as the catholic spirit lives in the church, she is continuously renewed through the impulses from her own past, and she will again and again face new and surprising aspects of the message which she has conveyed to the world for centuries.

One of the most bitter fruits of the division is that each subdivision of the Church and each sect is tempted to cultivate that portion of the truth which at one point in history was its own great discovery and then refuses to see beyond that. In a united church each new wave of life would be beneficial for the members of the body. It would become a part of the shared catholic faith. In a divided church the flows of renewal are often stopped already at the closest borderline between the confessions. They are not able to break through the old dams of distrust and disunity. Due to old grudges, one refuses to benefit from something that was discovered and loved in another part of Christendom. Therefore life easily stagnates in each isolated part of the church. That which in the first generation was a personal conquest, the great discovery of a half-forgotten pearl among the jewels of the gospel, in the second and third generations so easily becomes an inherited doctrine that no longer brings joy and liberty but is driven hard and narrowly, because it once became the particular characteristic. It really has become a barbed-wire fence with which one demarcates oneself from old antagonists. If such a tragedy continues, one can through spiritual inbreeding and narrow-gauge complacency lose so much so that one only would retain a few fragments of the Church's treasures, maybe not even enough for salvation.

3. Catholic is the Church because she is the mother of all the races and peoples on earth. Just as the seer saw before God's throne "a great multitude that no one could count, from every nation, tribe, people and language" (Rev 7:9), the Church already on earth unites a crowd of people more diversified than any empire ever was able to gather under its scepter. Already the account of the first Pentecost gives us the names of sixteen nationalities (Acts 2:9–11). Today the gospel is preached in more than a

thousand languages. Christ's Church builds bridges across gulfs of differences in customs and culture. People who otherwise would not be able to grasp anything of each other's ideas or conceptions are united in adoration before the Cross of Christ.

The catholic essence of the Church is in that way expressed in every nation. Yet, it is contrary to the catholic spirit to bind the gospel to particular kinds of personalities and attitudes, whether these are shaped by ethnic backgrounds, cultural expectations or personal disposition. Neither the emotional nor the reserved, neither the esthetic nor the ecstatic have a monopoly in forming the life of the Church. She defends herself against any truncation of her catholic richness. She is the Mother who has plenty of space and love for all her heterogeneous children.

4. The Church is called catholic because she channels the all-enclosing grace which stretches far beyond the uttermost measure of the sins of the world.

God has founded her in a fallen world, where we encounter everywhere the marks of a will that has rebelled against God. Therefore, "the Scripture declares that the whole world is a prisoner of sin" (Gal 3:22), a sentence that no one can avoid and that every honest conscience experiences.

When God calls us to His church, He has only unworthy to call on. "There is no difference. All have sinned and fall short of the glory of God" (Rom 3:22–23). But over all of us, the church lifts her arch as a shield of grace. The cross in the chancel glows over all who are gathered for worship. The lost glory of God comes to humankind again, shedding its light over repenting sinners. In our poor world, there is not a life so stained, not a crime so devilish, and not a secret so disgraceful that God's mercy cannot blot it out. And what is maybe even greater: there is not a relapse into our habitual sins so humiliating, not a fault of character or a bad habit so deep-rooted, that it cannot be turned toward forgiveness and ever new boldness for those sharing the life of the Church. After all, through the absolution she has God's command to pronounce forgiveness from the Almighty.

This is the Church's catholic, all-embracing message of grace for sinners. It is a break with the catholic spirit if we forget that in the church we all are completely placed on the same level as sinners under God's unmerited grace. As forgiven sinners we can hold out our hands to one another before the altar, and this in solidarity also with those who are still outsiders. "Are we any better? Not at all!" (Rom 3:9).

5. Catholic also means all-embracing concerning the equipment of human nature and the gifts of the Spirit. The knight and the friar, the hermit and the emperor, all of them were sons of the Church. Likewise she sees among her sons today researchers, in whose very being modern science is embedded, and academics at the height of contemporary learning. But in the same pew there may be a child, who is praying the Our Father as they do, and yet she is not even old enough to read. And worshiping with them might be an old tannery worker, who never was instructed in demonstrating a scientific theory but nevertheless has seen a wondrously great part of the fullness of Christ which surpasses all knowledge. They are all included in the same catholic fellowship. The Church has something essential to give to them all. They are all active in the great communion of the prayers and the doxologies. In the varied forms of the liturgy or in quiet meditation under the vaults, all of them find expressions for their longing and their joy, their concerns and their worries. Each of them has their favorite hymns and their dearest Bible passages. The one has seen that, the other something else, but the Church includes everything and everybody. She embraces their greatly diversified lives from cradle to grave, pulling everything in under her sanctifying realm.

This means that the Church throughout her history has a great throng of personalities with a brilliant richness of gifts of grace. "Now to each one the manifestation of the Spirit is given for the common good" (1 Cor 12:7). No one is able to grasp or to avail himself of the total catholic richness of the Church, at least not in this life. Each one must be content with playing his instrument in the symphony. There are those who seemingly play a more important part and are heard more than others. There are bound to be differences. But the Church bids us remember that she represents a kingdom where the first may become the last. The differences are a matter of serving according to the variety of talents and skills among the church members, not a matter of ranking order. God has arranged it in that way so "that there may be no discord in the body, but that the members may have the same care for one another" (1 Cor 12:25). It is contrary to the catholic spirit if anyone prides himself on his gift of grace, declaring it to be the most important and the greatest, and thus allows it to become a source of division instead of unity and richness. Sadly, this happens all too often. Various things may be over-emphasized at the detriment of other things: the pastoral office or speaking in tongues, faith-healing or social welfare activities, theology or administration. The outcome will be the same: as soon as one ceases to use one's gift of grace to serve and instead uses it to lord it over others, the gifts of grace become walls of separation. The blessing is changed into harm. This must not be allowed to happen. After all, Scripture expressly says about these gifts that not everybody can have them (1 Cor 12:27–30). We must learn to share them together, so that each one of us loyally presents himself with his particular gifts, serving the great fellowship of the believers and thus contributing to the overflowing richness of Christ's church.

6. We shall now add yet another point. When Cyril (315–386) wrote his catechism, Christianity could look back at a history of more than 300 years. Now another 1600 years of Christian history have been added. Therefore we are able to observe yet another essential feature of the Church's catholic character: she encompasses the centuries and extends over all ages. This contributes in a special way to her catholic richness.

When the Church emerged in the world, she already possessed everything in her Savior. She knew that she was called "to contend for the faith that was once for all delivered to the saints" (Jude 3). With a rigor which seemed intolerant to the outsider, she rejected all attempts to add or subtract anything from that faith. "Even if we or an angel from heaven should preach to you a gospel contrary to that which we preached to you, let him be accursed" (Gal 1:8). The apostle knew that would have been betrayal of God Himself and also betrayal of those who heard such a "gospel" preached.

However, this message is at the same time a sowing, a seed and a grain of mustard, harboring inside the mysterious power of growth and life. The message is continuously confronted with new circumstances and changing times. If the church only possessed a mechanically memorized gospel, and would she only be able to reproduce and repeat the past, she would soon be dead. But she is not a lecturer of ancient wisdom. In the Spirit's power, she *proclaims* from the fullness of Christ. The very life of Christ pulsates in her veins. In each new generation new people are received into this mysterious fellowship. And they are children of their time, filled with its questions and need. But they are also children of the Church, filled with the life of the Spirit and the power of the Word. Therefore they are able to present the old message as the innermost possession of their own being. And in the language of their own time, they will answer the questions of their own generation. Thus the church can handle ever new situations with an ever regenerated and refreshing gospel. Yet it always remains the same gospel. Therefore, during the course of the centuries she has gained a gigantic experience, embedded in dogma and theology, expressed in liturgical forms and church governance. This enormous collection of pastoral wisdom, of knowledge and of practical applications is what is known as *the tradition*.

Our evangelical attitude to the tradition is that nothing is necessary for salvation beyond that which has a clear foundation in the gospel. Scripture is the lord of the tradition, the original source of its norm. At the same time, knowing that the Church is Christ's body, the organ through which His will is done among us, we must with gratitude receive the experience of past generations for our enrichment. Acknowledging the tradition is therefore acknowledging the deeds of Christ in the past. Of course, errors occur and become part of the tradition. Many of them are revealed through God's judgments: mere human works did not last. Others became apparent through careful examination according to the measure of the Word. An oak-tree does not carry burdocks. No more can the church's tree carry all kinds of strange outgrowths. It can grow, it can push out new shoots. But the sap which rises in the new branches and the fruits which they yield must always be able show their unity of substance with the old stem from which they grew.

In many cases the tradition becomes decisive for our interpretation of the Bible. The New Testament Scriptures testify themselves that they are written for Christians, for people who already had received basic instruction (Luke 1:4; 1 Cor 11:2,23; 15:3; Heb 6:1; 2 Pet 1:12). We would in vain seek answers in the Bible about many things which were well-known and self-evident to them. There is so much concerning baptism and communion, teaching, offices, church discipline and worship, that we would like to know, but about which the New Testament is silent or at best gives us some hints. This is so because "the Christians in the New Testament congregations did not reflect upon the Church and the means of grace; they lived in them and of them" (Fridrichsen, Anton. *Kyrka och sacrament i Nya Testamentet [Church and Sacrament in the New Testament]*. Svensk Teologisk Kvartalskrift 1936, page 203).

This living and rich church life was of course inherited by the following generations. They taught the apostolic faith with the same words and terms that they themselves had learned. They celebrated the Lord's

Supper and baptized, they ordained men to the pastoral office and absolved from sin according to the lines of direction which they themselves had "received" (1 Cor 11:23, 15:3, cf. 2 Tim 1:13f, 3:14f). Faithfulness toward the tradition is always inculcated as a Christian duty (2 Tim 2:2, Titus 1:14, cf. 1 Tim 6:20, 1 Cor 4:17, Gal 1:8, Col 2:7, 2 Pet 3:2).

Much of the early Christian tradition is also preserved outside New Testament. The oldest non-biblical Christian writing, the so called First Letter of Clement, is from about the year 95. He was bishop of Rome 92–101. The Letters of Ignatius, bishop of Antioch, are from the beginning of the 100s. Clement of Rome, Ignatius, and Polycarp, bishop of Smyrna, have been designated, with a few others, as *"the apostolic fathers,"* since they personally had known and even been taught by some of the apostles.

Toward the end of the 100s we already find three great *"church fathers"*: Irenaeus, Tertullian, and Clement of Alexandria. The first of them was a Greek from Asia Minor, who became Bishop of Lyon. The second one was African, a resident of Carthage. The third one lived in Egypt and Palestine. It has rightly been pointed out that it is a good proof of the firmness and genuineness of the churchly tradition, that these three, although representing different languages, ethnic groups and continents, yet give such a unanimous picture of the apostolic faith and the apostolic church life.

Nothing can therefore be more natural than going back to this early tradition, when we need assistance in understanding the Bible. Even so, there are passages in the New Testament that remain inexplicable to us (e. g. 1 Cor 15:29). But it is also true that we in some matters obtain clear instructions concerning baptism of children and the offices of the church. We shall deal with those issues later in this book. Everywhere in the church we experience this broad and powerful stream of manners and customs, of prayers and hymns, of confessions and creeds, which wells forth from the early church and causes growth during all subsequent centuries. There is reason to rejoice that it still flows so mighty and undiluted in our own Church of Sweden. But all the same, we maintain our basic principle: only that which is founded in Scripture is necessary for salvation.

The church learns not only from her first centuries. Even thereafter Christ lives and is at work through His body. The church can never look at her history as something only belonging in the past. It also belongs to the life in Christ which fills us today. It becomes an always inspiring and renewing force, just as we may be affected by powerful movements in our time. When we learn from the past, we are learning from our brothers in Christ. The church lifts us over the limits of time. She places the generations side by side. The blessed saints are alive now. They are part of Christ's body. Thus Augustine, Chrysostom and Luther are our contemporaries in the Spirit. We live in fellowship with martyrs and reformers. Not everything which they have said or done was right. Therefore we must listen to them with an alert conscience, bound to God's word. The testimony of our forefathers does not place a new Bible in our hands. But it continually gives us new reminders of its richness. If we ourselves are bound to the Word, we can hear God Himself powerfully speak through the voices of our forebears. Deeply moved we see the infinity of His work throughout the history of the church. Humiliated we recognize our own limitations. Maybe we discover the frightening poverty of our own time, its spiritual impoverishment and one-sidedness. But at the same time we are caught by a sense of infinite jubilation. After all, this whole richness is ours! The past is not past, it is as real as it was on that day when it first emerged in history. We ourselves are partakers of it, as we truly live in an indissoluble connection with the Church which has these inexhaustible assets of faith and strength and willingness to sacrifice, of sanctified characters and burning spirits. In this catholic fellowship the paralyzing sense of weakness is overcome. In fellowship with the victory-crowned martyrs, we are always enabled to continue on the Way.

Thus the Church stretches her all-embracing band of unity through times past and into the future as well. She stands until the return of Christ and will receive as a mother in her arms also generations not yet born. This we only know as a presentiment. If that day, which the Father only knows, would not come for thousands of years, the Church would embrace new generations and extend to other cultures in order to sanctify them and fill them with the nearness of the Deity. And something remarkable will happen: these unknown will then recognize themselves in us, counting us as their own brothers and sisters, as their contemporaries in Christ.

We have now completed our attempt in expressing what the catholic thought means in its unspeakable richness. Meanwhile it has probably more and more become clear to us that the word "allmännelig" hardly is sufficient to cover its full meaning. We really should return to using the word *catholic,* and then of course in its correct sense. This has often been advocated by prominent leaders in our church. Many years ago Bishop

Aulén pointed out that there is no reason why "this glorious designation of the church should be applied only to the Roman Church." He adds, "Linguistic usage is not an indifferent matter. There is good reason why we speak about the power of language over thought. We need to be careful with our choice of words. Should we not then avoid giving Rome even an air of taking precedence over us concerning the church's catholicity?" (Aulén, Gustaf: *Evangeliskt och Romerskt [Evangelical and Roman]*, Uppsala 1922, page 101). He recommends the terminology that Archbishop Söderblom used to designate our branch of the Church, namely *the Evangelical-Catholic* as distinguished from the Greek-Catholic and the Roman-Catholic. (Söderblom, Nathan. *Kyrkan i Sverige [The Church in Sweden]*. Stockholm 1923, page 7.)

Calling ourselves evangelical catholics, we can even cite the reformers. They would never give up that glorious designation. "We all ought to be catholics," says Melanchton. He refers in a letter to that unity which consists of "the teaching of God's church, confessed both by the church in Sweden and by our churches in one spirit and with one voice *together with Christ's catholic church*" (Werner Elert: Morphologie des Luthertums. München 1931. Page 241). As already mentioned, Luther speaks without hesitation about his catholic faith, and another of the reformers, Jacob Heerbrand, says, "Never have I written, spoken or done anything against the Catholic Church. Far be it from me! Yes, I say, such blasphemy be far from me!" (Elert, page 245).

The reformers thus retained the old church's totally unanimous confession of her catholic essence, the confession which one of the church fathers in the fourth century formulated in a sonorous Latin sentence: *Christianus mihi nomen est, catholicus cognomen.* Christian is my name, Catholic my surname (Paceanus of Barcelona, Ep. 1 ad Sympron. 4). There is no reason for the church of the reformation in Sweden to depart from that confession today, unless she has ceased to be faithful to her own essence and begun to be ashamed of her origin from the times of the apostles, the martyrs, and the church fathers.

* * *

The catholic thought means that each congregation in its locality represents the Church with all her spiritual riches. What in history spans millennia, what on earth stretches over all the oceans and continents, yes even that which in the invisible world touches the throne of God's glory, it appears here, visible and concentrated at one point. The powers of the new era are at work in every small part of the Church. A part might only realize a fragment of its possibilities. And yet, everything belongs also to that congregation, even if some of it remains a hidden asset. Where Jesus Christ is, there is also the catholic Church. The essence of the Church lives also in the smallest of her parts, just as the same blood flows through all the parts of the body.

This does not at all mean that each individual congregation would be independent or autonomous. Rather the opposite: after all, it lives indissolubly grown together with all other congregations. This organic unity is bound to become organizational as well. Each part willingly integrates itself into the whole. What all the other congregations do becomes the evident rule. This was true already in the early church (1 Cor 14:34). Just as the apostles made up the decisive authority and the common tie for all Christendom, so their successors, the bishops, later on became the visible expression for the unity of the church.

For each individual Christian the catholic thought means a whole way of life. Being grafted into the Church as a member means to be an heir of her immeasurable riches. First of all it means a fellowship which lifts me out of the isolation of individualism. No longer is it just a question of the harmony of *my* soul or *my* happiness in life. I am now indissolubly united with my fellow Christians. They are with me members of the same Christ. I must love them as myself, see myself in them and them in me. It is all about *our* salvation.

Yet, this is not collectivism and self-effacement. On the contrary: it is self-realization. Strikingly it has been said that there are two ways to realize oneself: the individualistic and the catholic. The former means setting oneself free from God and neighbor. Man puts himself in the center and becomes isolated. He becomes his own master, proclaiming that he is in charge of his life, not acknowledging that it is a gift from God.

The catholic way is the opposite. Man gratefully acknowledges that he is totally dependent on his heavenly Father and indissolubly united with his brothers and sisters in Christ. He accepts the relationships where God has put him. He says yes to his baptism, to the promises of the gospel, and to the vocation God gives him. To some extent this means castigation and self-control. It means giving up everything that hinders the full fellowship with the Savior and fellow men. But at the same time it means a tremendous enrichment, it means that a whole world of beauty and strength and purpose opens up. It means that the soul at last will live and grow, that it can express its suppressed need of dedication and heroism, developing unimagined funds of tenderness and will-power. All this is successively stirred to life at the encounter with the catholic fullness of the Church. Time after another one thinks that the height now has been achieved, that faith has exhausted its possibilities, but again and again the Savior's promise comes true: You shall see greater things than these (John 1:50). The individualist can never quite understand that one can realize oneself and live in the deepest richness by being totally immersed in the fellowship of the Church. He immediately suspects that it must be a matter of masked egoism: "Surprisingly, there are some types who are so strange that they accept the church's straight-jacket." Jesus explains the deeper meaning, "Whoever loses his life for My sake will find it" (Matt 10:39). Since my life is a gift from God, it has only *one* purpose, namely God's purpose for it. As long as I try to wriggle away from God and His purpose in order to live according to my own will, I can at the best give my life a substitute kind of content that might suffice for a few years or decades. I cannot begin to discover the purpose with my life, until I lose my life, give up all demands, and acknowledge God's absolute sovereignty. Up till that point my life was like a languishing member of a body, but when it opens up for the divine flow of life, it functions in its rightful place. Thus it experiences at last its destiny, and my life is filled with its God-given purpose. This is so far away from feeling like a coercion that it on the contrary throughout the ages has been described as the most wonderful liberation: liberation *from* guilt and pangs of conscience, from disharmony and hopeless loneliness, *to* joy in one's work, fellowship, trust and confidence, and a strong prayer life.

Most Christians will probably never experience more than a fragment of the catholic richness of the church. But whenever the church is truly catholic, rich and all-embracing, and not sectarian, narrow and stingy, she releases precisely the deepest and most personal gifts in each person, helping her to find the purpose and destiny of her life. Each one of us must humbly acknowledge that we never are able to see more than in part. The portions of the church's legacy, of which some of us so far have been unable to avail ourselves, do not need to be worthless for that reason. Why should a doctrine, a rite or a part of the Bible be rejected or changed just because I personally do not understand it? Maybe my verdict will be different within a few years? Maybe I will not change my opinion, but I might live to see a whole new generation with palpable excitement testify that they have found something essential and liberating in that which I never was able to grasp.

A few have been privileged to assimilate so much of the richness of the centuries that they become one with the essence of the Church. Such catholic figures appear now and then in history. Their voices are heard through the centuries. When they speak, we listen to the genuine voice of the Church. In their lives we see the great miracle when a poor individual has been so filled with the Savior's pleroma and so grown together with his fellow believers of his own time that he embodies a whole epoch with its questions and conflicts, and at the same time conveys Christ's answers to his suffering brethren in such a way that they perceive God's all-embracing mercy and all-restoring forgiveness. Even when the catholic spirit thus triumphs by making an unworthy human being a saint in God, the personal is nonetheless not extinguished. Rather, it is increased to the height of power; the individuality has been most sharply chiseled out. No one can argue that *Bernhard* of Clairvaux, *Francis* of Assisi, and *Luther* of Wittenberg are impersonal. They are just the opposite! They embody the highest form of self-realization that the world has seen. It is a self-realization in the catholic sense: *God* has realized *His* intention with them in the great plan for His creation.

CHAPTER 4

The Church in Sweden

HERGEIR, ONE OF KING Björn's advisors in Birka, built in the year 830 the very first church in the Nordic lands. It was a small chapel in Birka, the Swedish capital on the Björkön island in the Mälaren lake. The first mass there was celebrated by Ansgar, a French monk who has been designatd as "the Apostle of the North." Most likely there were among the communicants some slaves who had been taken away from their Christian homelands during the expeditions of the Vikings. They may have been Greeks or Franks, Anglo-Saxons or Orientals, all of them could participate in the mass knowing that this was *their* church. This was so, because the One Holy and Catholic Church was yet extending herself from the outermost rocky islets of Ireland to the edge of the Arabian Desert. At Ansgar's mass she was now pushing forward her farthermost outpost to the North.

That time the attempt did not succeed in planting the church there in a lasting way. When the mission effort was resumed with great determination 200 years later, the situation had changed dramatically. The far-reaching schism between Rome and the East threw its shadow over the wilderness and the small settlements in Sweden. The pope sent missionaries from Hamburg. From England came mission bishops, more loosely tied to the pope's authority. The Varangians, armed Swedish tradesmen eastwards, returned from Russia and Constantinople with strong impressions of the Orthodox Church. This non-Roman influence was so strong that there is a bold hypothesis suggesting that one of the first known bishops among the Swedes, Osmund (Uppsala in the 1050s), actually could have been Greek-Orthodox (Schmid, Toni. *Sveriges kristnande [The Christianizing of Sweden]*. Uppsala, 1934). Whatever the case may be, in

Hamburg he was called an *episcopus acephalus*, that is a bishop who was not under the pope's jurisdiction, and because of him Rome's legates were sent away from King Emund's court in the 1050s.

Influence from Byzantine can also be traced in some of our oldest church architecture. Influences in the other direction occurred as well. A Swedish woman was revered as a saint in the East three hundred years before St. Birgitta (Bridget) was canonized in Rome. It was Ingegerd, daughter of Olof Skötkonung, who ruled Sweden ca. 994–1022 as its first Christian king, and sister of King Anund and King Emund, who ruled Sweden successively until 1060. In 1019 Ingegerd married Jaroslav the Great in Kiev. It was Christian Greeks who named her a saint and built churches in her honor! Jaroslav, who ruled all Russia 1036–1054, was the son of Saint Vladimir, the first Christian ruler of all Russia.

However, circumstances were such that the pope won a complete victory in the Nordic lands. The three new archbishoprics, Lund, Trondhjem, and Uppsala, were established in the 1100s as provinces in the Roman Church. Yet, the church in Sweden continued in many ways to do her own things. We ourselves chose our national patron saint, King Erik, who was loved by the common people because of his gentle rule and his sincere Christian piety. However, his opponents killed him in 1160 right after his having attended the mass. He seemed to have been displeasing to the pope and was never canonized, but the Swedes have always remembered him as Erik the Saint.

Ignoring canonical law, the parishes continued to elect their priests. The bishops were never able completely to enforce the demands of the Roman church. The celibacy was not at all accepted everywhere in spite of vigorous and threatening reminders from the papacy. Clergy marriages were commonplace as late as in the mid 1200s. There were clergy wives in most of our old parishes for centuries before the Reformation. Thus the church in Sweden followed, probably unknown to her the custom from the ancient church, such as it has been preserved outside the reach of Rome even in our day and time by the Orthodox Church.

The Roman leadership of the church carried with it many good things for Sweden. The total significance of the Cistercian monasteries to our people can hardly be appreciated enough. Even so, the system also led to unavoidable spiritual harm. It is true that the moral decline within the papal church was not so evident in Sweden. Toward the end of the Middle Ages, the church in Sweden seems to have been an honorable exception compared with the decline on the Continent. But the teaching of doing good deeds to earn your salvation was as massive here as elsewhere; the indulgence sellers traveled through the country; the intercessions of the saints were more valued than the merit of Christ; and the sacrament of Holy Communion was not celebrated according to the Lord's institution. Even at the time when Ansgar came to Birka, the Lord's Supper most likely was celebrated in the way of the ancient church with the laity receiving both the bread and the wine. Later the chalice was not given to the laity, and it became the general custom to commune only once a year, at Easter. All the other Sundays the priest celebrated the mass alone and offered the sacrifice of the mass, which was believed to be so efficient that masses for the deceased were said in great numbers for a fee, and this without any parishioners in attendance. Compared with worship practices in the ancient church with its strong fellowship, with frequent participation of the people in the Lord's Supper, its proclamation of God's Word in the sermon, its liturgy alive in the hearts and minds of the parishioners, the Middle Ages is characterized by a very deep decay. Christ's Church was on its way toward losing both the Word and the Sacrament of the Altar.

But God did not allow it to happen. When the debasement was at its lowest point and the very stones began to cry out, the great church renewal which we call the Reformation emerged.

What was the Reformation all about? We shall deal with that question considering primarily the developments in Sweden.

It has been said that the Reformation was established in Sweden by the parliamentary session in Västerås 1527. Nothing can be further from the truth. The Church in Sweden was not reformed through a resolution in the Parliament. She reformed herself, and it was a process that lasted for almost a century. The driving forces in this process belonged to the Church herself. They were her bishops and other men of God, such as Master Olof (alias Olaus Petri), all of them in the service of the Church. They were her diocesan chapters and her councils (that is: church assemblies), which continued to meet in order to make resolutions pertaining to the life and order of the Church. The resolutions in Västerås represented only a step in this process, which was followed by more decisive and significant steps at the many important councils during the 1500's.

Anyone who desires to catch a glimpse of the structure of the Church of Sweden during these years of transition should imagine himself present at the Council in Uppsala 1539, observing the church leaders gathered upon the summons of the archbishop. There they are seated, an incredibly diversified group and yet united at the same council meeting as sons of the same church.

Seated there is *Olaus Petri*, the genius and prophet of the Reformation, formally with a subordinate position in the church (he was a deacon, ordained a priest only later in that year) but the dominant figure through his religious charisma and his superior skills as author, jurist and historian. He has rightly been called "the Martin Luther of Sweden"! In the history of the Reformation he is the passionate, gifted and single-minded apostle of the Word, not without a slight drawing towards spiritualism. In fact, due to his excitement for the re-discovery of the Word, he had a certain tendency to underestimate the significance of the sacrament.

At his side we find his companion in arms, *Laurentius Andreae*, emerging from the old hierarchy, a scholar of superior learning, totally won for the evangelical faith, and with his whole being and intelligence dedicated to the cause of the Reformation. We honor him as being the first one, following the break with Rome, to advocate a free national church, governed by evangelical bishops. With impressive statesmanlike wisdom and great moral courage, he dared to promote this program for the church against Gustaf Vasa's (king 1523–1560) dictatorial tendencies. Andreae's struggle for the freedom of the church cut his career short already in 1539. And soon he came close to losing his life in it.

Seated with the reformers were also five bishops, of whom at least two clearly had their hearts on the side of the old faith. Even ten years later Rome counted upon having two supporters in the Swedish episcopacy, which probably was correct, as long as one realizes that these men were reform Roman-Catholics, that is belonging to the type of church leaders, who to be sure were faithful sons of the Roman Church but at the same time were deeply convinced of the necessity for a speedy and thorough reformation of the church. They had much in common with the evangelicals: they were warm promoters of the renewed urge for Bible study, they admired the church fathers and traced their ideals to the ancient church. Some of them warmly sympathized with Melanchton. Their evident leader was the bishop in Skara, *Sven Jacobi*, a "true patriot, who as a prominent church man during the upheavals of the Reformation period was able to combine faithfulness toward his Roman-Catholic convictions with faithfulness toward his country, which in the end became fully Lutheran" (Holmquist, Hjalmar. *Svenska Kyrkans historia [The History of the Swedish*

Church], III:1, page 224. Uppsala 1933). He served the Church of Sweden until his death in 1554, although during the last ten years he had to give up the bishop's chair for the deanship of the cathedral.

The center between these flanks and the man for the future in this diversified group was *Laurentius Petri*, our first evangelical archbishop, consecrated for his office by the bishops of the pre-Reformation period. No one has meant so much for our church as he. No one else is as he worthy to be loved and honored as our veritable Swedish church father. Wise and good, beloved and respected, he led during these fateful years the Church of Sweden in such a way that made her both genuinely evangelical and catholically rich. In his very character he combined the features which came to typify the Church of Sweden: steadfast evangelical faith and deep love for everything that was religiously of value from the past.

Among the churchmen seated at this council in Uppsala was also an outsider, the only man in the hall of the assembly whom one finds it difficult to appreciate: the king's chancellor *Konrad von Pyhy*. A Roman-Catholic from Bavaria, yet religiously indifferent, he was a suitable tool for the royal plenitude of power during these years, when Gustaf Vasa attempted to remold Swedish society with Germany as the pattern, making Christ's Church with the king as the head an instrument to serve his plans for the state government. If the aspirations that Pyhy represented had succeeded, the reformation of the church in Sweden would instead have resulted in an irreparable deformation, from Church to a state department. If we could imagine that we today in our country would not have any bishops with their chapters, that the king would be in the place of the archbishop, that the administration of the dioceses would be handled by the governors and their regional boards, and that a royal jurist or politicus periodically would arrange visitations in the parishes, then we would get an idea of the kind of disaster that would have befallen us, had Gustaf Vasa been able to carry out his will in the beginning of the 1540s. Here we are not talking just about some details of organization but rather nothing less than the freedom of the Gospel. This is clear from the king's own statements at this time, when he for example decrees that the citizens at the risk of his severe punishment and wrath must be obedient "both in worldly matters and in the religion, and do only what We through our ordinances prescribe in spiritual and worldly matters" (Hjalmar Holmquist: Svenska Kyrkans Historia III:1, Uppsala 1933, p.

272). This is pure caesaro-papism; the head of the state has become a new pope and a spiritual dictator for his subjects.

The reaction from the Swedish people to all this came hard and vigorously in the Dacke rebellion. A peasants army in the province of Småland, under the strong leadership of Nils Dacke, defeated the king's troops in several battles, thereby forcing the king to lower his tone. Yet, he did continue his attack on the office of bishop, attempting to reorganize the dioceses and trying to substitute superintendents for bishops. He refused to approve the church order that the archbishop had worked out on the basis of Swedish church practice. If he could not exercise command over the church, he would not in any case acknowledge her independence. But even in the face of royal disfavor, Archbishop Laurentius calmly continued to work for reform in the church. He saw to it that improved editions of the liturgical manuals were produced, he issued ordinances and memorandums for all facets of church life in the parishes, he looked after the schools that the state had allowed to deteriorate. All this was done quietly, without the formal sanction of the state, in virtue of the archbishop's moral authority and the loyalty of the priests toward their leaders. The Church lived her life, at times under great distress but internally with increasing stability.

It seems as if God had chosen and equipped Archbishop Laurentius to be the rescuer of our church during these fateful years when everything more than once was within a hairbreadth of being lost. Personally unassuming and free from matters of prestige, he managed to preserve the king's personal confidence in the midst of disfavor. He understood to hold back when needed and to humble himself as a person without giving in on the heart of the issues. For more than forty years as archbishop, he battled for the freedom of the Church and stood at last as the victor, revered and loved in the whole nation. During the difficult years, when the papists could still threaten with violence, the king once offered him an escort of body-guards. He did without that protection and instead arranged so that the money thus saved would be directed toward supporting poor university students preparing for the priesthood. He willingly accepted the risk of assault, if he thereby could help the Church in getting well educated and dedicated servants. It was in that spirit that he laid the foundation for the future of the church in Sweden.

Next to his concern for the main article of the reformation, justification through faith alone in Christ alone, was his deep dedication to the liturgy, his desire to promote a sound, evangelical and catholic way of worship throughout the church. Musically well-educated and with an unusually good ear for the language of liturgy, he was suited as few others to lead the formation of the reformed rituals, as they slowly were introduced in Swedish fashion and with purified contents.

The renewal continued year after year. It was not a revolution, no sharp and sudden breaks. Everything occurred from the inside and little by little. Nobody was out to create a new church, driving away the old priests. They stayed on and served side by side with the new, often in the same parish - and some even in the same diocesan chapter. The new orders that were introduced were prescribed by bishop and chapter in accordance with the resolutions of the Church Assemblies. No schism occurred, no persecution, no mutual anathemas declared. Even when church leaders expressed differences of opinion, they all knew that they belonged to one and the same church and answered to one and the same bishop and chapter in their own diocese. *There has never been more than one church in Sweden*, the one that Ansgar and his successors planted in the North, the one that under the most able leadership of Archbishop Laurentius (the Latin form of his Swedish name Lars) went through her great improvement and reformed herself from having been a province in the papal church with its many abuses to becoming a pruned branch on the tree of Christ's Church, faithful both to the Gospel, to the legacy of the Church, and to the Swedish people with its national needs. The Reformation was in Sweden a process of healing *within* the Church, a recovery from papistic errors to new evangelical health.

As on the national level, the changes took place in the parishes very gradually. In many of our churches you will find in the sacristy or maybe on the back wall of the nave a *Series Pastorum*, the long list of pastors who served the parish through the centuries. Usually the list begins way back in the Middle Ages. As you get to the first half of the 1500's, you find that it continues in unbroken succession with the same Latin forms of names and the same kind of titles for the office holders. Usually it is impossible to decide from the information on the list who was the first evangelical pastor in the parish. Often the parish itself could not tell. The change was so gradual, and when it was completed, one still worshipped in the same church, the priest kneeled at the same altar with the same antependium, the same crucifix, and the same candlesticks. The priest wore the same chasuble, the same bells summoned the parishioners to the high mass, and just as in the past the same church wardens served in the Lord's House. The difference was that the people could understand the whole liturgy since it was now in Swedish, that there was always a sermon, that congregational hymn singing had been introduced, that the laity received the chalice as well, and that people more frequently partook of the sacrament of the altar. What the people noticed and that was something that caused furious anger (expressed for example in the Dacke rebellion) was that the churches were plundered of many of their old and beautiful inventories, which had been a delight to the eye, contributing to making the mass a pleasant break from the dullness of everyday life. This pillaging was the work of the king, a way for him to enrich the state treasury. It was an economic reduction. It had nothing to do with the purpose and aim of the Reformation.

The classic document of the Reformation in Sweden is Laurentius Petri's famous Church Order. After the state at last gave up its resistance toward this expression of the Church's independence, it was sanctioned by the Church at a council in 1572. It is usually referred to as *The Church Order of 1571*, the year it was printed and made available to the clergy, the politicians, and the general public. It is not a church constitution in the common sense but rather a treatise on the life and essence of the Church of Sweden with practical applications and examples. It has always been looked upon as a confessional document for our church. Of course, some practical provisions have been changed over the many years, but The Church Order of 1571 in its principal view of the Church and in its basic provisions for the life of the church remains binding on all her leaders and members.

In the well-written preamble, the character of the Church of Sweden is clearly defined: She is a true evangelical Church that maintains a right *Via media* (middle way) between the erroneous doctrines of the papists and the Calvinists.

The Church Order forcefully deals with the accusation from the papists that the reformed church is not Catholic. To the extent that the Church of Sweden "abolished ordinances and ceremonies of the Roman Church," she has done so because they cannot be harmonized with the right and pure evangelical teaching. Such abuses as sorceries, worship of saints, the sacrifice of the mass, "sales of indulgences, and accepting payment for saying mass for the departed" have made it impossible for our church to be one with the papal church. "And this is in short the reason why we in our Church Order to such great extent have severed us from the Roman Church and her ordinances."

But the Church of Sweden has thereby in no way broken away from Christ's Catholic Church. We reject in no way the orders of the ancient church as do all "these Enthusiasts, Anabaptists, defilers of the sacraments, Zwinglians, Calvinists, and so many others." On the contrary, we desire to keep many "orders which have been in use not only under the Pope but elsewhere in all Christendom," first of all our holy days and our churches, our bishops, priests and deacons, our masses with their firm rituals, our churchly acts and ceremonies and much more, which we by no means must "reject just because they were used also under the Pope." Neither do we want to "throw away the good with the bad as the iconoclasts do." We want to keep the church of our fathers after having corrected the abuses with Christian instruction. Thus we retain paintings and sculptures, the prayer hours and vestments, altars, paraments, chalice and paten; likewise we call the Lord's Supper the mass "as it was always called in Christendom."

The line is thus clear, and the front is maintained unbroken both against Rome and against the Reformed. We reject the former because they do not proclaim the gospel in full measure, the latter because they have thrown away the good with the bad and unnecessarily severed themselves from the church catholic, depriving the Christian life of its old time-tested forms without having been able to replace them with something of equal value. Distinguishing herself from these opposite traditions, the Church of Sweden desires to be both truly evangelical and truly catholic. With address to the papists she confesses the pure and full gospel, ready to test everything in its light. As Laurentius Petri says in his Church Order, "We are willing to stand corrected and be taught with reasons from Scripture" concerning any point of doctrine. But the Church of Sweden desires just as clearly, and here she addresses the Reformed, to uphold the connection with the church catholic. In doctrine and liturgy she wants to remain a genuine branch, now pruned and renewed through the Reformation, of Christ's Holy Catholic Church.

The Council held 1593 in Uppsala concluded the Lutheran Reformation in Sweden. It was a traditional "concilium" with all the bishops and representatives for the parish priests participating. Due to the complicated political situation, governmental leaders were also present.

At this council the Church of Sweden acted on its own accord and with great independence from the state. Sigismund, the lawful king of Sweden, also king of Poland, was Roman-Catholic and spent most of his time in Poland. The virtual regent in Sweden, Sigismund's uncle Duke Karl, sympathized with the Calvinistic cause. The council dared to defy both of them, keeping the Via media laid out in the 1571 Church Order. The subsequent development consolidated the Church's victory: the resolutions made at the council were generally accepted, and the council was thus acknowledged as the supreme authority in spiritual matters. The apparent danger for the church during the reformation period to be swallowed up by the state had finally been successfully avoided!

The 1593 Uppsala Council adopted these confessional documents: (1) The three Catholic or Ecumenical Symbols: The Apostles' Creed, The Nicene Creed, and The Athanasian Creed [named after Athanasius (ca. 293–373), Patriarch of Alexandria]; (2) The 1571 Church Order; and (3) The Unaltered Augsburg Confession (Augustana Invariata).

Herewith the character of the Church of Sweden was once again affirmed. The three ancient creeds mark the indissoluble connection with the ancient church. With their very wording we confess our belonging to the One Holy Catholic and Apostolic Church of Christ. The new documents clearly pronounce on the one hand that we want to be evangelical. We can under no circumstances diverge from Scripture and its message of salvation. We count as one of the most unalienable treasures of Christianity the truth on righteousness through faith as Paul proclaimed it and as Luther again brought it to light. But these documents declare on the other hand just as clearly that we in no way have formed a new church but that we remain a branch of the church catholic. Just as the Swedish Church Order of 1571, the Augsburg Confession underlines the unbroken connection between the church catholic and the church reformed, pointing out (as already quoted) in the summary following the twenty-one positive articles, "As can be seen, there is nothing here that departs from the Scriptures or the catholic church or the church of Rome, in so far as the ancient church is known to us from its writers. --- The whole dissension is concerned with a certain few abuses which have crept into the churches."

Nathan Söderblom was altogether in the right when he said, "The catholic church in Sweden, that's we." The Church of Sweden is Christ's Church in Sweden, the Swedish branch of the whole world-embracing catholic Church. We have not renounced the legacy from the Church. We do not need to surrender the designation catholic to the church of Rome. The life of the great world-wide Church is preserved in our country by the Church of Sweden. Our high mass is to the spirit but in some ways also to the form more like the ancient liturgy than the Roman mass is. Our bishops are the rightful successors to those in the old church. They stand in the unbroken chain of church leaders since the days of the apostles. The archbishop of Uppsala is the primate of the same church province that was established 800 years ago. Yes, Archbishop *Nathan Söderblom* knew what he was talking about. When he ordained pastors for his diocese at the high altar in the Uppsala Dome, he held in his hand the crozier that was carried not only by *Johan Olof Wallin* (archbishop 1837–1839; the foremost Swedish hymnwriter, represented with 30 hymns in the Augustana Hymnal and also in other American hymnals, e. g. the LBW and the LW), *Haquin Spegel* (archbishop 1711–1714, also in the Augustana Hymnal), and *Laurentius Petri* (archbishop 1531–1573). And the same crozier was used back in the Middle Ages as well! It has thus been held also by *Jakob Ulfsson* (archbishop 1470–1515), the founder of Uppsala University in 1477, and it was most likely given to *Stefan* (1164–1185), when he in France was consecrated Sweden's first archbishop in 1164. This shepherd's staff for the archbishop is the same now as it was then. And so is the office of the archbishop: the same now as it was then.

During the manifold events of history the Church in Sweden has been intimately joined to the people and to the state, sharing bad and good times. And yet, she remains something else than an agency of the state. Even during the reign of *Gustavus Adolphus*, while remaining loyal to the king, she uncompromisingly maintained her independence in that she frustrated his plans on subordinating the Church under a governmental department. The church was strongly opposed to the idea "that the highest matters concerning God's congregation would be in the hands of politicians so that they would be the highest rulers and judges of God's congregation, quite contrary to God's order and the rightful custom of the congregation" (Söderblom, Nathan. *The Body and Soul of the Swedish Church*. Page 14).

The term "state church" is therefore misleading in reference to the Church of Sweden. Clergy salaries are not paid by the state. Buildings in the parish for worship and other purposes are either financed by the parish itself or by a cluster of smaller parishes. Normally, there is no money allocated from the state treasury. It does happen that a small parish receives financial support from the state to maintain a church designated as a historic landmark. All expenses to run the parish are paid for through two sources: the church tax levied on the parish members by each parish council and therefore varying from parish to parish, and by the yield from the ecclesiastical domains. Each bishop is sovereign in deciding whom he shall ordain to the pastoral office. The main rule is that the parishes elect their pastors. However, there are exceptions when the government indeed has the privilege to appoint a parish pastor, yet among those nominated by the church. The government appoints all bishops, yet among the three who received most votes from the diocesan clergy. The closest connection between church and state in our country is that the records the pastors for centuries have kept of all residents in the parish are utilized by both the local and national levels of government.

There is another side of the relationship between state and church that we dare not forget. The Church is the conscience of the state. By means of her close relationship to the state, she has been given a position by God to expose sins committed by the governing authorities and subsequently call them to repent.

Johannes Rudbeckius said in a sermon, while serving as the court chaplain for Gustavus Adolphus during the Russian campaign in 1615, that the servants of the Word just as the Old Testament prophets should not allow themselves to overlook the sins, consenting to evilness and wrongdoing, but they should expose the sins without favoritism. It was not long before this fearless chaplain learned that the king himself had lost his temper and thereby badly insulted one of his officers. Rudbeckius did not keep quiet. In June 1617, on the national Day of Penance, he gave before "the just victorious and at times dangerously hot-headed young king" an admonitory address, which was both austere and fatherly,

> "Your Majesty has transgressed God's commandment, thereby arousing his wrath and also causing no minor stain on Your laudable name. I ask Your Majesty to seriously consider these things in Your heart, repent without delay, and be reconciled with God, so that Your Majesty will enjoy God's grace and friendship once again . . . With the authority of God's Word and because of the loyalty I owe Your Majesty as your chaplain, it was my duty to speak thus today." (Holmquist, Hjalmar. *Svenska Kyrkans Historia,* Vol. IV:1, p. 148, Uppsala 1933).

Gustavus Adolphus accepted the reprimand, and when Rudbeckius fifteen years later (then Bishop of Västerås) gave the sermon at the king's funeral, he praised the king "for having given us a safe and free pulpit so that we have been able freely to preach the truth, exposing the sins of Israel and the misdeeds of Jacob's house, and yet nobody dared to impeach or persecute us" (Holmquist, IV:1, p. 149).

As long as the Church in Sweden is allowed freely to preach the full gospel toward judgment and grace, and as long as she is allowed freely to administer her sacraments and her ancient and authentic rites, she can safely remain in that close connection with the state, in which she was led during her history, which certainly did not come about without God's rule and guidance. However, if a secularized state would try to meddle in matters which are sacred to the church, she need not fear to live her life completely released from the association with the state. After all, for hundreds of years in the past, the Church in Sweden was not associated with the state, just as the Church is not today in many countries. The Church existed long before the Swedish state, and she will outlive it as well. The Church is the Body of Christ, and the Body of Christ never was an agency of the state, nor will she ever become one.

* * *

This is thus the crown of honor for the Church of Sweden: She is solidly evangelical and therefore also firmly anchored on the foundation of the ancient church. She can never part from that foundation without being unfaithful to her own Lord and to her own essence. To be sure, more than once she was actually slipping away from that old bed-rock foundation, and maybe she has never been so close of losing her crown of honor as during the past 50 years. Ever since the 1700's strong forces have been in motion which did not want to acknowledge the church's past and instead more or less intentionally aspired to attain a new reformation.

The secularized mentality, which has its roots in the age of Enlightenment and which yielded a strong influence during the 1800's, was not able to appreciate much of the classic Christian faith as received from the ancient church. Cultural life was characterized by faith in man, technology, natural science, and reforms. If there was still some interest in religion at all, then man again was in the focus. His inner experiences, his feelings and personal convictions took the center stage. Anything that could restrain individuality was rejected. The Bible and the church with her doctrines, sacraments and orders were re-interpreted or pushed aside altogether as irrelevant. One could accept the Reformation to some extent, because it was regarded as a step toward the emancipation of modern man. Homage was given to Luther as the great apostle of freedom of conscience. And it is indeed true that Luther taught that it is not wise to act contrary to one's conscience. However, he was talking about the conscience, which is totally dedicated to God and firmly anchored in His Word. What the new age had in mind was autonomous man's own judgment and sense of right. Freedom of conscience became the same as each man's right to be saved in his own way. From within himself, from his heart, was man to find the norms for his life and for his beliefs. But Jesus says (Mark 7:21f): "From within, out of the heart of man, come evil thoughts, fornication, theft, murder, adultery, greed, malice, deceit …." No wonder that the world has been so dreadfully battered during the past fifty years under the rule of the self-glorifying human reason.

This mentality had of course its stronghold outside the church. It often ended up in pronounced hostility toward the church. But with the power of the "zeit-geist" its influence reached far into the Christian camp. Without realizing it themselves many "protestants" lived with a faith that had very little to do with Luther and his church. While Luther knew that reason is blinded and the will is in bondage, it was now said that reason is the right guide and that man's will is a wonderful power of creativity which in an ever ascending curve leads the development of culture upwards. For Luther everything had to do with Christ's work of atonement and with forgiveness. For the "enlightened" mind everything had to do with culture, progress, and the human mind. If religion was given any place in this system, it was as one of the forces that would promote the new liberated view of man and culture. Religion was defended as a factor that was necessary for man's deepest harmony and the richest development of culture. It was a fatal shifting in the understanding of Christianity. Thus far the Christian had been God's servant and slave, a fighter "against the spiritual forces of evil" (Eph 6:12), ready to suffer and die only and solely for the glory of his Lord. Now God was turned into a servant of man. He was supposed to improve the moral standard in society and with a sublime message of the immortality of the soul give something of the glow of eternity to the proud building of culture. For Luther it was all about finding a gracious God. For contemporary man interested in religion, God must be acceptable to his reason. Previously, the great question was how man would be righteous before God. Now man questioned God Himself. God must meet these or those demands to be acknowledged in our modern times.

God's church and His Word were summoned to answer before man's court. The Bible was degraded, its authority disappeared in the jumble of voices asking the church to adjust to modern thinking. Reservations were made everywhere in the creed. The sacraments were beyond understanding. All too palpably, they indicate the necessity of salvation, proclaiming that God came to earth to save and redeem us lost and condemned beings. One ceased kneeling and making the sign of the cross at worship. The creed was no longer said in unison. The children were no longer baptized at the services, or at church at all. Even the dead in the casket must turn right about face! Previously, he had during his funeral service been facing the altar, that is toward the east, toward the risen and coming-again Jesus Christ. Now he was turned toward the mourners so as to have a last glance of his earthly life. This change is symbolic. The funeral service is now perceived in a different way by the people. From having been the pilgrim's jubilant departure to meet his Lord, awaiting the resurrection day, it has become a dismissal, a solemn time for mourning, a last farewell to a loved one who has gone away - *who knows where?*

During this crisis in the church, that began already 150 years ago, was wasted much of that for which our reformers had fought and faithfully preserved of the Church's legacy. The old vestments, which can be traced back to the days of the apostles, went out of use more and more. In a strange way, one began already in the 1700's to lose the sense of the joy and solemnity of the liturgy. Maybe that happened because the mass no longer was the heavenly feast of joy, where the congregation meets her King, but rather an occasion for enlightenment of the people. One also preferred to alter the nave so as to more resemble a high school auditorium. Many of the old churches built in the Middle Ages when Christianity came to Sweden were torn down. In the zeal of neo-protestantism one lime-whitened the old paintings that Laurentius Petri had protected with fatherly hand. "Stubborn ignorance which knows everything hangs on to the opinion that it was the Lutheran Reformation which lime-whitened the churches," says Nathan Söderblom. "One should rather learn that a great many of our church paintings have been added after the Reformation. The lime-whitening actually was a result of the scientific and utilitarian mind-set during the Age of Enlightenment" (Söderblom, p.77). Even the liturgy was "lime-whitened." The liturgy of the eucharist during the 1800's has never been as impoverished in our country, before or after.

During this period of decay the very name of our church was changed. Of course she should not be called catholic. One had just about forgotten that the evangelical church ever had called herself catholic. For the mind-set of enlightenment, catholicism became the quintessence of everything backward and wrong, and the word got that bad ring to it that it still has to so many people. Even the word evangelical was often avoided. Maybe it reminded people too much of the forgiveness of sins and the atonement in Christ, too much of man's helplessness and too little of his freedom. *Protestant* was the preferred term because it means someone who protests, thus someone who wants to have his own opinion, someone who speaks out rather than giving in to authority. In its negative sense, the word protestant suited the attitude of individualism. But it obtained a meaning that is totally incompatible with the essence of the Christian church. The Church does not teach man to go his own way or arrange his life according to his own understanding. No, the Church proclaims, as commanded by God, that Jesus is the way, the truth, and the life. He and no one else!

This "neo-protestantism" represents in comparison with the faith of the reformers nothing less than a new form of Christianity. In a striking way it has been said that if the gulf between Rome and Wittenberg was a few yards, then the distance between the authentic evangelical faith and the neo-Protestant culture religion equals the distance between sun and moon.

If the reformers would see the current state of the church in many parts of the Protestant world, they would be filled with real anguish for our souls. Maybe they also would teach us a lesson in holy wrath. Because *this* certainly was not what they had fought for. They wanted once again to set the candle on the candlestick, they wanted the Word to have the prominent position and to be preached in its purity and clarity. But what is the use of the Word being preached and heard, if it is received not as God's Word but as more or less well-compiled thoughts of men? And the reformers also restored the Sacrament of the Altar so that the people once again received the chalice and also once again would commune frequently, even every Sunday, and not just once a year, at Easter, as had become the general custom in the Roman church. If they would see the situation in all too many of our congregations, where more than 90 percent of the parishioners in reality have excommunicated themselves by never attending a service and where those who do attend receive the sacrament very seldom, maybe even just once a year, they would weep with grief and wished the Middle Ages back again.

We could continue point by point and ask ourselves if the situation is better now than in the year 1500. The state of morality in large numbers of our people give us hardly any right to be horrified at the licentiousness in monasteries during the Middle Ages. The deplorable decline of prayer discipline in our lives should call us to self-reflection, before we pride ourselves on not using the rosary as Catholics do. And what about righteousness through faith alone? Where is the rightful appreciation of this chief article of the Reformation? How many would be able to give even a scanty explanation of what it means that faith justifies? If one asks an average "Lutheran" member of our church what it is that separates us from Rome, he will predictably answer by pointing out some purely external things. In fact, to a great extent he would mention things which for the reformers themselves never were a dividing-wall but on the contrary belong to great treasure of shared Christian legacy, that only were dropped first by enthusiasts during the Reformation period and later by the new-Protestants. Thus it is being said that private confession, making the sign of the cross, and kneeling are Roman characteristics. That would greatly have surprised Luther! He went to private confession at least every other week; the sign of the cross is part of the daily morning and evening prayers included in the original version of his small catechism; and kneeling during prayer whether at home or at church was for him so obvious that he would have had a hard time to accept our modern pews without kneelers.

* * *

What we have said here does not give in any way a complete picture of the recent developments in our church. There are many other currents which are both deeper and stronger. The revival movements, the leading theology, and the efforts of renewal within the church, e. g. in the area of works of mercy, have been borne by forces of genuine Christian faith. Even so, with the pressing power of the diffuse "zeit-geist," the new-Protestant superficiality has been able to intrude the church and influence much of her everyday life as well our own opinions.

In this situation we must rally around totally different banners. Using all the strength of authentic Christian faith that the Church still has within herself, she must offer resistance against that internal break-down which threatens to destroy her. She must discover anew her true essence and her commission. She must bring forth her half-forgotten treasures. She must proclaim the Word without excuses and reinterpretations. She must again rejoice in her sacraments instead of being somewhat embarrassed by them. She must openly and with infinite gratitude be dedicated to be what God has planted her to be among us: the Swedish branch of Christ's One Holy and Catholic Church.

Everybody has noticed how the wind has changed the last 20 years. The young-church movement emerged with a powerful appeal to the church to bear in mind her mission. It caused a mighty wave of joy and enthusiasm in the church, not at least among the young people. The ecumenical movement, especially through the Ecumenical Meeting in Stockholm 1925, raised a new awareness in Sweden concerning our place in the global Church. And in thousands of Christian homes, both among pastors and parishioners, a new and deeper love grew for our Mother the Church during the spiritual winter, the bleak days of ridicule and indifference. Maybe the day is dawning when the wonderful prophecy we listen to at Epiphany shall become a reality in our parish churches,

> *"Lift up your eyes round about, and see;*
> *they all gather together, they come to you;*
> *your sons shall come from far,*
> *and your daughters shall be carried in the arms.*
> *Then you shall see and be radiant,*
> *Your heart shall thrill and rejoice."*
> Isaiah 60:4–5

Chapter 5

The Parish Church

THE SUNSHINE REFLECTS ABUNDANTLY from the white walls of the parish church, while the ash-trees rustle in the summer breeze. Here she stands. It was here that we began our walk, and now we are back. Our inquiry concerning her essence has led us across the millennia and has invited us to extend our search throughout the whole world. When we now stand before the parish church again, the perspectives open up anew. Maybe it is 800 years since the foundation of the church was laid here on the ridge. Eight hundred years! The thought of this time span is overwhelming. Birger Jarl was not yet born! He ruled Sweden as regent 1250–1266. Among his greatest accomplishments was the founding of Stockholm in 1253. Maybe it was Inge the older or Halsten or Sverker, who then ruled these parts of the country. Inge and Halsten competed for power approximately 1080–1110; the first monasteries were established in Sweden during the reign of King Sverker, 1130–1156.

The parish church up here embodies even greater perspectives than the mere national ones. It was not a new-born community that took on a visible form, when the grey-stone walls of the church began to rise over the area. It was a more than a thousand year old stream of life, that had come to our shores as well. God's house in my parish is a child of the Church that was a reality already when Titus's legions destroyed the temple in Jerusalem. She has seen the great cities of antiquity, now long since in ruins, at the height of their glory and power. She preached the gospel in Carthage, Caesarea and Antioch, while the smoke rose from the sacrifices offered on the altars of Apollo and Minerva. She heard learned debates in high-sounding Greek in the pillared halls of Alexandria. She saw Diocletian and Constantine, Odovakar and Attila outside her walls or under her arches. When our forefathers here in the North still placed children in the woods and sacrificed horses to Tyr, the hymns of the Church had already sounded for hundreds of years in classic beauty on the other side of the forests of Germania, and the words of the creed had been recited on three continents in Latin, Greek, and Syrian, as well as in the Abyssinian and Coptic languages.

    Then she came here too. And now she stands here, that church which for us always shall remain the church of our fathers, those who worshiped here before us. Imagine if we just one time could see what these walls have seen! We would then know more about the life of our forefathers than ever will be known by any researcher. These white walls have seen peasants who still wore belts adorned with runic meanders. Their shaggy horses were harnessed to primitive sleighs outside the church's gateway. Their spears and swords have been put against the narthex wall, and long-ago extinct words from the language of the Vikings would have filled the air. The changes of history have been flitting past in fast-moving scenes. Common men summoned to arms and powerful great men have passed by on the road. Maybe *Karl Knutsson Bonde* and his escort rested in the church yard. A member of the prominent Bonde clan, he ruled Sweden for a total of fourteen years during four different periods beginning in 1436 and ending in 1470. Maybe *Saint Birgitta* (ca. 1303–1377) kneeled on the chancel floor. Founder of the Order of the Most Holy Savior, she is the only Swede ever to be canonized by the pope. It is a certain thing that some of the old bishops in my diocese have said mass at this altar, maybe *Ricardus, Gislo* or *Kol* who all occupied the Linköping chair in 12th century. One of them marked the consecration crosses with holy oil on the newly-plastered walls. If the old stones in the church walls could echo what they since have heard, chances are that we would hear the sound of *Nikolaus Hermanni's* voice or hear *Hans Brask* warn of Luther's heresies, bishops in Linköping 1374–1391 and 1513–1527 respectively. We would hear the first ungainly sermons in the Swedish language. The grand chorales from our Great Power period (1611–1718) would reverberate around us. We would listen to decrees for observance of national days of prayer, to thanksgivings for victories, and to regulations and advice concerning famine and pestilence. The proudest memories and the deepest sufferings of our nation would give a thousand-fold echo of voices in prayer and song inside the church and in conversation outside the church.

Thinking of all this, I almost want to walk up to the church and caress the rough stone wall. These stones are living links which palpably bind me together with the past. My forefathers are dead and rest, no one knows where. But our Mother the Church, who has embraced generation after generation of my people, still stands as a bride in white, eternally young, with the same open gates. It is not just dead stone, where so many prayers have risen toward heaven and so much heavenly reflection has radiated from God's people singing His praise. I can stand with my ear against the stone and hear the eternal pulses of life in the flow of centuries.

The flow of centuries? There is something more. The pulse-beats vibrating in these old walls and the flow of life filling the temple with its warmth, all this is really a flow of that inexhaustible stream of renewal and life, which comes from the very heart of existence, from my Savior and Redeemer. He is the beginning and the continuation and the end of that stream of life, that welled forth in the Holy Land and after a thousand years reached our shores. He gives life also to the old parish church.

Therefore, there is a deep truth behind the beautiful scenery, when she in the evenings reflects the whole vault of heaven on her white walls, and when she stands there shining in the dusk as if she were filled with a mystic internal light. She is really the earthly reflection of a heavenly clarity, she radiates something that is not of this world, she conveys the invisible and imperishable life in Christ's body.

Now I have a vision of the Church such as she really is. High above us is the Heavenly King, the Savior, on His throne of glory. He is surrounded by the heavenly choirs. I cannot see them, and I would not be able to endure their radiant light. But I know that up there is the heavenly stronghold of the Church, the Redeemer Himself with the overwhelming fullness of salvation and with the inexhaustible well of life. From Christ broad rivers of light are now pouring down into our existence. As clusters of sun rays penetrate the clouds, so the light from Christ descends from His throne in heaven into our world of death and corruption. This brilliant light from heaven is caught up by earthly vessels, by external insignificant things which God Himself has chosen to reflect the glory of God's kingdom. This brilliant reflection meets the eye everywhere in the parish church. A Bible is placed on the pulpit: its pages are suffused by this invisible splendor. There is the baptismal font of grayish red stone: it shines in the light from above as an enchanted flower-cup with the sap of life eternal in its stalk. There are the altar books with the prayers of the

Church: they too reflect God's brilliant light. Most clearly I see this heavenly light reflected in the silver chalice and in the wafers on the paten.

Here that light converges, in which Christ descends to be present in our midst. The rays of this light break together as in a prism in the old parish church. This is a holy place, God is present here, heaven is open above us, and we enter into the eternal flow of light. This is what makes the parish church God's Church. Her life is gathered around the altar, the font, and the pulpit, around the Word and the Sacraments.

I do not hesitate for a moment in making this confession: the church here on the ridge is Christ's Church, an expression of God's presence on earth, a revelation of the salvation in our sinful existence. Therefore I shall thank and praise the All-Merciful for raising the church of the apostles here in our northern lands, descending with His saving presence among us Swedes as well.

* * *

Now we stand once again on the church slope looking out over the valley. We are looking over the village and there we see once again the yellow-white gable of the Mission Covenant chapel and the red meeting house of the Pentecostals.

What are we to think about them?

We leave that question in God's hands. To be sure, the sin of division is burning in our conscience. As Christians we must grieve every day that the Body of Christ is broken in this way. We must confess our own fault in this sad drama. If our church had managed her God-given commission as she should have done, the situation would have been different. We are now called upon to pray and work toward the goal that our church once again shall be filled with the fullness and richness of Christ's life. We believe that the old church up here is Christ's Church, founded by Him, and that she owns God's promises, if she only would act on them. As far as other Christian groups are concerned, it is not up to us to make any judgment on them. That they through baptism, just as we, are members of Christ's Body, by God Himself received into His Church, we cannot for a moment doubt that. As their brethren and fellow Christians we wish from our hearts God's blessing upon them. We wish for both them and us the grace to grasp the whole richness of Christ's fullness in such a way that the final re-unification shall be possible, not as a compromise but as a great step forward toward the truth. We cannot but in hope and prayer look forward to a day, when as in the past all genuinely Christian spiritual life shall dwell under the same church vaults, and when Christ's Church shall anew realize her catholic essence, so that all that is now divided into denominations and sects shall worship and serve God within one and the same Holy and Catholic Church.

Waiting for that day, we shall do everything in our power to live in peace with Christians in other traditions. We are determined to manage our legacy faithfully, extending our efforts to make its richness come alive in our nation. We also want to listen carefully and be humbly ready to learn, if we will be shown that we have forgotten and neglected something that is of great value in the life of Christians elsewhere. We Christians have enough to do in heeding Christ's commission to His Church to make disciples of all people; we cannot afford to spend any time and energy in fighting each other.

We can clearly see it in front of us as we walk down from the church. We see the many homes in the village, the new settlement further down the road, and all the farmhouses in the valley. There are the real challenges: we think of all those who live and die without perceiving the light from heaven, which has come into our existence to lead us home to God.

In these times of indifference it is tempting to console oneself with thinking that the large crowds are not necessary: the church is Christ's true Church, no matter how many desert her. The crowd of believers may be large or small. Whatever the case, Christ's true Church is amongst us, as long as the sacred texts are recited and as long as the Sacrament of the Altar is celebrated.

This is indeed all true. And yet: even if the Church remains, we cannot be at peace when so many stay away. What we have envisioned of the essence of the Church: the Savior on His heavenly throne with all the treasures of grace and the light that flows down from Him and takes on visible form and shape among us in the means of grace, all this is calling out for a continuation. It seeks *faith* on earth, it wants to gather us all in this light, which only for our sake is shining forth in the world. The Church is the vehicle for an infinite love, God's love, stretching out to reach His lost children. It would be treason if the Church kept that love for herself, so that she began to love her ancient liturgy, her hymns and her customs, but forgot the people that she has been sent to save. Precisely because she is God's visible presence on earth, she must love all the people with God's own love, also the most scornful and rejecting, also the most lost and repulsive. Her constant and burning longing must be to reveal the heavenly glory to the blind and insecure and straying, and convey the atoning love to the suffering and the oppressed.

Can she do this?

Yes, she can, *if God may be at work in her.* It means: if God may speak through His Word and act through His means of grace. Our interest now turns to them. They demand a special main part of our presentation.

Part Two

The Presence of the Holy One

Chapter 6

God Is In Our Midst

GOD IS IN OUR midst! All Christian life is characterized by this overwhelming truth, the whole existence of the church is carried by this jubilant certainty: God is present here! God who is invisible, unreachable and incomprehensible has descended to us. His incorruptible and imperishable glory has entered this world marked by death, has become embodied in the only begotten Son, has overcome death, and has established that community of victory, redemption and salvation, which is named God's Holy Church.

God is in our midst! At one point the wall of separation is broken. All glory of heaven is now flowing into our existence. The morning has dawned and the Good News is now resounding on earth:

We have seen His glory! The eternal life which was with the Father was made manifest to us! That which we have seen with our eyes, which we have looked upon and touched with our hands, this we proclaim. The light has come into the world, the darkness is passing away, and the true light is already shining (see John 1:14; 1 John 1:1–2; John 3:19; 1 John 2:8).

Even more: From His fullness have we all received grace upon grace! In Him we have redemption, the forgiveness of our sins. In Him we are blessed with every spiritual blessing in the heavenly places. In Him we are partakers of the fullness of deity, of the unspeakable, incomprehensible and incorruptible glory of the heavenly realm (see John 1:16; Eph 1:3,7; Col 2:10).

> "All preaching in the early church is carried by this experience of the fullness . . . of the richness that has been revealed and given to us, of the treasure that we carry with us in jars of clay, of our death

with Christ which we take on, so that His life may be revealed in us, and of the break-through of a new life. Hence this joy, this transfigured light even in suffering: we rejoice in our sufferings (Rom 5:3), as sorrowful, yet always rejoicing (2 Cor 6:10), because our Lord Jesus Christ will change our lowly body to be like His glorious body (Phil 3:21). It seems that words do not suffice for Paul when he describes what has happened in Christ: the revelation of the fullness, of the grace and of God's mystery, which is Christ in us, the hope of glory (Col 1:27). For all the promises of God find their Yes in Him (2 Cor 1:20). The apostle himself is won by Christ (Phil 3:12), he is overwhelmed by the new life, he is a slave of Jesus Christ. Again and again he must witness to the unsearchable riches of Christ (Eph 3:8). He speaks about God's glorious grace, the riches of His grace (Eph 1:6f). He lifts up the riches of His glorious inheritance in the saints and the immeasurable greatness of His power in us who believe (Eph 1:18f). And this God's unspeakable glory has come to us in the fullness of time and in the fullness of Christ. For in Him the whole fullness of the Godhead dwells bodily (Col 2:9)." (Arseniew, Nikolaus von. *Der urchristliche Realismus und die Gegenwart*. Kassel 1933. Page I:9).

God is in our midst! Also today. Because what happened once in history is not only something in the past. The connection that was then opened between earth and heaven has never since been broken. The same Lord, who came to dwell among us, also built His Church among us. He is still active there through His Spirit, in the external forms of the word and the sacraments. The new life still descends into this world of corruption. The eternal light is still being revealed. Christ is still doing the work for which He was made man.

To be sure, we do have the treasure in jars of clay. Just as many rejected God, because He came in the form of insignificance, the self-glorifying human will is still blind for everything except for the jars of clay. As long as man is enough unto himself and lives in the closed sphere of his own will, behind an impenetrable shell of his own thoughts, his own desires and his own helpless corruption, he can never see God's glory in the Church. "But he who does what is true comes to the light" (John 1:21). He who hungers and thirsts for God will soon notice where the wells are.

God is in our midst! Just as Jesus once entered the world as God's outstretched hand, as a visible revelation of God's invisible being, and as an audible message of that which no ear has heard, so God's hand is still stretched out at the baptismal font and the communion rail, and so the

Word still sounds, not as a mechanical repetition of what the Master once said but as a continually repeated message from the mouth of our Savior. The Word is not only a teaching but a living call, an offer from God, a herald's summons, that the Eternal One issues to us and that again and again requires from us a response. It is the same way with the sacraments. They are not symbols and metaphors but Christ's way to deal with us today, just as real and tangible as He once dealt with people on the fields in Galilee and the streets in Capernaum. Thus He has given us baptism in order still to receive people into the Kingdom and into the fellowship of His followers. Thus He is still at the table with us in the Lord's Supper to make us partakers of His atoning sacrifice. He has not left the world, where He once was born for our salvation.

The miracle that took place in the incarnation when the Word became flesh continues in the church and the sacraments. He who does not understand the sacraments will not understand the depth of what Christ has done for us. Faith becomes a philosophy. Jesus becomes a moral role model. The Spirit is replaced with the idealism of good intentions. But faith in God's world-embracing liberation deed in the incarnation, the jubilation in God's having come to us in His Son and freed us from sin and death, everything that is part of the great drama of our salvation, it all is obliterated, forgotten or reinterpreted. Thereby Christianity itself is dissolved. Living and genuine Christianity is in its innermost essence faith in the incarnation and the atonement. It is in its innermost essence sacramental, it is the message of God's real and wondrous presence in the midst of the fallen creation, in the Lord Christ and His Church.

The means of grace is of old the designation for the vehicles that God has chosen to realize His presence in our midst. We shall now deal with them in proper order. Everyone knows three of them: The Word, The Lord's Supper, and Baptism. But our church owns yet a sacrament that needs to be acknowledged and fully appreciated. Our church owns an office that is instituted by Christ in order that the Word shall be proclaimed and the sacraments administered. The sacraments belong together, they are interconnected. They are the Church's external, visible organs, the earthly vessels in which the flow of life from above is channeled and brought into our everyday existence. They are externally insignificant. Yet, they are holy for the sake of God's promises. It is because of them we have the right to say with steadfast certainty: God is in our midst. God is present *here*.

Chapter 7

God's Word and Promise

"The Christian faith in the authority of the Bible, I have tried to render as a statement of confession: I believe that the Bible tells us what God through the Bible wants to tell us, or: I believe that God has given us His word in that way that He wanted us to have it" (Wallerius, Ivar. *Kristendomens självständighetskrav [Christianity's Quest for Independence.* Göteborg, 1927. Page 31). That is the way "a right teacher" from West-Sweden has worded his faith in God's word and promise. That wording essentially says what the Church always and unanimously has taught concerning Holy Scripture.

The Church never adopted a doctrinal statement of inspiration. The ancient church never for a moment questioned the Bible as God's word, but it never felt the need to determine the nature of the inspiration. Various possibilities were left open. However, the inspiration itself was and remains one of the unwavering truths of the Church.

The Bible is *God's address to man,* God's authoritative message about my sin and His grace. This message is not negotiable. The Bible has come from God such as it lies before me. When I open it, I can do it in the full assurance that here God wants to speak to me in order to tell me something that I otherwise could not know, something that I for the sake of my salvation *must* know.

In the language of ancient piety this has been worded in this way: the Bible shall be read *with the intention to learn about salvation.* It means that I should read it to get this question answered: How shall I gain eternal life? Any other use of the Bible is an abuse, because it would be using it for something that God never meant. If my curious mind attempts to use the Bible as an oracle that for example would tell me how the stock market would turn out next week, or as a convenient encyclopedia to find out how long the world has existed or how the digestion of the hare functions, then I can only blame myself. Maybe I will get some answers, but I have no guarantee that those answers are from God. He has more important things to speak about with me.

Just as the Son of God lived here on earth, the word of God also has its earthly and insignificant form. Just as many were offended that the Son of God appeared among them as a simple carpenter with callous hands, many are also offended that the word of God here on earth has the same form as common human words. Just as God allowed that we humans maltreated his Son and spat Him in the face, nor does he prevent us when we maltreat the Word by nailing it to the cross of criticism, spitting on it and scornfully saying: May it now step down to us and answer our questions, showing us that everything in it makes sense, so that we can believe in it!

Both word and sacrament are vehicles of the living God. Both are expressions of God's innermost being. God is that love that could not remain on His throne in exalted peace, when His children on earth perished. He intervened, He descended to us, He spoke to us, and He dealt with us. Just as the hand of God then reached into the visible creation, He still intervenes, speaks and deals through His visible vehicles: word and sacrament. Just as the sacraments are carriers of the heavenly life that God only can give, and gates through which the glory of grace descends into our existence, the Word also is filled with the Spirit and the life that proceeds from God himself. Both word and sacrament are thus a stream of life from another world, coming forth into our fallen creation. In the sacraments the emphasis is on the real act that God does. In the Word it is on the speech that proceeds from God's mouth. But it is only a difference of degree, because the Word is filled with might, loaded with God's power. It strikes down on earth as a strong hand; God sends it against His adversaries as a mighty army (cf. Isa 9:8, NRSV). Just as we can say that God *acts* through the Word, we can also say that He *speaks* and *preaches* through the sacraments, not only through the Word that is always in them but also through the very act. Word and sacrament are of the same essence, because it is the same new era that is at work in both of them. It is the same God who intervenes through them in this world, and it is the same salvation that they mediate.

The church is therefore obliged to care for the Word with the same commitment as she cares for the sacraments. God has given both of them to us because both are needed. If we neglect the preaching of the Word, it is a sign that we have a false understanding of the sacraments. If the sacraments are pushed aside, it is just as much a sign that the Word no longer is received in the right way. In the former case one tries to avoid God's judgment upon our sins and His demands for repentance and instead put one's trust solely in the sacraments, as if they would work *ex opere operato,* that is merely by the external mechanical use of them. In the latter case, when the sacraments are pushed aside, it often seems to be a sign indicating that the Word also has lost its sacramental character: it is no longer received as the living Word of God, which judges and transforms, but as a kind of "view of life," that engages man's thoughts and feelings but not his total being and everyday life. Just as the rationalism of the 1800's could not understand the sacraments, because it did not want to see God so really present as He is, nor could it understand the Word, because it did not want to receive it as an irrevocable authority with power to judge and restore. This is in both cases due to the same reinterpretation of Christianity: a slipping away from faith in the incarnated God who in boundless love became man to save us, to faith in the mild Father who in exalted majesty rules through the laws of nature and quite graciously looks down at His capable children, as they are helping Him to correct the antiquated doctrines and the unhistorical view of the Bible, the legacy from a less enlightened era.

The Word works sacramentally. It emerges from God as a flow of life. When this flow reaches and surrounds a human being, God is near her whether she wants that or not. Just as a person at the Lord's table totally apart from her state of mind or of her faith receives the body and blood of Christ, for life or for judgment, likewise she hears God speak in the Word totally apart from her feelings, her thoughts or her faith. And when God speaks, it is not theoretical teachings that He sets forth, but it is a *commandment* or an *offer* that He issues. Therefore, man must take a stand before the Word. He will respond *either* in faith, gratitude and obedience, *or* in indifference, impenitence and defiance. In the former case it means life, grace and forgiveness, but in the latter case guilt and judgment.

All that the Church does is based on the firm faith that the Word is efficient and that without the Word there is no salvation for this suffering world, since it does not know God. Nothing but God's word and sacrament can make a person a Christian. If the Word does not have any effect on her, nothing else will help. In times of decline, when the crowds are thinning seriously, the Church must only ask herself if she has rightly administered the sacraments and if she has proclaimed the Word purely and clearly and lovingly. If she has done that, then she has also done all that is in her power and all that God has commanded her to do for the conversion of man. He who hardens himself before God's word rightly proclaimed has therewith said no to God Himself. Our heavenly Father must again and again experience that grief. The Church too must live with that grief, in prayer and patient waiting, without giving up hope, without getting weary in deeds of love, and without ceasing to proclaim the Word just as purely and clearly and lovingly as always. But woe to her if she thinks that adding human means will do it, where God's word was rejected, and sevenfold woe to her if she, fearing to lose also her last hearers, attempts to keep them with human ties but neglects to preach the Word for judgment and grace, purely and clearly and lovingly! It can be very tempting to do such a thing. When people are not coming to church, God's word is being diluted with lots of other things that are attractive to sinful human nature. The methods vary according to the taste of the people that one is eager to reach. But the consequences are just as disastrous in every case. One gets a public instead of a congregation. One substitutes religious interest for faith. One connects the people to activities, projects and entertaining events, but not to Christ. Of course, it is quite possible to get a lot of people to come together! Captivating speakers and popular musicians will often attract large audiences. Hundreds of examples of the entertainment offered by the churches are frequently advertised in the newspapers, on community bulletin boards, and on bill boards along our highways. That is the way the churches go, when they no longer dare to trust only and solely in God's word and sacrament.

This is not meant to be an anathema upon all the many necessary attempts to reach those who from bluntness or under the pressure of a secularized environment are kept from hearing God's word. It is meant as a reminder to all the Church's friends and servants in the young generation. We must wake up and seriously defend ourselves less God's word shall be drowned in a wave of spiritual diversion. *We must do the work of the Reformation once again.* As once before, at the Reformation, the Word must be lifted up from its degradation, it must again be preached and received as GOD'S WORD, so that it once again will produce conversion and new life. If an event is published as "of the church," everyone should know for certain: *there,* for sure, we will hear the truth, purely and clearly and lovingly proclaimed.

During the Middle Ages, when the Word was obscured, the church life was going on with magnificent masses and with delightful outdoor processions, which captivated the minds and the hearts of the people. We rightly criticize much of this and call it estheticism. But it is not at all any better to keep the church life going with our modern methods of entertainment, and then add a "sermon" crowded with anecdotes but with God's word inserted here and there. The whole system is an appeal to natural man's need for fellowship, to his romantic and sentimental inclinations. *This is also estheticism,* but in coarser and simpler form. If something like this would be done very occasionally in order to reach totally indifferent people, it might be defensible. The serious thing is that sensational methods have a definite tendency to be used in all activities of the churches to reach out. The result is obvious: people become fastidious. They won't show up unless something "special" is offered. By offering something "special," churches are actually unintentionally (or is it intentionally?) causing people to drift away from the very foundation in all Christian life, the clear-as-day duty to use God's word regularly and to receive it for its own sake, on its own terms. The very word "edification" has taken on a different meaning. Nowadays when someone says about a sermon that it was edifying, he means that it was a moving message; the preacher had had the ability to captivate the hearers, putting their feelings in motion. Our forefathers had quite different expectations for an edifying sermon. It should "cause repentance, faith, and sanctification." There should be *results* from it. The results depend on two things: first, the sermon must be in accordance with God's word, it must be *right,* secondly, the hearer must in faith and obedience surrender to the word that God speaks. Then one has reason to say, "This was edifying," and this regardless of what one felt or did not feel concerning the preacher's delivery.

Thus what is needed once again is that the watchword from the parliamentary session in Västerås 1527, by which the Church in Sweden began her Reformation, might be heralded with new power: *God's word must be preached purely everywhere in the kingdom.* All of us in the church need to acknowledge that our salvation stands and falls with the right proclamation and the right reception of the Word, and not with any other procedures or movements or organizations or reforms.

This causes another intrusive question. There used to be in the tree of the Church a sound and strong heartwood, an uncompromisingly faithful kind of people, called "church readers." They were referred to with this honorable designation because of the holy persistence with which they clang to the Bible and books of sermons, to family devotions and the high mass. Where are they now? Who will take their place? If we are to experience a new reformation, which will lift the Word up from its degradation, then we must revive the personal study of the Bible. In caring consideration for the eternal welfare of her children, the Church cannot be silent on this issue, because without the regular use of God's word, the matter of repentance, faith and sanctification will not take on the urgency that it should have in our lives.

Reading the Bible on your own is no easy undertaking. The Church has therefore always referred the beginner to the preached Word. It is offered to him expounded and explained, in a definite order, which during the course of the liturgical year systematically leads the listener through all the main articles of the creed. It is in every aspect easier to assimilate than the read Word. And yet, it cannot replace it. Therefore the Church tries to see to it that every church member, and of course prospective members as well, has her own Bible and exhorts her to read it.

What is needed for a profitable Bible study is first of all an honest intention and a good portion of holy persistency. One must set aside a certain time every day, reserved only for prayer and Bible study. And one must determine a plan for the reading. Reading the whole Bible in just one year is not possible for most people, especially if due time is given to meditation on the reading for each day. Some of us need two or three or even four years to read all the sixty-six books of Holy Scriptures. Each daily reading should include a passage from both the Old Testament and from the New Testament (see Appendix with a flexible plan for reading the whole Bible at your chosen pace). Most hymnals include a lectionary, usually following the liturgical year, which means that the readings cover the main tenets of the Bible's message.

Most important: we should always read the Bible with the intention to learn about salvation. As already pointed out: you can always open the Bible with the certain assurance that God wants to speak to you in that Scripture that is your chosen assignment for the day. He who listens in faith with this prayer in his heart: "Speak, Lord, for your servant is listening" (1 Sam 3:9), will realize most often with great certainty what the

Lord wants him to know through the Word that day. It often penetrates one's conscience as glowing iron or gushes as a stream of strength and assurance into one's heart, helping a Christian to overcome perplexity by answering his questions pertaining to his life and faith. Every Christian has marked passages in his Bible that in times of adversity were messages from God, intended just for him on days when he dearly needed them.

Yet, we must always humbly remember that the Word accomplishes what *God* desires and achieves the purpose for which He sent it (Isa 55:11). Since the Bible is God's word for all generations and all nations, it hardly means that each verse and each chapter has a message just for me today in my particular situation. If I stand *under* the Word, ready to receive what God wants to give me, then I can trust that God shall open my eyes so that I can see what He wants to give me today. What I am unable to apply to my own life or even understand at all, that I must just pass by for now. It does not cease to be God's word, just because I cannot understand it today. I shall save it in the safe assurance that I have yet much left to discover in this inexhaustible book.

We shall now conclude as we began, with a quote, this time from the Word itself. It is a promise that once was given to the old Israel but it is also intended for the new Israel. It was given in a period of disasters, in a context of threat and judgment, and yet at last it is turned into a promise of restoration. We believe that this Bible passage applies to us as well, conscious of the judgment that now befalls us because we have despised the Word, but also trusting in the promise which in spite of all stands firm. Under that promise we gratefully continue our service in the Church, without looking to the right or to the left, knowing well that the time of its fulfillment is coming:

> "Behold, the days are coming," says the Lord God,
> "when I will send a famine on the land;
> not a famine of bread,
> nor a thirst for water,
> but of hearing the words of the Lord."
> Amos 8:11

Chapter 8

The New Covenant

There is a story about a Norwegian man, who was in Stockholm to see some good friends of his. He was deeply affected by the Oxford Movement, so he shared with his hosts his desire to attend church on Sunday morning. He especially expressed what a joy it would be to partake in the Lord's Supper together with his Swedish brethren. The Swedes looked at one other somewhat embarrassed. Partake in the Lord's Supper, that was not exactly what they had in mind. However, they decided to check the church ads in the newspapers. They looked for a service with the sacrament included, but without success. Finally they had to state the fact: the Lord's Supper was not celebrated anywhere in all of Stockholm on that summer Sunday!

Maybe the story is legendary, but it is in any case typical. This is what a Christian from almost any other country would discover, when he gets acquainted more closely with church life in Sweden. We do not need to go further than to Oslo or Copenhagen to find out that the Lord's Supper has a totally different position. And if we would travel around the world or back through the centuries, we would see that the Lord's Supper ever since the earliest times of Christianity as a matter of course was and remains the main divine service, celebrated every Sunday in the overwhelming number of locations where the Church is present.

How could it be in any other way? After all, the Lord's Supper is the only service, that Jesus Himself expressly has prescribed when he said: *Do this*. No matter what opinion one would have about the essence of Christianity, one must reasonably say: *This* at least belongs to the foundations, this is an inescapable element in a Christian life.

That is why the neglect of the Lord's Supper in so many of our congregations seems so frightening. It is so strange that even people who still want to be counted as Christians dare to stay away from the sacrament year after year. This feast, the purest well of joy in life, that ought to be the central point in all Christian life, has become something that all too many people recoil at, something that one partly fears and partly is ashamed of.

We are now called upon to help our fellow Christians to find their way to the Lord's Table. Then I think we should not begin with doctrines and theological distinctions concerning this sacrament but rather with the graphic reality in the night when the Lord Jesus was betrayed.

* * *

In our imagination we move back to that first Maunday Thursday evening, finding our way on the narrow and dirty streets in the holy city. Around us the last daylight in the sky is fading, a pale glow lingers along the copings of the walls, but down in the narrow lane the darkness of night is already thick. We walk through a pitch-black archway, cross the built-in square, and go groping up a steep stairway. A fluttering shining light guides us into a large austere room with lime-whitened walls. The oil-lamps on the table light up a circle of weather-beaten faces. They are men of the people with calloused hands, gathered around the paschal lamb. They have been gathered many times before around their Master. But this evening is something special. They all have a sense that this is the last time they are together. The tension in the struggle with the leaders of the people has unbearably increased. Ill-omened clouds have been gathering above them. The deadly hatred of the Pharisees is evident. The enemy can strike at any time, and he is going to strike hard in order to silence once and for all the offensive prophet from Nazareth.

Their Master is at table with them. He knows that His hour has come. Now the dark gate to the suffering that He must undergo is being opened. Now He must leave them, these inexperienced and injudicious apostles, who are going to be the leaders in the new Israel, the foundation for the Church that shall stand to the end of the ages. Just days ago they were debating which of them were the greatest. Now only a few hours remain for Him to be together with them.

What did the Master do at this hour that marked such a crucial time in His mission here on earth? He did something so infinitely common and yet so sublime. He made their table fellowship into a divine service, indeed something more than a divine service.

Table fellowship is in itself something holy for the Orientals. An Arab would not in the slightest way harm a stranger, with whom he has shared a piece of bread or a pinch of salt. The Jews hallowed each meal with prayer and recitation of the Psalms. Jesus did the same as the head of His family, consisting of his chosen apostles. It is not hard for us to imagine the significance of table fellowship between Jesus and the Twelve and others of his disciples in their everyday life together. Their wanderings were at times full of hardships. The land was poor with many areas where water was scarce. When the band of disciples toward evening-time rested in the shade of a big rock and the Master gave thanks to God, broke the last loaf of bread and distributed pieces to everyone, while the disciples shared the remaining water in the leather skin seeing to it that everyone got some, even if nobody got enough, such evenings they certainly experienced the table fellowship as a bond of union, hallowed by God himself.

In this last night, the Master did something that He had done so many times before: He gave thanks to God, broke the bread, and gave it to the disciples. But this evening He said: *This is My body given for you.* In the same manner He let the cup with the red wine be passed around the table and said: *This cup is the new covenant in My blood, which is poured out for you for the forgiveness of sins.*

What were the disciples thinking at that moment? They would hardly have been able to give an account of it immediately afterwards. They felt that they had experienced something that words could not describe sufficiently. They were standing before a mystery, the depth of which they only vaguely could imagine, an act so expressive and comprehensive that it would take them years to understand its meaning.

They must have been shaken by the expressive power in that symbolic act that the Master had carried out before their eyes. When He broke the bread, the tough unleavened bread that had to *be torn* into pieces, they saw how His body would be torn and broken down in death. When He handed them the red wine and spoke about the blood that would be poured, they understood that death and the bloody reality of martyrdom already was waiting at the door.

However, it was not all that they understood. The Master had told them that all this happened for *their* sake. And yet more: He had mentioned *a new covenant*. They all knew the old covenant. They were gathered this night to observe its remembrance. God had made it with Israel, when He delivered His people out of Egypt. Was God now about to make a completely new covenant? Was maybe a completely new era to break into the world this fateful night? They remembered that everything that the Master had done had always been pointing forward, toward a new Israel, toward that Church that would prevail against the gates of hell. Now He was again speaking about what was to come, about the new covenant that would embrace not only Israel but also the many who previously had been excluded, and He commanded them to celebrate this meal anew, again and again, in His remembrance. Was God thus about to intervene in this night to accomplish a new deed of salvation, greater than any of those that He had done in the old covenant?

All this could hardly have been more than a premonition and vague expectation in their minds and hearts that evening. But one thing was certain: when they received the bread that the Master gave them, a fellowship was established so real and living that it was better than all theoretical clarity. The most important thing was beyond any doubt: the invisible God was mysteriously present in His chosen Messiah, in the Master and Son of Man, sitting there in their midst, and it was into His fellowship that they now were included. They had been so powerfully overcome by that fact that one of them in victorious jubilation later on proclaimed with these words, "That which we have seen with our eyes, which we have looked at and our hands have touched, this we proclaim concerning the Word of life. The life appeared; we have seen it and testify to it" (1 John 1:1–2). This life, the mysterious and divine, that they had seen in the Son of Man, was given to them here. They received it as a gift from His hand, as He had said firmly and authoritatively: This is My body. This is My blood. Now they knew that they were one with Him, in a covenant and an essential fellowship that would hold in life and death.

Then came the disaster: the cross. The faith of the apostles faltered. That was not the way they had fathomed God's great deed of salvation. They fled. But God had still something in store that they had not expected: the resurrection. Here they stood before something that confirmed and sealed more than they ever would have dared to hope. Their faith was firmly fortified. They came together again, to conquer the world!

As they now took on this seemingly preposterous task, they would experience in earnest what the Lord had given them in the night when He was betrayed. The memory of all the times that He had broken the bread in their midst was woven together with the remembrance of the last supper and His sacrificial death. Now they understood more and more why He had said that His blood was poured out for many *for the forgiveness of sins*. They had all forsaken Him that night. It was also for their sake that He had suffered. But they too were included in the atonement and the new covenant. They owned the seal of forgiveness in that cup that He Himself had handed them. They knew that a new era had broken into the world! They themselves had witnessed how the Life that was in Him had overcome sin and death. They knew that it was that life and that victory, which He wanted to be theirs as well, when He before His suffering took them up into the new covenant. Thus they celebrated the Lord's Supper with joy and jubilation as one celebrates a great victory. "They broke bread in their homes and ate together with glad and sincere hearts, praising God" (Acts 2:46–47). That tone of triumph, of thanksgiving and liberation, which sounded through the celebration of the sacrament in the early church, belongs to the basic tone of the Christian message.

* * *

As we have seen, the Lord's Supper was in early Christianity most of all *table fellowship,* by which the great brotherhood of the Church was made manifest in a simple and palpable way. Here new converts were indissolubly included in the Christian fellowship. They were taken up into the circle of those who had listened to the Savior Himself and walked with Him on the byways of Galilee. They ate at the same table and drank from the same cup as the Lord's apostles. It could not be stated more plainly that they too were partakers of that covenant and that salvation which had here been established. There was never more than *one* communion table with only one chain of communicants. Wherever the sacrament was celebrated, there was always someone at the table who had communed elsewhere side by side with someone else, who in her turn with other believers was associated with the first Christian congregation in Jerusalem, with its communion table and with its circle of men who had been at table around the Master in the night when the Lord's Supper was instituted. Thus the holy table fellowship became one of the strongest bands in holding the early church together. "Because there is one bread, we who are many are one body, for we all partake of the one bread" (1 Cor 10:17).

This table fellowship was at the same time *a fellowship in and with Christ*. It was a partaking "of the table of *the Lord*" (1 Cor 10:21), where He Himself was present. It conveyed all that the fellowship and life-giving connection with Him could give a disciple. As we have already seen, this kind of fellowship the early church understood as a *fellowship in the Body of Christ*. "The cup of blessing which we bless, is it not a participation in the blood of Christ? The bread which we break, is it not a participation in the body of Christ? ... we are one body" (1 Cor 10:16–17). That divine reality, that revelation of life and light and truth, which in Christ Jesus has appeared on earth, has sacrificed itself on the cross, has conquered death, and has risen in glory. All this descends anew here in our world, pouring itself as a flow of life upon the faithful, making them parts of the new creation that now has its hidden beginning in the Church, visible only to the eyes of faith. But on the strength of God's unfailing might, it shall all appear when the Lord returns in glory and power. And yet, this coming Kingdom is revealed to the believers at every celebration of the Lord's Supper, to be sure in insignificance and poverty, yet overshadowed by the glory of the world to come. "For as often as you eat this bread and drink the cup, you proclaim the Lord's death until He comes" (1 Cor 11:26).

* * *

Considering this background, we shall think about what the Lord's Supper means for us today.

1. The Lord's Supper is **confession**. Walking the few steps from the pew to the altar rail conveys a message, noticed down to the last pew under the balcony and maybe to the farthest corner of the parish, that one wants to belong to the Lord who for our sake offered His life in death and rose again and lives eternally. It does not mean that one is claiming to be more special or further advanced in Christian knowledge. One only confesses about oneself that one is a sinner. About Christ, one confesses that he is the Savior without whom one cannot live.

2. The Lord's Supper is **remembrance**. Coming to the altar rail and kneeling there, I am at that Lord's table that once was set in the upper room in Jerusalem. Here I experience a definite historic reality with simple and powerful signs of remembrance. On the altar is still the com-

mon meal of the Orient: bread and wine. The pastor still wears the garment that in spite of the liturgical design reveals its unbroken connection with the cloak and tunic which were worn by the Lord and His apostles. The hand that gives me the bread is only the current link in an unbroken chain that through 19 centuries of ordinations stretches back all the way to the apostles in the holy city. All this tells me that the Savior once lived in our midst, that He ate and drank as one of us, and that here I am observing the remembrance of an event, which was just as real as other historical events, for example the death of our King Gustavus Adolphus in the battle of Lützen in Germany on 6 November 1632, which we call into remembrance by having designated that day as a national flag day here in Sweden.

3. **The Lord's Supper is *communio*, fellowship.** Kneeling at the altar rail, I am very close to the other communicants. Maybe I don't even know their names. And yet, I know that we are tied to one another in a fellowship that is stronger than any family ties, more intimate than any kinship. We are limbs in the one and same organism of the Spirit. The blood from the one and same heart flows through each one of us. If we would not see one another again in this earthly life, we know we shall meet again at the same heavenly banquet.

This fellowship is experienced through the whole circle of communicants. Where the circle ends at the chancel wall, the fellowship still continues; in the church yard is the resting place of the dead, the Lord's faithful, who now are partakers of the great banquet in heaven. They are with us as a great cloud of witnesses, they continue the small circle of people around the altar in my parish church, a circle that widens and is extended both back in time through the centuries and forward into the eternal world. It is a table fellowship without end. Shoulder by shoulder are they with us: our own faithful ancestors who once received the sacrament here at this altar, saints and martyrs elsewhere through the ages, and finally the Lord Himself and His apostles in the glorious kingdom in heaven above where the circle comes to its conclusion.

This is *communio sanctorum*, the communion of saints in Christ's kingdom of grace. Celebrating the Lord's Supper with my brothers and sisters in Christ, I am connected with the saints who sit at the Lord's table in the heavenly kingdom. I am counted as one of God's Holy people. Is that really possible, is it really true? Yes, it is, because

4. The Lord's Supper is God's visible seal of the forgiveness of sins! When the pastor comes closer to my place at the altar rail, I hear again and again: For you ... For you ... For you. Yes, this sacrifice was given also *for me*, for forgiveness of sins. Here I let go of all doubts. No longer do I anxiously ask myself if I was sufficiently attentive during the confession of sins, if I am sufficiently repentant in my heart and sufficiently focused in my intent to improve my life. I *have* not deserved this and I *can* not deserve it. But my Lord comes and he says: For you ... For you! I cannot doubt that He knew what He did when He instituted this sacrament. I cannot not doubt that He meant what He said. And yet, He must have known that His disciples just a few hours later would forsake and deny Him! Thus I stand before the fact and must believe it: Although I have not deserved it, He loves also me and has given Himself also for me. So I commend myself into His hands and entrust my future to His mercy and supreme power.

5. The Lord's Supper is *unio mystica*, the mysterious union with the Savior. If we could see the invisible, we would see the Lord Himself standing at the altar, shining in heavenly transparency, just as real as any of us and filled with a glory that none of us possesses. That was the way He had shown Himself to the disciples after the resurrection. Gathered at the altar rail, we would see Him lifting His hands and blessing the bread and the cup, as He did in the night of the institution of the Lord's Supper. We would see Him walking along the altar rail and Himself handing us His gifts, and we would see how the gift itself, the white bread in His hand and the dark wine in the chalice, would begin to shine with the same heavenly transparency, conveying the same transcendent life that was in Him Himself.

Therefore we bow our heads in reverence at the altar rail, trembling before God's miracle. This gift comes from the Savior Himself. The outpouring of His heavenly glory that once surrounded me in baptism comes here to me anew. The atoning blood and the irresistible life stream of the resurrection from my heavenly Lord are flowing into me, just as the heart at every beat of the pulse drives the warming and renewing life stream of the blood through my limbs. Thus I am one with Him and live with Him in a mysterious, indissoluble and intimate union, in an *unio mystica*.

6. The Lord's Supper is *a sacrifice*. This sacrament is altogether an overwhelming proclamation of the Lord's death, a dramatic presentation of that sacrifice that was given and poured out for the atonement of the sins of the world. This sacrifice of Christ's, which is the central point of world history and which reveals the innermost meaning of existence, overshadows us all, as the benefits of it is offered to all people through the ages. In the Lord's Supper this offer comes to us as a penetrating appeal, "Be reconciled to God!" (2 Cor 5:20).

When this appeal takes hold of a Christian's heart at the Lord's table, then he himself, included in Christ's atonement, becomes a sacrifice, dedicated to God. This is the only proper response that he can give to God's great act of atonement and to His abundant mercy: he falls down before Him, commends himself to Him, rejoices before Him and dedicates himself to serve Him with everything he is and owns. Thus man comes to the sacrament with his sacrifice, presenting his body "as a living sacrifice, holy and acceptable to God" (Rom 12:1). He puts himself and all his plans, his wishes and his will, his mental powers, his time, his worries and impulses as a gift before the altar, dedicating it to God as a thank-offering of the soul.

The Lord's Supper is therefore also *eucharist,* thanksgiving. Who could hold back jubilation when the heart is filled with the glory of God, when the soul perceives that God is near? This jubilation flows as a roaring wave of praise toward us ever since the days of the early church. It sounds endlessly throughout the world today in the joyful rhythms of the liturgy, and it is thousand-fold answered in the innermost prayers of the faithful. This we shall return to in another chapter in this book.

* * *

No matter how boundlessly one can speak about the riches of the Lord's Supper, that still does not mean that its true value is depending on the communicant's feelings and experiences. An old wise saying tells us that it is on Thursday rather than on Sunday that one will know the true blessing of the Sunday communion. The real benefit of having received the blessed sacrament is not the emotions at the communion itself or the pious sentiments afterwards. Even if one does not experience anything of all that, one has still met one's Savior and received His gift. It is in the long run, during the strains of everyday life, in moral conflicts and in the many decisions, that the true power of the Lord's Supper is revealed. When communing becomes an inescapable part of my Christian life, when there is a quiet and obvious certainty in my soul that I just recently was present at the Lord's table and soon will be there again, then all my deeds and all my words will slowly begin to be marked by the nearness of the Holy One.

Communing just once or twice during the whole year is therefore spiritually living on minimum ration. This is actually contempt for the Lord's Supper. "When a person, with nothing to hinder him, lets a long period of time elapse without ever desiring the sacrament, I call that despising it," says Luther in the Large Catechism (V:49). It may be caused by the stingy and ungrateful attitude that always objects to all God's offers: do I *have to* do that? It can also be due to a wry and misdirected reverence. One believes that the Lord's Supper is something so holy that one dares not approach it without first having thoroughly polished up one's feelings and thoughts. One prepares oneself for a long time, gets wound up in a mood of great solemnity, wants to be very moved at the altar and tries to keep the mood from the communion to stay as long as possible afterwards. When everything is over, then one has overdone oneself for yet another year. The months pass by, one is back again in the triviality, and not until next Maunday Thursday is one about to make the same strenuous effort.

This is altogether wrong. Not getting ready for the Lord's Supper! That certainly should be done. But the preparation does not consist in creating some level of feelings but it consists in examining oneself, one's thoughts, words, and deeds, and then confess one's sins. If one dares not commune because one was not able to produce the "right" mood, then one has actually put one's feelings and one's experiences higher than God's forgiveness and His aid toward sanctification. One regards partaking of the sacrament rather as an achievement, not as a gift to sinners. Here we have again reason to listen to Father Luther, "It is certainly true, as I have found in my own experience, and as everyone will find in his own case, that if a person stays away from the sacrament, day by day he will become more and more callous and cold, and eventually spurn it altogether. To avoid this, we must examine our heart and conscience and act like a person who really desires to be right with God. The more we do this, the more will our heart be warmed and kindled, and will not grow entirely cold" (Large Catechism V:53–54).

It is a great mistake to believe that the Lord's Supper is profaned by being celebrated often. If it were a mobilization of human feelings or a beautiful spectacle, then we had all reasons to rarely celebrate it, because all stirring up of human feelings and all spectacles are boring in the long run. But Holy Communion is something completely different. It is God's dealing with the soul, something that we need continually and that will increasingly become a blessing to us the more often it happens. God's work never becomes boring, and His holiness does not decrease as the years pass by.

No one doubts that we daily need to receive forgiveness of sin. Isn't it then also appropriate that we often receive this gift at the Lord's Table? Every Christian knows that we should be prepared to meet our Savior any minute. Why wouldn't we want to meet Him then every Sunday at the altar? "Indeed, the very words *as often as you do it* imply that we should do it often," says Luther in the Large Catechism (V:47). For those who yet hesitate and wonder if they really should commune often, we want to add yet a few words from the Large Catechism (V:61), "It is the highest wisdom to realize that this sacrament does not depend upon our worthiness. We are not baptized because we are worthy and holy, nor do we come to confession pure and without sin; on the contrary, we come as poor, miserable men, precisely because we are unworthy."

There is a word that once was thrown into our Master's face as an invective, but it was remembered by His disciples rather as a word of honor. It should be widely announced when the Lord's Supper is celebrated. It is a promise and an invitation from God. It is recorded in Luke 15:2,

"This man receives sinners and eats with them."

Chapter 9

The Second Birth

Properly speaking, we should have started with this chapter and placed it before both the Word and the Lord's Supper. But life has its own strange logic. Although baptism comes to us first of all God's means of grace, it is often the last one I discover. It is so far away in the past, beyond every conscious thought that I have had, beyond every memory that has engraved itself in the soul.

Just as I in life first meet everyday realities with its concerns and joys and only slowly, little by little, begin to widen my horizon so that I can see forward and backward, asking: Whence and whither?, so I meet also in the sphere of faith first the issues of the present, the simple questions of rights and duties, of guilt and remorse. But little by little the horizon widens. I look forward, and I begin to grasp more and more of the immense reality of the resurrection from the dead. I also begin to look back, searching the traces of God's merciful presence in my own life. Then I notice all the invisible threads by which He has guided my steps before I myself knew it.

As I thus look back at my life, I cannot avoid noticing at the very beginning a fact that emerges as a monumental gate of entrance. Maybe it at first appears mysterious and unfathomable. But I cannot get away from it: *I am baptized.*

I am continually reminded of this fact. It appears over and over again in the Bible and in the hymnal. It follows me through life and demands reflection on my part. Maybe I interpret it symbolically as the first sign of God's grace, coming to me even before my asking for it. Maybe I think of it as the solemn ceremony through which I was received into the congregation. However, those interpretations could not suffice at length. They contain only a portion of the truth. Baptism is something far more.

The day comes when I begin to realize that. Maybe it happens when I am holding in my arms my own little child, a crying tiny bundle, the most defenseless of all defenseless. A wave of a sense of responsibility rises within me. This perception of responsibility stays with me wherever I go. It puts new questions in my mind. It is not easy to be a human being today, not at least being a parent. What kind of future is there for our children?

The morning paper comes every day with the echo of guns in many corners of the world. The airplane, which passes by with its cargo of mail to distant places, reminds us how far we can reach not only for peaceful purposes but also for destruction. And behind the obvious manifestations of human evil I perceive what is the very context of Evil: that entire brokenness in creation, that tragedy in our existence which has driven us out of paradise and filled the earth with thorns and thistles, with tears and pain, with curses and hatred.

I walk through the fields, where the sunshine glitters upon the grass, and the branches of the birches play in the summer breeze. But even here the questions follow me. I just saw a viper between the stones and began to think of my little daughter who enjoys running around here barefoot. And over there a butcher-bird flew out of the shrubbery with a green worm in the bill. It gives me the unpleasant thought of how she impales her prey on thorns, storing it in nature's own torture-chamber. In the midst of the many delights of summertime, I cannot get away from the fact that nature is not good and not merciful. It emerged once harmonious and beautiful from the Creator's hand. But creation has rebelled against its Creator. Through all its beauty, it has a satanic streak which expresses itself in history with double brutality. The great guilt, the tragic curse, throws its dark shadow across all existence. It is painfully perceivable also in the delightful wind and scent of a beautiful summer day. It takes hold of us as the news of wars and conflicts, persecutions and acts of terrorism, reaches us, and also when tragedy in many shapes hits our own neighborhood. Is it right and defensible to kindle new human life in such a world?

But now I see the church again, beyond the fields, with its steeple constantly pointing toward heaven. Now I become calm. God has not left us alone. He is still here, He who once broke down the wall of separation and descended here to live as a brother among siblings and as a Savior among the lost. Yes, the world has the marks of sin and Satan. But God is also present here. In the church on the hill over there, He has established the visible proof of His presence. He has come to our cursed world with His salvation. Here is healing. Here is life and forgiveness.

There will be baptism in the church on Sunday. Now it has become so very simple and clear to me what that means. I will carry my child into the church to the baptismal font. This means: I carry my child from the world out there, where everything is strife and danger, where temptations and suffering lie in wait behind every stone, into God's world, in under the father-hand of the living God. From one world into another. From sin and death, corruption and suffering, to the heart of creation, to partaking in that life that can never die and to that atonement that opens up the gates of forgiveness in the midst of a world of guilt.

Atonement? Yes, even a child needs atonement! If I am naïve enough to believe in the idea of "the innocent little ones," I will realize that I have been out of touch with real life, when it falls on me to rear children. I soon discover that they are no angels. On the contrary, they are very much human; just like all of us they are full of selfishness and willfulness. They can quarrel and be envious long before they can speak a full sentence. "By nature" they are not fit for God's kingdom, no more than we grown-ups. But the unfathomable depth of God's mercy and atonement is revealed precisely here: I can look at my playing child and know that it too partakes of Christ's life, that the seal of the cross is marked on its forehead, and that the guilt that follows us because of our perverted will is removed. Baptism is God's own proof of that fact.

But even more: "by one Spirit we were all baptized into one body" (1 Cor 12:13). In baptism we are thus joined with Christ, a union with that spiritual organism which is His body, the Church. It means a living and real participation in the Savior's own life. That stream of life that flowed down to the dried-out desert of the world when Jesus was born and that ever since powerfully rushes forth through the ages, that stream reaches here a new heart, embraces and flows through a new human being, carrying her with itself on its way toward the eternal goal. As the Savior said in the night when Nicodemus came to him, "Unless a man is born anew (or: *from above*), he cannot see the kingdom of God" (John 3:3). And when Nicodemus could not understand that a man can be born a second time,

Jesus added, "Except a man be born of *water and the Spirit*, he cannot enter the kingdom of God" (John 3:5, KJV).

"Of water and the Spirit" means: in Holy Baptism. Thus a new birth happens. Here the Almighty deals with a child of His a second time. It was born with groaning and pain, the first birth, into a fallen world with guilt and suffering. *"That which is born of the flesh is flesh"* (John 3:6). It is inexorably under the dominion of sin and death and corruption. But in Holy Baptism God intervenes with a new act of creation, a miracle just as great as when He kindled human life in the first birth. Here a human being is born a second time, now with solemnity and holy joy, into that world where God has re-established the covenant which we broke, a redeemed world with atonement and mercy. In the midst of this fallen world we are incorporated into a new creation and become heirs of the era to come with its glory and joy. The baptismal act itself is the meeting place, that sacred act, which God has chosen for this miracle.

But why did God choose this means? He could have chosen any other means! But He chose this one. And that is not arbitrariness but mercy. I must remember that it is not Himself but us that he has tied to this external means. Beyond this He may have hundreds of ways and means to reach souls whom we in our blindness regard as hopelessly lost. About that we know nothing, because God has not revealed it to us. We have to be careful concerning what to say about what will happen to a child if he would die without yet being baptized. But one thing we do know, and that is what is truly important: the child that *is* baptized belongs to God. He is a member in Christ's glorified body, partaking of that life which in ever new pulse-beats flows from the very center of existence, from the fountain-head of Grace and Truth at God's heart. That is why I carry my child to the baptismal font with such immense gratitude and with a security that this world never can give.

* * *

There is also a completely different way through which I may discover baptism as the most personal and precious thing in my life.

If it is risky to be a human being, it is all the more risky to be a Christian. Maybe I have sincerely tried. Yet, I fail to be a better person. The more sincerely I try my hardest to obey God in everything, the deeper I look down into that abyss that separates my poor and powerless life from the ideal of Christ's wholeness and strength. Finally I totally despair. I am ready to give up. But I cannot. Erasing God from my life, consciously shutting the gate of heaven, becoming alone in this world, and teaching my poor children that this existence of hatred and cruelty and arrogance and folly is all we can hope for? No, I cannot do that! My full conscience and my innermost sense of truth rise in protest. I have seen enough to know: God *is*. But I am not a man of God, no real Christian. My will is full of self-interest, my disposition is full of loveless capriciousness, and my heart is full of pride and introspection. I have seen enough of that as well.

God up there in holiness and perfection, and I down here in helpless imperfection. It's an abyss between us. But, no! The fact is that there is for me a bridge across that abyss, and it is *my baptism*.

When I discover that fact, it has unimagined things to tell me. It says: You foolish man, complaining about your hopeless attempts to become a man of God, see how He made you a child of His in your baptism. And since God already made you a child of His, you no longer need to try to become a child of His. Now you understand that His mercy is greater than all your weakness. You also understand that it would be ingratitude on your part to remain in despair. Instead now you must rise and thank God that He is so incomprehensibly good and infinitely great in grace that He for the sake of His mercy already has made you a child of His!

Here baptism opens a gate to all God's gracious promises. I read them in His Word and I am filled with wonder anew,

> *"Fear not, for I have redeemed you;*
> *I have called you by name, you are mine.*
> *When you pass through the waters I will be with you;*
> *and through the rivers they shall not overwhelm you.*
> *When you walk through fire you shall not be burned,*
> *and the flames shall not consume you.*
> *For I am the Lord your God, the Holy One of Israel, your Savior."*
> (Isa 43:1–3)

Here a new world opens up. I leave my human limitations, I forget my powerlessness. I know that nothing of this depends on my efforts and power. Behind my feeble attempts, behind my faltering will is God's immoveable faithfulness. The promise of baptism shines above all my sin: the atonement is also for me. Fire or water, temptation and fall may come. But the Creator and Redeemer is with me. He is holding me in His all-powerful hand and has embraced me in His high-as-heaven mercy. Then everything will be well with me, through defeat and struggle, through fall and restoration. That is what God wants for me. I know because he says, "My grace is sufficient for you, for my power is made perfect in weakness" (2 Cor 12:9). All this becomes more clear, more true and more tremendous, the more I contemplate my baptism.

* * *

Because baptism in its essence is not a deed that we do but God's unmerited election, it has been a natural thing from the earliest times of Christianity that also the children were baptized.

Already during the second century, baptism of children was administered throughout the church. *Irenaeus* (born c:a 140), who had been taught by *Polycarp*, a disciple of the apostles, obviously presupposes baptism of children when he says in *Adversus Haereses* (II:22,4) that Christ came to save all ages, even the small children, by regenerating them for God, that is through baptism. *Origen* (born c:a 185), the most learned man in the early church, expressly states (in Rom 5:9), "The church has from the apostles received the tradition that baptism shall be given to the small children." That Origen is right here and that baptism of children was practiced already in apostolic time is confirmed from that circumstance that *Justin Martyr* around the year 140 writes (in *Apology* I:15) that he knew people in their 70's, who had been Christians since childhood.

Tertullian (c:a 200) is the only one among the great church fathers who has expressed some apprehensions about baptism of children. He too knows it as the common custom. It would not occur to him to deny that it was apostolic and valid. He is not suggesting that anyone baptized as a child must be baptized again as an adult. His apprehensions were a consequence of his rigorism, that is his (erroneous!) opinion that a baptized person could not receive forgiveness for any severe sin. Therefore he advised that baptism should be delayed until after young people had gained more stability. A couple centuries later, the custom of postponing baptism, even to the deathbed, was practiced in some places. That was an unfortunate practice that the church forcefully opposed, teaching the people that baptism is not the atoning conclusion of a life in sin, but it is the holy dedication of a life in sanctification and obedience to God.

Thus we can affirm baptism of children with gratitude and joy. It is not expressly mentioned in the New Testament. It is probably indirectly referred to in Acts 16:15 and 16:33 as well as in 1 Cor 1:16, where baptism of households (most likely including children) are reported. We must remember that the first generation of the Church which we meet in the New Testament was a mission church, where normally adults were instructed in the Christian faith and then baptized. This is exactly the way it is today in our mission fields in Africa and India. We need first Christian parents and homes before children can be baptized.

It is not defensible for Christian parents to refuse baptism for their children with the argument that "the Bible does not say that children shall be baptized." Then we would also exclude women from the Lord's Supper, because nowhere in the Bible is it commanded or granted that women shall commune. Such absurd interpretation of the Bible is only possible if one seizes it from the Church. It is the Church the Mother who gives us the Bible. She has determined which scriptures are holy, and it is she who aids us in understanding them. If we ask her, we will get a plain and reliable answer: women have always communed, and children have always been allowed to be baptized. When the Bible became the Church's holy book, there was no doubt about these two issues. Why? Because the Church knew best what the apostles had said and intended. It is only when one leaves the fellowship of the Church or seizes the Bible from her hands, trying to expound her on one's own, that uncertainty becomes a factor. We become blind and helpless, beginning unknowingly to read in our own favorite ideas and our modern conceptions into the classic timeless Christian message.

It goes without saying that baptism of children is rather offensive for our "natural" way of thinking. It inexorably refutes the vague ideas of God which are so common. A generally religious person thinks of God as the supreme being, an abstract "spiritual reality," an impersonal origin to "moral principles." But God has never called Himself the highest Being. He calls Himself Father. It would be very odd if a father was never to see his children. And only an unnatural son would be content with the knowledge of having a father, whom he owes some gratitude, but to whom he really does not pay any attention. That is exactly the way that most "generally religious" people function. But the true parent/child relationship is always living together, just as all the members do in a loving family. That is how our relationship to God should be. He has clearly made known to us that He seeks the fellowship of His children and that He is in our midst waiting for us. And yet, when He comes to us as palpably as He does in baptism, then we step back, somewhat embarrassed. He must not come *that* close!

The great hindrance here is first of all man's incomprehensible religious pride. To call oneself born again, when one has sincerely battled with sins, confessed them and obtained peace, is acceptable. To agree that everything depends on grace, if one at least may keep the consciousness of dramatic experiences and a splendid conversion, that is not repugnant either. But this: to admit that I am *so* powerless and that God is *so* powerful that He could intervene in my life and make me a member in Christ, when I did not even know it, that is too much for my self-reliance. I cannot believe it, not until God has crushed the last remainder of my trusting in my own deeds to be right with Him. Therefore it often takes a long time before one discovers the gift of baptism and begins to thank God for it. Because I cannot do otherwise when I finally have discovered that this is the depth and height of God's mercy, that which most of all reveals to me the love of my Father in heaven, giving me something unshakably firm both to live on and die on. As Scripture assures us, "When the goodness and loving kindness of God our Savior appeared, He saved us, *not because of deeds done by us in righteousness,* but in virtue of His own mercy through the washing of rebirth and renewal in the Holy Spirit" (Titus 3:4f.).

As long as anyone trusts in his own deeds done in righteousness, he would rather repeat his baptism to make sure that *he* had done something, wanted something and intended something with his baptism. Or maybe he would accept his baptism as a child but trusts in something "more certain": his repentance, his faith, his feelings, his commitment, or his conversion, as if there would be anything more certain than God's faithfulness and His election! But all our own "certain" foundations crumble sooner or later for us. Blessed are we then, if we begin building on the true Foundation. When we once again have become as helpless and dependent as we were as little children at our baptism, then we have at last become as children and may enter the kingdom of God (Matt 18:1–4).

It is thus to turn things upside down to demand that children first must grow up and become like adults, become wise, mature, and responsible, in order for baptism to be of value for them. It is precisely the other way around, says Jesus. It is we big, wise and self-sufficing grown-ups, who first need to be helpless as the little children, poor in spirit, completely depending on that which we neither have nor are able to get on our own in order to be fit for the kingdom of heaven. Therefore Jesus took the little children in His arms and blessed them (Mark 10:13–16). The disciples objected when the children were brought to Jesus. They represented reason: What could these little ones understand of the great Master's message? But Jesus had a different opinion, "The kingdom of God belongs to such as these." We would rather turn those words upside down as well, saying, "Such belong to the kingdom of God." Then the glory of man is barely salvaged, since at least the little children have been declared to have a *right* to God's kingdom, in virtue of some innocence or some purity or some other good quality, supposedly part of human nature from the beginning. But Jesus said the exact opposite: God's kingdom belongs to them too. Our Savior came to earth with the great undeserved gift, the new life which cannot die. That gift is also for the little children, because they too are born of the flesh and belong therefore to the world that is under the tyranny of sin and death. Here it is a matter no longer of an unrealistic and romantic view of children but of the blessed reality that God's salvation reaches also those who can neither contemplate nor understand what happens to them in baptism. "And He took the children in His arms, put His hands on them and blessed them" (Mark 10:16).

This was the first occasion of children's baptism. The Savior did the same here as when He otherwise with His calling, His forgiving of sins or His laying on of hands admitted somebody into the kingdom of salvation. As we know, He never baptized anyone (John 4:2). There was no need for Him to do that, because in His very person He was the salvation, He was the kingdom in heaven revealed on earth. Where He was received in faith, where people in adversity in some way came into contact with Him, be it only by touching His garment as He made His way through the crowds, there salvation was a reality, there the Church was already established. Baptism is the means by which the Lord still is present, the means through which He after His departure still receives people into the kingdom of salvation. Thus when a child today is being baptized, the same occurs as when Jesus blessed the children. He has in baptism reached with His hand yet another human being. He has joined yet another member into His glorious body through the miracle of a new birth.

Once I discover what is greater than any hymn of praise can celebrate in song and deeper than any thought can fathom, namely that the Holy

One has entered this world to make us partakers of His Holiness, that His glory has been revealed, and that His salvation is now in our midst, then I realize that I can never fully appreciate and ponder my baptism.

My baptism means that I myself am joined to that flow of life that God sent to earth in Christ. God "who lives in unapproachable light, whom no one has seen or can see" (1 Tim 6:16), has come to his rebellious creation to regain through His Son that which has gone astray and is lost. In my baptism God made me his possession, He lifted me with my soul and my body into His realm. His flow of life has filled me, making me a partaker of the redeemed creation, of the regained humanity that is consecrated anew to serve Him in eternity. I am born from above (John 3:3), seated in the heavenly realms (Eph 2:6), the fore-court of which on earth is the Church. I have been united with Christ; I have died His death in order to rise to His new life (Rom 6:3–5). "I no longer live, but Christ lives in me" (Gal 2:20), I have clothed myself with Him, I am a living member in Christ's body consecrated for God in order to live for Him.

Nobody can be forced or commanded to believe this. But when the greatness of God becomes evident, so that you understand that you cannot but believe it, then your heart begins to sing for joy. You begin to understand how tremendous it is to be a Christian!

Maybe at first I will bend under the responsibility. From my baptism I learn that there is no way to escape the call for amendment of life. After all, I belong to God! I have been consecrated for Him. I am filled with Christ. I am a temple built to glorify God. I am a living monument to God's victorious intervention in this sinful world! How have I managed God's temple? How have I been a witness to Christ as a member of His body? How many times have I desecrated that which was consecrated for God? Yes, the call for amendment of life is overwhelming!

But even more overwhelming is the gospel made manifest in my baptism! "God's gifts and His calling are irrevocable" (Rom. 11:29). He does not revoke the consecration that He once gave me. Because of my baptism I dare believe that the work of Christ was also for me. Because of my baptism I dare come forward to the Lord's table.

Chapter 10

A Neglected Means of Grace

> "When I kept silent, my bones wasted away
> through my groaning all day long.
> For day and night Your hand was heavy upon me;
> my strength was sapped as in the heat of summer.
> Then I acknowledged my sin to You
> and did not cover up my iniquity.
> I said, I will confess my transgressions to the Lord;
> And You forgave the guilt of my sin."

THE ANCIENT WORDS IN Psalm 32, verses 3–5, point to the solution of a very common problem today. The problem is embedded in the words: *When I kept silent . . .*

On the surface everything is just fine. We are up to date, standardized modern people, externally polished as the most popular living-room furniture. We laugh and we joke, we discuss and are social, not indicating with the slightest facial expression that we inside are bothered with unsolved issues. Nevertheless, behind the polished surface there are painful memories and sensitive problems, which we anxiously hide away. Not everything is fine. Scripture is right: Each one will have to bear his own burden. One bears the unsolved conflicts in his marriage, another struggles with dark and half oppressed pangs of conscience because of his business methods, and yet another suffers from an awkward relationship to a fellow worker or to a relative. Old conflicts, humbling memories, and painful episodes lie there as half healed wounds. And behind all this that we call "problems" and "troubles" and "vexations" lies something else which we rightly should call: *guilt*.

Whoever is not willing to acknowledge this only needs to make a little mental experiment. He can imagine himself at an upbeat dinner party. You are there with some really good friends and also some not so good. There is maybe somebody looking at you in a somewhat disapproving way. Also there is maybe some influential superior before whom one automatically behaves correctly or tries to show one's most favorable sides.

However, an unexpected mishap occurs. Suddenly the door opens. An uninvited guest is standing there. He is your most candid enemy, who really would enjoy seeing you humbled and dishonored. He looks at you with triumphant malice in his eyes. He has power over you this evening. In his hand he is holding a bewitched knife: you are now defenseless in his hands. He can open your soul and lay your inner man bare at his will. With a quick incision he has already cut through the surface, through all that you want everyone to see, because you take pride in it. But he cuts down deeper, into your life's most intimate and private sphere, which you possibly in deep confidence would entrust to a good friend. And then he cuts even deeper, reaching down into the deepest cellar vaults of your soul, where you behind double locks and impenetrable walls keep that which you would like to forget altogether. He reveals your most deplorable secrets, your most humbling memories and most shameful intentions, things that you would not entrust to a page in your diary but which nonetheless are dreadful reality. There he digs down with his eager fingers, makes a malign grip, pulls out a handful of the squalor, holds it for all to see and hollers triumphantly: Look here! *This* is who he really is!

More than one of us would rather be devoured alive by the earth than experience the shame of having all our sinful secrets be displayed for everybody to see. This is *the guilt*. After all, *God* has seen all this all the time. Day after day his piercing eye sees even the most secret and darkest corner at the bottom vault of my soul.

Remaining silent is a severe and constant pain for anyone who knows God's presence in his life. And even so, all too many persist with their silence when it comes to those things stored away deepest in the soul. Otherwise they can ask God for forgiveness of sin in a general sense. But they do not dare to come to God with their shameful secret sins in fear of his judgment and his commandments. They know that it all is wrong but they feel that they won't be able to promise any change. And they think that they do not have the strength to turn things right again. But continuing being silent means a constant accusation in the conscience and a constant consumption for the soul: *"For day and night your hand was heavy over me; my strength was sapped as in the heat of summer."*

There is only *one* remedy here: to speak out, to break the chains of reticence, to prostrate oneself before God, confessing even the innermost sins with unrelenting, clear and candid words. *"Then I acknowledged my sin to You and did not cover up my iniquity."*

Did not cover up . . . Now the cover is torn away, everything is laid bare in the light. Just to be able at last to talk about life's most deplorable "problems" and call sin for what it is, all this thaws the ice in the frozen soul. And then comes God's verdict: *"And You forgave the guilt of my sin."*

Somebody may say: Sounds fine, if I just could believe it. But I have not clearly heard that verdict for me. What I clearly hear is the verdict of my conscience. I also clearly see my sin. But my remorse and my repentance are fragmentary, strong at times but sometimes almost gone. Neither do I dare to talk about victory or about giving any promises for the future. How then can I believe in forgiveness?

Yes, that is the way it has always been, not only in our modern and complicated lives. This simple fact: *And you forgave the guilt of my sin,* is for a remorseful and wounded conscience the most difficult of all things to believe. How could it be any other way? God is not one to be trifled with. Your conscience which knows God's holiness also knows what guilt is. Your conscience is totally right when asking this question again and again: Do you really believe that the uncompromising and holy God would accept you such as you are today?

The answer to the tormenting question from your conscience, the answer to all the uncompromising demands from righteousness, God could only give by coming down to the earth, by allowing the Son to suffer and die and as a sacrifice give His life a ransom for many. God's answer to all the rightful accusations of justice is the mystery of the atonement.

Yet, it is difficult for the soul to be certain about God's grace, to be personally convinced. Where are you, God? So far away, so unreal. On my knees I have asked for forgiveness, but I have not looked into the kind eyes of the Father. I am crying out into the empty space.

Once again, God's answer to the soul's cry is given in Christ. God came down to the earth, so that we could behold Him and hear His voice. "No one has ever seen God; the only begotten Son, who is in the bosom of the Father, He has made Him known" (John 1:18). There is the answer to the soul's question. He walked around among us "and dwelt among us, full of grace and truth, and we beheld His glory" (John 1:14). And He *forgave our sins,* and said: Take heart. Go in peace. Your sins are forgiven.

Again, the doubting soul may say: That was said *then* to *those* people. But *I* have never met Him as surely as they did, *I* have not felt His hand on my head and heard the word of forgiveness spoken with God's authority to *me.*

Jesus anticipated that difficulty as well. Even if He did not stay with us here on earth in the same way that He was with His first followers, He did not leave us alone. He promised, "I am with you always, even unto the end of the world" (Matt 28:20). For that purpose He gave us meeting places, where He himself would be present and act with us in all generations "unto the end of the world" in just as real a way as when He once acted with and among the people in Galilee. He gave us baptism. He gave us the Lord's Supper. And He also gave us the absolution by which He still lays His hand on your head and tells you personally, audibly and inescapably: Your sins are forgiven. When Jesus sent out His apostles in the world, He gave them this command and promise, "If you forgive the sins of any, they are forgiven; if you retain the sins of any, they are retained" (John 20:23; see also Matt 16:19 and 18:18). These are the Words of Institution for the Sacrament of Absolution.

It is truly amazing that Jesus has given such power and authority in human hands. Yes, indeed it is! But as a matter of fact, it is the same unprecedented reality, as in the other sacraments: God's powerful presence in our midst. This is one of the core truths of the entire Christian faith. Christ is still present, the Invisible One takes on visible form in the sacrament. The voice of Christ is still heard in the proclamation of the gospel and in the words of the absolution. Thus God still reaches His lost children in this world. The Exalted One comes humanly near to us.

* * *

At a summer meeting for young people a few years ago, some of the leaders were gathered informally one evening conversing on the Lord's Supper. They recalled a communion at a meeting the previous year, one of those unforgettable highlights, when table after table of young men filled the altar rail, thereby conveying a vision of that church which we pray for and that we at least by glimpses begin to see as a reality in some of our parishes. That communion had been a very moving experience, both for the leaders and for the large number of young men participating. There was an unusual factor that contributed greatly to the celebration of the Lord's Supper at that occasion. A young pastor explained it in this way to his fellow leaders that evening,

"Before that communion, private confession was available, and we listened to the confessions of these young people and brought them absolution of all sin in Christ's behalf. At the following administration of the Body and Blood of Christ, we pastors were almost leaning on each other so as not to collapse under the burden of seeing such young people carry such loads of terrible guilt . . . Something we knew for sure right there was that here were lost souls who really had gained peace with God."

It hit me that this statement of his experience was quite striking. If it had been made just ten years ago, we would all have been quite surprised. Now it was something that could be expected . We all knew: *Private confession has begun a come-back in our church.* It simply could not be held back, especially within some branches of the youth movement. It is not talked about a lot, which is actually a good thing. The veil of unswerving silence covers absolutely everything that is said during private confession. That is why it can never be just another "church activity" to talk about in the same way as about confirmation retreats or mid-week Lenten gatherings.

However, it is about time that it would be made very clear that private confession indeed does exist in our church and that Swedish church law instructs every pastor to receive any parishioner for private confession and at the risk of being defrocked keep totally secret what was said. Ignorance about this is both common and dangerous. A well known author shared in a magazine interview recently the plight of a friend of hers,

"Full of sadness she once said to me, 'I wish there were in our church something like the Catholics have in private confession: Someone you can talk to, knowing that he could loose and bind, in God's stead, so that I would know that my sin against my neighbor is forgiven. So that I would become free . . . If I would go to a pastor in my parish, which I have actually wanted to do many times but never dared to do it, there would be something uncertain about it. Neither the obligation to observe secrecy is there, nor the authority . . . I have no one, no one . . .'"

The most remarkable thing in this interview is that the author herself obviously shares her friend's total ignorance about the existence of private confession in our church. And this is not at all the only example of an amazing ignorance concerning Swedish church life that can be found in the newspapers. When we encounter these proofs of unfamiliarity with what the church does and stands for, rather than be indignant we should improve the church's way of providing information to the general public. And of course, we should teach and instruct the faithful in our church about the Sacrament of Absolution.

Now it needs to be said anew in all seriousness and with great zeal, that Jesus Christ has given us too that which our forefathers called *the office of the keys,* the authority to loose and to bind, so that a poor human being would know where to go in order to be loosened from her sin. It also needs to be said that private confession is not only for great sinners. It is a way out of the bondage of sin even for very common "average" sinners, bearing fruit in a strengthened faith, sanctification and peace with God. Very tiny and commonplace everyday sins can also become walls between the soul and God, or become mountains of burdensome problems, which one tries to deal with in vain. But when God's own voice pronounces the absolution for a dejected sinner, then the mightiest walls will fall just as they did at Jericho when the priests blew their trumpets of rams' horn.

* * *

We shall now proceed to some particular questions that usually are asked when private confession becomes the subject.

IS IT EVANGELICAL TO GO TO PRIVATE CONFESSION?

That question ought to be superfluous considering what has been said so far in this chapter. However, since it should be altogether clear that the reformers too loved and honored private confession, a few quotes will be added here. Our Lutheran confessional documents bring it out clearly in many passages that "private confession should be retained and not allowed to fall into disuse" (Augsburg Confession, Article XI). "Private confession has not been abolished in our congregations. The custom has been retained among us of not administering the sacrament to those who have not previously been examined and absolved. At the same time the people are carefully instructed concerning the consolation of the Word of absolution so that they may esteem absolution as a great and precious thing. It is not the voice or word of the man who speaks it, but it is the Word of God, who forgives sin, for it is spoken in God's stead and by God's command" (Augsburg Confession, Article XXV); and "since absolution and the power of the keys, which was instituted by Christ in the Gospel, is a consolation and help against sin and a bad conscience, confession and absolution should by no means be allowed to fall into disuse in the church, especially for the sake of timid consciences and for the sake of untrained young people who need to be examined and instructed in Christian doctrine" (Luther in the Smalcald Articles , Part III, VIII:1).

Luther himself practiced private confession frequently. He appreciated the absolution as the sweetest means of consolation when sin and guilt brought him into deep agony. He said in his sermon on Palm Sunday 1529, "If I were offered all treasures in a world where leaves on the trees and all the grains of sand in the ocean were gold, if I would abstain from private confession, I would immediately turn down that offer."

There is thus no doubt that a faithful Christian in the Lutheran tradition not only may but also ought to practice private confession. The reformers did reject the mandatory requirement to do it, but they certainly thereby did not mean that just because we no longer are forced to go to private confession, that we would never do it.

The Lutheran reformation stated right from the beginning that *absolution is a sacrament.* We quote from the Apology of the Augsburg Confession, Article XIII, "If we define sacraments as rites which have the command of God and to which the promise of grace have been added, we can easily determine which are sacraments in the strict sense. --- The genuine sacraments, therefore are Baptism, the Lord's Supper, and Absolution (which is the sacrament of penitence), for these rites have the commandment of God and the promise of grace, which is the heart of the New Testament." This article is even willing to count ordination as a sacrament, "since the ministry of the Word has God's command and glorious promises." Thus our church counts *three* or even *four* sacraments, not two, as it is often said.

How self-evident it was for the reformers to count Absolution as one of the sacraments is seen in the Augsburg Confession. The articles on Baptism and the Lord's Supper are followed by the articles on Confession and Repentance, and then we find immediately the article on the Use of the Sacraments. This is just as clear in the original Small Catechism with its six main sections. Between the fourth section on Baptism and the sixth section on the Lord's Supper is the fifth section on Confession and Absolution. Here we find a brief order for confession and absolution beginning with this explanation, "Confession consists of two parts. One is that we confess our sins. The other is that we receive absolution or forgiveness from the confessor as from God Himself, by no means doubting but firmly believing that our sins are thereby forgiven before God in heaven." In conclusion the confessor says, "Be it done for you as you have believed. According to the command of our Lord I forgive you your sins in the name of the Father and of the Son and of the Holy Spirit. Amen. Go in peace!"

TO WHOM SHALL I CONFESS?

Of course you can go to any devout fellow Christian. "The mutual conversation and consolation of brethren" (Smalcald Articles Part III, Article IV) is regarded as a form of the gospel by our confessional documents. We can hardly enough appreciate the spiritual aid and guidance that are conveyed from soul to soul between fellow Christians. If the walls could speak, they would give us eloquent and moving testimonies about it. However, as we just were reminded, both the Augsburg Confession and the Small Catechism teach us that private confession consists not only of confession of sin but also of the very essential element of the Absolution. When it comes to absolving a person and thus in God's name forgive someone his sins, our lay people have always been very restrictive in doing so between themselves. They rightly recognize that it is here a matter of administering a sacrament, something that belongs to the ordained servants of Word and Sacrament to do.

This restrictiveness is sound and right. But it should not be taken too far. If a newborn child is dying, it is the duty of any Christian to baptize her and thus administer the sacrament of Baptism. Similarly it would be the case, when someone is in deep distress concerning his salvation, especially if he is on his deathbed and no pastor is available. Why should not a sincere Christian then resolutely intervene, recite the Word of God, pray for the sick person, show him God's grace in Christ, and even in God's name assure him that his sins are forgiven for Christ's sake? When doing so, a Christian would be a Christ for his neighbor, which we all are called to be through our baptism.

However, the normal and natural thing to do is that one would make private confession to the parish pastor. One can go to him in the safe certainty to be protected against indiscretions. The law is exceptionally strict when it comes to the confidentiality of private confession. If a pastor would break the seal of private confession, revealing even the slightest information that he received in private confession, he would be defrocked from the pastoral office. It is therefore of decisive importance that the private confession be handled as a sacrament. If it is regarded merely as a conversation between pastor and parishioner, it may be tempting for the pastor to share with others a portion of what he heard. This was one of the ill-fated results of the dissolution of ecclesial forms through pietism in the 1700s. As a German writer has pointed out, "Soon one could no longer actually speak about a real absolution" (Quade, page 263). Even from the pulpit it has happened that stories are told beginning somewhat like this, "This past week a middle-aged man came to me wanting to speak to me on a private matter . . ." Such punishable and reprehensible loquaciousness is devastating not only for the pastor's own reputation as shepherd of the souls, but what is worse: it leads to a lack of credibility toward the whole Church.

The danger of tampering with the confidentiality is averted when it is clear both to the pastor and the confidant that their time together is an involvement in the Sacrament of Private Confession with Absolution. Here is drawn a distinct line, marking an insurmountable wall of absolute silence around *everything* that will be said from the moment that the confessant arrives until he leaves in peace. It all belongs in a special compartment in the pastor's soul, not to be opened until Judgment Day and not to be connected with anything else that he knows or may talk about.

WHEN SHALL I GO TO PRIVATE CONFESSION?

For an evangelical Christian there is no coercion and there are no binding rules concerning the frequency of private confession. However, there are two situations in life where I would counsel fellow Christians to shrive (see *shrive* and *shrift* in Webster's Dictionary, words that are related to *skrifta*, used here in the Swedish original; these words are related to the English *Scripture* and the Swedish *Skriften*; thus *to shrive* is to examine one's thoughts, words and deeds in light of *Scripture,* the Word of God).

One situation is what I would call *the turning-point.* When someone has been indifferent to God for a long time but through the work of the Holy Spirit has come to the point where he desires to make a decisive break with the past and begin a deliberate Christian life, then it is a great blessing to mark that turning-point in the Sacrament of private confession. Whether the desire to break with the ungodly past is a sudden experience or the outcome of years of searching does not make any difference. This person needs to confess sins in the past, be absolved and get advice for the future. Receiving this Sacrament soon followed by participation in Holy Communion, and with the sincere intention to pray daily and to worship and commune as often as possible, is the way to mark the turning-point and begin the new life in the Church.

Other occasions when private confession is very helpful are those *crises* that sooner or later come precisely upon someone who no longer wants to live an ungodly life. She realizes that she does not always live the way she ought to do. She sees clearer than ever all the short-comings in her everyday life. She struggles in vain to fulfill the commandment to love her neighbor as herself. She begins to doubt her right to be called a Christian. It is absolutely necessary in such crises that one does not get overwhelmed by the difficulties. One needs to open up one's heart in private confession, get helpful advice for one's life in the world and in the church, and in the absolution receive forgiveness of all sin for Christ's sake.

Yet, private confession is not only a blessing at the *turning-point* and at *crises.* Just as the Lord's Supper, it becomes a rightful blessing only when we begin to use this sacrament *regularly.* The Church has two great seasons of penance, when she admonishes us to examine ourselves: Advent and Lent. During those weeks, it should be a natural thing also for anyone who is not bothered by particular pangs of conscience to make a thorough self-examination, for example in the light of the Ten Commandments with Luther's explanations. The secret and half excused everyday sins need to be identified and confessed. That which one once in mortification confessed as *sin,* divested of all euphemisms, one is not so likely to relapse into.

HOW SHALL I MAKE PRIVATE CONFESSION?

It is simply a matter of contacting the parish pastor and agreeing with him on time and place, which could be the sacristy, the parish office, or the pastor's study in the parsonage. Some churches also announce a regular time, often once a week, when the pastor is available for private confession.

During the first part of your time with the pastor, you will tell him about those sins that have burdened you lately. Your pastor will mostly listen but also give some advice. If he is convinced that you are truly sorry for your sins and open for God's forgiveness for Christ's sake, he will invite you to receive the Sacrament of Confession and Absolution.

Kneeling you will confess your sin with words from the Service Book to which the pastor will guide you. You may mention in your confession specific sins that have caused you anxiety. Then the pastor will absolve you in the name of the Father and the Son and the Holy Spirit. This absolution you shall accept "as from God himself, not doubting, but firmly believing that by it your sins are forgiven before God in heaven" (Luther's Small Catechism).

WHY SHOULD I GO TO PRIVATE CONFESSION?

Why is it not enough for me to confess my sins before God in my privacy? What can the Sacrament of Confession and Absolution give me that I would not receive just through a silent confession before God? We shall answer these questions, considering the three parts in a complete confession before the pastor: (1) the confession, (2) the absolution, and (3) the advice given by the pastor!

Already making *confession* of your sin to a fellow human being can be immensely helpful. It allows you to get a hold on your sin, nailing it to the pillory and often showing amazingly clearly where the cure is needed. Yes, it is humiliating but also liberating. As long as you keep your sin secret to yourself, it has the upper hand in your struggle. But at the very moment that you dare to reveal it to someone else in confidence, it loses its grip. Your confession is the right way to master the memories which are the nightmares of your soul and the extortioner of your conscience.

The *absolution* is the crown of this sacrament, its most important and sweetest part. Christ our Lord would not have given it to His Church, if He had not known and understood what it means to have the forgiveness of sin declared to us personally in this way. All experience shows that while it is easy to believe that God is good and forgiving in a general way, it is terribly hard to believe that God really forgives *me*, especially sins with which I have struggled for a long time with little success. Absolution is here the out-stretched hand of Jesus to the poor in spirit, His own word to the heavy laden.

The pastor mediates the absolution, but he also gives *advice*, sometimes including suggestions for *penance* and *satisfaction*. This advice is some of the most beneficial in a complete confession before the pastor. A person may be entangled in such moral conflicts that life becomes almost unbearable. She might have no one in whom she dare to confide. What if she then would realize that her pastor is a shepherd of the souls ready to meet with her in private confession and obligated to keep to himself everything that she has told him! It should really be a normal thing for our teenagers in their difficult years of transition to avail themselves of this sacrament. In fact, every pastor ought to teach his confirmands that it is here for their benefit as well. Many lonely desperate struggles, which in worst case scenarios have resulted in permanent spiritual illness and in desperate actions, could in this way have been prevented or relieved.

When it comes to penance it must be said immediately with emphasis that no penance in the world can earn forgiveness of sins for us. We receive forgiveness of sins *only* for the sake of Jesus Christ, by grace and without anything that we do. If we would *earn* forgiveness with our penance, we would be lost beyond hope. This would anyone keenly experience who imagines that his satisfactions are some kind of payment to God. If he is an honest soul, he will never obtain peace with God, because he realizes again and again that something is still missing. He must acknowledge that he neither had been as contrite as he should have been nor had done enough to put relationships right with fellow men whom he had insulted in the past and, truth be told, still insults with envious and demeaning thoughts. Nor dare he claim that he has such disgust at sinning as he ought to have or that he has such firm determination never again to commit the same sins that he on that ground dare believe that everything now is well and the sins removed.

The alternative to that kind of honest despair is to fool yourself in really thinking that you indeed have done well enough, of course not perfectly well, but whatever might be lacking, God who is good will look upon with leniency. Then your situation is infinitely worse, because you have become a genuine Pharisee living on a false righteousness and an equally false faith.

Thus penance is not a means for us to make us deserve forgiveness. But what then is it? Penance is *one of the fruits of the faith*. It is not a condition for our receiving God's forgiveness. It is a consequence of the forgiveness. After all, it is faith that justifies, faith in what Christ has done for me. When I look at the cross, I hear God saying to me, "Look here, my child, this I have done for you. Look here, your sin is forgiven, you are partaking in this covenant of the atonement, you may be a member of my holy Church, of the body of Christ." When I *believe* this, when it takes hold of me, when I am overwhelmed and ruled by Christ's love, then are opened to me the first possibilities for a new life, for a grateful and joyful and willing obedience. I have then become a living member in Christ. The blood, the warmth and the power of life from my Savior's heart are flowing through me. Only this power of life, this love, received in faith through the Word and the blessed sacraments, can make me good. And only a good tree can bear good fruit.

How penance is a fruit of faith is strikingly set forth in the story of Zacchaeus, the tax collector in Jericho known for his greed. He was despised by all the townspeople, but when Jesus came to Jericho He first of all paid a visit to Zacchaeus, who confessed his sinful love of money and was fully forgiven by Jesus. Zacchaeus said, filled with the jubilant joy of faith in his Savior, "Lord, I will give half my belongings to the poor, and if I have cheated anyone, I will pay him back four times as much" (Luke 19:8).

That is what penance is! When Zacchaeus embraced in faith the gift of forgiveness, he immediately felt that he just could no longer live in the same way as before. Everything in his rich home reminded him that he had been living for his own benefit at the expense of others. If there possibly had been some secret anxiety in his heart concerning his dishonest ways of dealing with people, then he probably would have told himself that there was no way he could make things right again, at least not without risking his position as director in the Jericho customs department.

But today, having received God's forgiveness which was given to him through Jesus, everything was possible for him. He had found the precious pearl, peace with God. Now he was ready to thoroughly amend his ways with fellow men. And thus he made penance, joyfully and with generosity toward those he had wronged, and all this without any fear of the consequences. The tree had become good. And thus it bore good fruit.

The Spirit and the Word will often drive a person who is penitent to do the penance that God expect from her without her being guided by anyone else. However, every Christian knows that it is not always easy to understand what kind of penance God wants him to do, even if he dearly desires to do His will. This uncertainty can be totally devastating for the peace of the soul. Maybe the memory of something wrong that I caused someone torments me. Maybe other people are involved? If I seek reconciliation with the person whom I wronged, maybe I will hurt the relationship between him and others whom I mention to him? And then I might think that those thoughts are just excuses so I don't have to do any demanding amendments in my life? I am probably not penitent enough! I want God's forgiveness, without obedience! It all becomes cheap grace!

To anyone who recognizes himself in that kind of experience, there is only one thing to say, *"Remember: for you too there is the Sacrament of Confession and Forgiveness!"* Let go of this skein that you can never untangle! Let God take care of it in this blessed sacrament! If you want real cure for your tormented conscience, there is one thing to do: to lay everything bare for your pastor, confessing your sins and receiving in the absolution the gift of forgiveness, and also accepting his advice for your spiritual journey. Your father confessor may then ask you, as a sign of your penitence, to agree to do the penance he suggests without your knowing what he is going to ask you to do. Those who are really penitent usually agree with visible joy, thereby showing that they more than anything else desire to obey God in everything, as they accept the advice from a servant of God's Word as from God himself. And indeed, the pastor being impartial in the penitent's broken relationship with others is better suited to recognize that which are the vexations of a sensitive conscience and that which are attempts by our sinful nature to avoid the road of obedience and amendment of life. When you thus have placed the matter in the hands of him who in your midst is the ordained servant of the Word and to him honestly have confessed everything, you shall firmly believe the words of the absolution, never under any circumstances doubt that your sin is and remains forgiven for Jesus' sake. And then you will eagerly do the assignments which your pastor gives you, firmly convinced that the atonement of Christ covers all your sin. God's grace is now fully yours. It is a sure thing that He will not ask for any other sign of your genuine faith and penitence than your joyful acceptance to do your assigned penance.

We may think of three kinds of penance. It may be a simple and honest matter of *restitution*. After all, it is a general rule for all Christians that we are called upon to compensate our neighbors for any harm we may have caused them. A lie or a false testimony shall be admitted, so that the one who was harmed will be fully righted. Stolen property and embezzled money shall be returned. Those obvious cases any penitent person will acknowledge and take care of in a Christian way. But there are a lot of complicated cases where my conscience does not give me sure guidance. Shall I report myself to the police for a theft or may I anonymously return the money to the rightful owner? What shall I do if I by cheating or by presenting falsified documents was awarded a degree or was accepted for a position at the expense of others who really were more qualified? How can I rectify the harm I have caused others through selfishness, dishonesty, or unfaithfulness in dating or marriage? There are more such questions than people on this earth!

Here I give the same advice as before: place the matter trustingly in the hands of your pastor. Behind him is the rich experience and the merciful love of the Church. She is the mother who tenderly handles that which her children have broken. If it is stolen property or money, the pastor might return it to the owner with the information that this comes from someone who through the power of God's Word has decided to be an honest person from now on. When it comes to broken marriages and other hurting relationships, the pastor will offer advice and guidance. Leaning on God's Word and the collected experience of the Church, he says with authority to the penitent concerning the penance: *You shall*, and one is wise to obey that assignment without compromise.

There is also a penance that serves as a *pedagogy*, as an aid in a person's spiritual discipline. Above all, three things are necessary in the life of all Christians: to pray regularly, to frequently be guided and nurtured by the Word, and to continually fight against the temptations to sin. It is easy to begin the day without prayer. It is even easier to skip reading the Bible. It is easy to find excuses to stay away from Sunday morning worship. But it is not an easy thing to cut off the connection with all that which pulls me away from God, be it books, friends, entertainment events, or even an "innocent" hobby.

Every Christian knows how often we have to confess such sins before God. Every Christian also knows that we cannot rightly receive God's forgiveness without a sincere willingness to fight against the sins we have confessed. And yes, in the blessed moment of the absolution, we are full of good intentions for the future.

What happened to those good intentions? Maybe they were realized a day or two, or even a week, maybe longer. Every Christian has experienced too many good intentions which failed. Is there anything we can do about it? A big factor is that all too often I cannot command myself to do the right thing. But the astonishing fact is that I can do it if someone else commands me, someone who in a solemn moment told me what I should do, someone I respect and revere as God's spokesman.

This is the benefit of the penance that is assigned to the confidant in the Sacrament of Confession and Absolution. No one will be commanded to do more than he will be able to do. A basic rule is that the penance shall be merciful. Each one will be assigned to do precisely that which in his particular situation is most necessary and best for his soul. The one who tends to neglect his morning devotions for the newspaper will be asked for a determined number of weeks to get out of bed at a determined hour and do his devotions, before the newspaper has been delivered. The inert Bible reader will be assigned to rigorously follow a reading plan for a month, devoting a set hour every day for that purpose. Anyone who has been foolish in the choice of literature and entertainment will get assignments to read two or three books with sound contents and to attend specific Christian events within the next few months.

Those who have been truly penitent and have been longing for forgiveness usually do such exercises of penance with great joy and in gratefulness to God, and even continue doing them beyond the determined time span. Such penance has of course nothing to do with the idea that we can earn God's forgiveness through our so called good deeds. In this sacrament we have already received forgiveness. The exercises of penance are aiming at keeping the soul in the state of grace, just as our catechism answers the question, "What must the believer do to be kept in the faith? The believer must abide in God's word, earnestly watch and pray, frequently commune at the Lord's table, and lead a godly life." (The Catechism of the Church of Sweden, Paragraph 155. Also in The Catechism of the Augustana Evangelical Lutheran Church, Paragraph 85.)

Finally, penance may also serve as a *thank offering*, as a fitting channel for the joyful and grateful service that a person who has been absolved from his sin is eager to do. People are rarely filled with such childlike and pure joy as when the heavy load on their conscience has been removed by

God. But how shall this joyful longing to serve be realized? Someone who is timid and introverted will not change personality even in this new-found joy. For such a person it is very helpful simply to get an assignment: you are now to call on someone who is old or sick or home-bound, and see if you can help that person in some way. Or: you shall write to three of your relatives or friends whom you have neglected for some time. Or: you shall consider if there is someone in your neighborhood or in your work place whom you can assist with your special talents and resources.

The fulfillment of such penance usually brings a quiet joy to us. It is a pleasant secret that we share only with our Savior. Nobody else knows what it is that moved those forces. But such penance often opens new and unexpected avenues to friendship and fellowship with people whom I previously had neglected or not even known.

* * *

A renewal of private confession and absolution is not an end in itself. On the contrary: its renewal is a deed of mercy, to which we are driven by love of humankind. What is so deplorable is not primarily that this sacrament has become a forgotten means of grace, but that this indicates that people so seldom think about the eternal well-being of their souls, and that those who do often live without the blessings of this sacrament. When people wake up and want to live as children of God, the Church must help them to use this sacrament. Otherwise the risk is great that they may not really enter the gate of forgiveness in such a way that it leads to the rest in Christ's atonement.

The renewal of the Sacrament of Private Confession and Absolution is a necessary part of that church renewal, to which we are driven by love for fellow men. In just the last ten years there has been in our church such a significant increase in the use of this sacrament that only those of little faith would deny the possibility of a deepening renewal of the private care of souls. Those of us who are pastors must frequently preach and teach about the meaning and availability of this sacrament, not at least in those parishes where there as yet no one has asked for it. We must be ready when they do come, so that every member in the parish knows that this means of grace, this means of help and blessing, is there for them.

A final word to my fellow pastors: let us dig deeply into Scripture, into the Book of Concord, and into the Church's treasury of care-of-souls literature, so that as we battle to enter the narrow gate we may obtain advice and guidance and comfort from the old sources of life. For those who are to guide others, I cannot recommend enough a thorough study of Schartau's *Letters of Spiritual Concerns* or Fresenius's *Communion Book* and a frequent use of private confession for the sake of your own soul. If you yourself have struggled with your sins, yourself said confession and done penance, and yourself have a Bible with God's promises well-marked, then you can be an authentic tool in guiding others to the peace in Christ.

Chapter 11

The Ministry of Reconciliation

1. CHRIST'S COMMISSION

"*I* MAGNIFY MINE OFFICE" (ROM 11:13, KJV). Paul is referring to his office as an apostle, the great commission to be *"an apostle to the Gentiles"* (same verse). This is *"the ministry of reconciliation"* (2 Cor 5:18), which he received "not from men nor by man, but by Jesus Christ and God the Father" (Gal 1:1) and which he therefore recognized as belonging to the foundation of the church (Eph 2:20).

In order to find out what the New Testament teaches about the Holy Ministry, also called the Pastoral Office, we do best by starting with the apostolate. Of all the offices in the early church, this is without comparison the one that is most often mentioned in the New Testament. There are those who deny that the early church had any real offices. They claim that there were no such things as ecclesiastical law, organization, and hierarchy in the first Christian congregations. The apostolate had thus no character of office. Instead the authority of the apostles was completely due to their personal qualities: they were the oldest members of the church, they had personally seen Jesus, they had the greatest gifts of grace, they were the most appreciated preachers of their time. Therefore they enjoyed a moral authority but they had no real office, especially not one that they had received from Jesus himself.

However, careful linguistic scrutiny has made this idea impossible. Scholars have been able to conclude that the very word apostle (in Greek *apóstolos*) is a direct translation of a Jewish term, *schalíach*, which means *authorized representative*. At the time when Jesus called disciples "*and chose from them twelve, whom He named apostles*" (Luke 6:13–16), this term was among the Jews an established legal institution. Through a schaliach one could be represented at just about any function or ceremony with the same legal effect as if oneself would have been present. What a person's schaliach had said, done or written was just as binding as if oneself had done it. One could even get engaged through such a representative; and a Jewish engagement had the same binding consequences as a wedding ceremony among us.

The word apostle is used also in the New Testament in this general sense: "An *apóstolos* (= messenger, schaliach) is not greater than he who sent him" (John 13:16). The word can also be used with the meaning authorized representative of a congregation; see 2 Cor 8:23 (*apóstoloi* is there rendered messengers by the KJV and the RSV and representatives by the NIV). It may be surprising that this word that was the title for the highest office in the early church also was used for relatively insignificant representatives for congregations. This could be done simply because the meaning of the word as such is "one who is sent to act with authority on someone else's behalf." The sound that the word apostle has to our ears and also very soon had in the early church was because *the Twelve were the Apostles with the authority of Jesus Christ.*

Jesus had indeed chosen twelve among His disciples and named them apostles (scheluchim), as recorded in Matt 10:1–4, Mark 3:13–15; 6:7, and Luke 6:13; 9:1–2, CEV (based on Codex Sinaiticus). He had given a special commission to these twelve men. Only they became His authorized representatives! He gave them His own power to cure the sick in His name and proclaim that the kingdom of heaven is near. Their authority came from being Christ's apostles, not just disciples as many others were. Their message was to be accepted as the very words of Jesus, "He who hears you hears Me, and he who rejects you rejects Me, and he who rejects Me rejects Him who sent Me" (Luke 10:16). Their presence was the presence of Jesus, "He who receives you receives me" (Matt 10:40).

However, this commission seemed to have been for a limited task and for a limited time. Then we learn that they who were sent out return to give a report (Mark 6:30; Luke 9:10; cf 10:17). In any case, upon the death of Jesus the disciples were totally paralyzed and perplexed. They did not seem to have any authority to go on speaking in His name. If they once had had it, it was now forfeited, because they had all denied and deserted Him. Their Master had been publicly executed as a false

Messiah, an unmasked beguiler of the people. To go on preaching in His name was impossible.

But the event that changed everything was the resurrection of Christ! An event that transformed the hopeless situation and set the pace for all future. Now the apostolate is renewed by the Risen One Himself, and this for all future until His return in glory. He gives the apostles a new mandate: they are first of all going to be witnesses of His resurrection. They are being equipped with the Holy Spirit (John 20:22; Acts 2:4) and vested with the power to do miracles. That they really did so is beyond any doubt. Paul refers as a matter of fact to the "signs, wonders and miracles" he had done in Corinth, and he calls them "the signs of a true apostle" (2 Cor 12:12). On behalf of Christ, the apostles are also to beseech the people to be reconciled to God (2 Cor 5:20) and to forgive sins in His name with the same validity as when He himself forgave sins (John 20:23).

Historically, the first office of the Church is thus *the commission to be Jesus' authorized representatives.* This commission is issued by Jesus Himself. That is why there are no apostles except in the first generation. Only The Twelve were named apostles, and yes, Paul as well. Indeed, it took some time before the early church acknowledged him as "an apostle, not from men nor by man, but by Jesus Christ" (Gal 1:1). The title of apostle was also used about a few others, who probably like Paul had a personal commission from Jesus. If one had no such commission, one would not be recognized as an apostle, even if one was ever so important as a leader in the early church. Men such as Apollos and Timothy were never spoken of as apostles, nor any of the many who had seen the Risen Lord *without* having received His commission.

There was no fixed church order in the early church, neither was there any need for it, because the apostles were there. They were Christ's authorized representatives: the Lord Himself had vested them with His power! Their words are referred to as having binding authority (Jude 17), their teaching belonged to the foundations of the Church (Acts 2:42), they were a channel for the Holy Spirit (Acts 8:14–17; 19:6). Even when they chose to use the means of persuasion, they knew that they could "have made demands as apostles of Christ" (2 Thess 2:6) and that they had the right to command obedience (Phlm 8–10, cf 1 Cor 7:17; 11:34; Acts 16:4).

Thus the matter of authority was not an issue in the early church. The apostles were the obvious leaders in the Church. But how did things turn out in the next generation? Who took over after the apostles? The answer given by the early Christian tradition is: those who were chosen and authorized by the apostles themselves.

We learn this already from the oldest Christian document outside the New Testament. Clement of Rome writes (c:a 95 A.D.) in his Letter to the Corinthians (chapters 42 and 44),

> "The apostles have preached the Gospel to us from the Lord Jesus Christ; Jesus Christ from God. Christ therefore was sent forth by God, and the apostles by Christ. . . . And thus preaching through countries and cities, they appointed the first-fruits [of their labors], having first proved them by the Spirit, to be bishops and deacons of those who should afterwards believe. . . . Our apostles also knew that, through our Lord Jesus Christ, that there would be strife on account of the office of the episcopate. For this reason, therefore, inasmuch as they had obtained a perfect fore-knowledge of this, they appointed those already mentioned, and afterwards gave instructions, that when these should fall asleep, other approved men should succeed them in their ministry."

Clement clearly points out, and this already in the generation immediately (!) succeeding the apostles, that the office of the church originated with the apostles of Christ. The chain is clear: Christ sent out His apostles who installed the first bishops and deacons. They in their turn gave the office to a new generation, all this as commanded by the apostles according to the commission of Jesus.

One can see the beginning of this development in our New Testament. Besides the apostolate, there are a number of offices that gradually emerge. Some of them are "prophetic"; they depend on a vision or a prompting of the Spirit. Others are offices in our sense; they depend on a commission or a consecration. And it was the apostles who presided at these rites. They both chose the seven "deacons," whether thus titled or not, and then installed them in their office with prayer and laying-on-of hands (Acts 6:1–6).

During their missionary travels, the *apostles* installed presbyters in the congregations (Acts 14:23). The *apostle* Paul writes to Titus, "This is why I left you in Crete, that you might amend what was defective, and appoint presbyters in every town as I directed you" (Titus 1:5). Timothy was also installed into his office through prayer and apostolic laying-on-of-hands, through which he received his "gift from God" (2 Tim 1:6; 1

Tim 4:14). Thereby he also was vested with the authority to pronounce judgment on presbyters and to entrust the apostolic message, with which he had been entrusted, "to faithful men who will be able to teach others also" (2 Tim 2:2).

The apostolic succession in the sense of an office *received from the hands of the apostles* has obviously right from the beginning been of the greatest significance in the Church. The three offices, which the Church has kept up till our time, were there already at the time of the apostles. Even the New Testament words have been maintained from generation to generation and are used in our languages today, in English and Swedish respectively: *bishop* and *biskop* (epískopus), *priest* and *präst* (presbýteros), *deacon* and *diakon* (diákonos).

How the duties were divided up between these offices in the early church has not been solved and cannot be solved. The Bible does not provide enough material to answer that question. However, we learn with certainty that the deacons then as well as now primarily did work of mercy, while presbyters and bishops proclaimed the Word and generally handled the administration of the church. But it is very uncertain whether there was a clear distinction between bishops and presbyters. It is simply impossible to determine, based only on the Bible, the structure and organization of the early church. In all attempts to do so, one has been forced to fill in essential parts according to one's own assumptions or certain modern ideas. The order that we have in the Church of Sweden is not built only on the Bible but also on the development such as it occurred in the Church during the second century. That which could not be clearly determined from the New Testament, we have not complemented with our own additions but with those orders, which were documented as existing in the generations immediately succeeding the apostles, and with the information, which the early church fathers have given us concerning the intentions and prescriptions of the apostles.

Ignatius, the famous martyred bishop of Antioch, developed already in the beginning of the second century the concept of the bishop's office which has been kept till this very day. His letters inform us about the situation in Syria and Asia Minor shortly after the death of the last apostle. Every major town with surrounding area has now its bishop. Nothing may be undertaken without the bishop and the presbyters. They are to be obeyed just as the Lord and his apostles. Ignatius writes in his Epistle to the Ephesians, Chapter 6, "We ought to receive every one whom the

Master of the house sends to be over His household, as we would do Him that sent him. It is manifest, therefore, that we should look upon the bishop even as we would upon the Lord Himself." Here is applied on the bishop the same view as that of an apostle as the representative of Christ.

When the sources toward the end of the second century begin to flow more richly, we found as accepted tradition that bishops and presbyters are considered to be the successors of the apostles. Irenaeus (born c:a 130), the church father, through his mentor Polycarp, himself a disciple of John the apostle, had thorough knowledge about the apostolic period. He underscores again and again that the offices of the Church have an unbroken succession from the men "who by the apostles had been installed as bishops in the churches" (Adversus haereses, III, 3:1; see also IV, 26:2).

All this is nothing else than what one would have to assume, even if the sources did not directly say so. Since the apostolate was a commission *with authority*, it is in the nature of things that the authority of the apostle would be transferred to those whom they in their turn authorized. The offices of the Church as we know them today have organically emerged from the commission that the Lord Himself once gave to His apostles. The substance of the office was there right from the outset. It was just the forms which needed to be shaped. It seems to have taken a couple generations until the arrangement of duties between the three offices was fully established. In the next generation after the apostles, there seems to have been men such as Timothy and Titus, who as commissioned by the apostles handled the office, which most closely corresponds to the office of bishop as it took form already in the next two or three generations. At the same time some functions, such as evangelists and teachers, seemed to have been integrated in the office of the presbyter. It became rather soon the generally accepted order in the whole church that only bishops were allowed to ordain, that is to consecrate someone for an office in the church. Thereby was that order completed that has been kept for almost two thousand years. An unbroken chain of bishops has been preserved through a never-ceasing row of consecrations, and this also in that branch of Christ's Church which is known as the Church of Sweden.

The offices of the Church have thus emerged from the apostles and through them from Jesus Himself. It was clear to the early church that the apostles acted on behalf of Jesus and according to His will, when they saw to it that their commission would be handed to others in the succeeding generation. It was just as clear that the Holy Spirit who is at work in the

Church was the driving force in the development of the offices, which already in the immediate generations after the apostles led to the shape of the offices that we have today. This view is maintained by the church of the reformation in Sweden in its Church Order of 1571, "Therefore, since this order with bishops and priests was quite beneficial and *without doubt given by God the Holy Spirit, who is the giver of all good things*, it was throughout Christendom generally approved and accepted, and has ever since remained, *and will remain even as long as the world stands.*"

There was in the early church also another altogether different kind of office, namely the *prophetic,* not given through the apostles but directly through the Spirit. In the first generations, there appeared "charismatics" and "pneumatics" claiming immediate mandate from Christ. The New Testament prophets were highly esteemed, usually named right after the apostles. However, one learned soon from bitter experience that some were false prophets: impostors who claiming inspiration from the Spirit as well found ready listeners in the congregations. Already around the year 100, the young Church had to struggle for the very gospel with those who advocated a view known as *gnosticism.* In fact, the beginning of that struggle is reflected in Paul's advice to Timothy, "Guard what has been entrusted to your care. Turn away from godless chatter and the opposing ideas of what is falsely called knowledge (in Greek: *gnosis*), which some have professed and in so doing have wandered from the faith" (1 Tim 6:20–21). During that struggle the Church learned that the survival of the authentic gospel depended on its being proclaimed by those whose commission and loyalty were beyond all doubts. This was the first great encounter that the Church had with a false spirituality without firm norms. Thereby she gained soon enough the insight into those things that serve as a bulwark against all subjective re-interpretations of the gospel: the external authoritative Word, the Rule of Faith (Regula Fidei), and the fixed confession, and alongside them the three-fold office with its unbroken succession from the apostles.

Of course, this did not mean that the free prophesying ceased. It has never ceased and can never be abolished. Whenever it pleases God, He can call people to come forward and speak in His name. The Church should listen to such prophetic voices of men and women, but she should also test their message according to the Word which has been entrusted to her. We must not confuse this prophetic office with the ordinary offices of the Church. The prophet speaks as directly called by the Spirit and delivers a message as long as the inspiration lasts. Whoever speaks based on such a personal call, must again and again search himself in order to be sure of the Spirit's guidance. An ordinary office is different. It is a commission based on consecration. Then it is a not a matter of speaking in power of your personal inspiration but of faithfully presenting the old message such as it once was given and received. That is what Paul expects from a bishop, "He must hold firm to the sure word as taught, so that he may be able to give instruction in sound doctrine and also to confute those who contradict it" (Titus 1:9). Of course, also this office must be carried out in the power of the Spirit and with the guidance of the Spirit, but its foundation and authority are not the private experience or feeling of a calling, but it is the gift of the Spirit in the consecration and the presence of the Spirit in the Word and the Sacraments. The prophetic office is a consequence of God's extra-ordinary intervention at special occasions. The ordinary office is a form of God's continuous activity by which He builds up the Church (Eph 4:11–112).

* * *

The ordinary office of the Church is, as we have seen, founded on a commission from Christ. It is not founded on the personal skills, faith, zeal or the feeling of being called which the office holders have. The significance of the apostles was based on the power of Christ's authority, not on the strength of the human characters. Personally they were just common human beings. The sources acknowledge this with a candor that surprises those holding a heroic and humanistic view of the apostles, seeing them as prominent personalities, as religious geniuses or admired moral role models. They were not much of that. What they were, they were through the power of having been called by Christ to be His authorized representatives.

However, this does not at all mean that it is unimportant what kind of person the office holder is. In the areas of business and politics, authorized representatives may turn out to betray their company or party. This is true about the apostles as well, as we see from the example of Judas. The faithfulness of an apostle is therefore an absolute requirement. It is true that he did not receive the office based on excellent personal qualities. However, once he has accepted the office given to him, his total loyalty is demanded. The concept of the office ever since the early church has thus a two-fold focus: the commission from Christ and devotion to the commission.

The commission rests altogether on Christ's calling. Nobody enters the office through his own decision. Behind the apostle stands His Lord with His commission. Only in the power of this commission dares the apostle to go forth. He gets his boundless forthrightness from this commission. He never needs to wonder whether his personal qualities will suffice. He does not need anxiously to ask himself if his talents or will-power or eloquence are good enough for him to succeed. He can say: *The Lord wills it.* "We are ambassadors for Christ, God making His appeal through us. We beseech you *on behalf of Christ*, be reconciled to God" (2 Cor 5:20). The power and certainty in this conception of the office is enveloped in these words of Jesus to the apostles, "You did not choose Me but I chose you. And *I appointed you* to go and bear fruit, fruit that will last" (John 15:16).

Devotion is the other side of the same thing. There is no room for the apostle to master or sift, to adapt or improve the message he has been entrusted to proclaim. It may cause offense or be regarded as foolishness, but the apostle will not fall back, "Woe to me if I do not preach the gospel" (1 Cor 9:16). He has neither any obligation nor any right to seek any other legitimation for the message than this one: *The Lord has commanded it.* "Think of us in this way, as servants of Christ and stewards of God's mysteries. Moreover, it is required of stewards that they be found trustworthy" (1 Cor 4:1–2). An apostle would never usurp any honor or privilege for himself: the office he has is not his but the Lord's! The Lord of the commission is the center around which everything in the administration of the office revolves. "For if I preach the gospel, that gives me no ground for boasting . . . For if I do this of my own will, I have a reward; but if not of my own will, I am entrusted with a commission" (1 Cor 9:16f). "Not that we are competent of ourselves to claim anything as coming from us; our competence is from God" (2 Cor 3:5).

The apostle is thus *one* with his Lord. His life is no longer his own. He knows that the apostles are "God's fellow workers" (1 Cor 3:9), consecrated and set apart to proclaim the gospel in God's plan of salvation. This consecration is also a *consecration for suffering*. "It is enough for the disciple if he is treated like his teacher, and for the servant like his master" (Matt 10:25). Flogging, prison and hatred belong to the consequences of the office. "This man is My chosen instrument . . . I will show him how much he must suffer for the sake of My name" (Acts 9:15–16). That is what the Lord said referring to Saul who was about to be made the Apostle Paul.

That is why a true apostle does not run away from suffering. When some of the apostles had been imprisoned in Jerusalem and were flogged before being released, they "left the Sanhedrin, rejoicing because they had been counted worthy of suffering disgrace for the Name" (Acts 5:41). Referring to bodily abuse Paul wrote, "We always carry around in our body the death of Jesus, so that the life of Jesus may also be revealed in our body" (2 Cor 4:10). Whatever the circumstances, "in honor and dishonor, in ill repute and good repute" (2 Cor 6:8), one thing only is important: the commission entrusted to the apostle. "For we do not preach ourselves, but Jesus Christ as Lord, and ourselves as your servants for Jesus' sake" (2 Cor 4:5).

There is no right administration of the office without this devotion, without this uncompromising obedience to the commission such as it is given, and without this whole-hearted trust in the Lord who gave it.

* * *

When the apostles gave to their successors the commission that they had received from Christ, the apostolic office did not change its character. In virtue of his office, Timothy too can appear with an authority that his young age otherwise would not have allowed him to do (1 Tim 4:12). The early church knew that the leaders were appointed by God (1 Cor. 12:28). Paul thus said to the presbyters of the church in Ephesus who had been installed by the apostles in their office, "The Holy Spirit has made you overseers" (Acts 20:28). The commission is to be *shepherds,* "not by constraint but willingly, not for shameful gain but eager to serve, not lording it over those entrusted to you" (1 Pet 5:2–3). The authority is guided by the duty to serve. The purpose of the office is not to glorify the office holder but to glorify his Lord.

* * *

How then shall we understand the general priesthood, the priesthood of all the baptized? If the pastoral office is a holy commission that first was given to the apostles and then has been entrusted to every new generation to this very day, is there then any purpose in acknowledging a general priesthood? Yes, it is! The priesthood of the baptized is in its own right a very vital concept in the Church.

When Luther revived the neglected biblical concept of the general priesthood of all God's people, he used the word in contrast to the Roman priesthood. The Roman Church regarded the priestly office as a sacrificial office; the foremost task of the priest was to present the sacrifice of the mass, the atoning sacrifice of Christ, that was repeated every day at the altar. Since only the priest could celebrate a valid mass, he became the indispensable mediator between the people and God.

Luther's teaching on the general priesthood is to show the falsehood of the Roman understanding of the priesthood. Since Christ has died for our sins once for all, His sacrifice never needs to be repeated. Forgiveness is open every day for all who believe. Each believer can therefore at any time come to our gracious heavenly Father and receive full forgiveness. Every Christian has the same possibility as the priest (the pastor) to approach God in the name of Jesus. (The Lutheran churches in Scandinavia usually refer to a pastor as priest, in Danish præst, in Norwegian prest, and in Swedish präst.)

In his Apology of the Augsburg Confession (XIII:7–11), Philipp Melanchthon points out that the priestly (pastoral) office does not have a sacrificial purpose but a very different task: it is a preaching office:

> "Our opponents do not interpret the priesthood in reference to the ministry of the Word or the administration of the sacraments to others, but in reference to sacrifice, as though the new covenant needed a priesthood like the Levitical to offer sacrifices and merit the forgiveness of sins for the people. - - - Thus priests are not called to make sacrifices that merit forgiveness of sins for the people, as in the Old Testament, but they are called to preach the Gospel and administer the sacraments to the people. As the Epistle to the Hebrews (chapters 7–9) teaches clearly enough , we do not have a priesthood like the Levitical. If ordination is interpreted in relation to the ministry of the Word, we have no objection to calling ordination a sacrament."

The priestly office thus understood does not become superfluous because of the general priesthood of all the baptized. We underscore that this office is not about offering sacrifices to God, but it is an office for the administration of the means of grace to God's people. It is not the bridge by which humanity comes to God, but it is one of the tools which God has designed to speak and act in the world. Its purpose is not to appease God, but He needs it to reach His creatures, the refractory and forgetful human family, and He does that by having His Word preached and His sacraments administered.

Just as Christ sent His apostles in order to continue His work by proclaiming the gospel, baptizing, forgiving sins, and being shepherds for His Church, so the apostles in their turn chose others to continue their work, and thus emerged, as we have seen, the offices of the Church. The tasks of the priestly office, the holy ministry, are still the same as they were for the apostles: to proclaim the Word and administer the sacraments, wield the power of the keys, and be shepherds of the flock. No one can take on this holy ministry on his own, as is taught by the Augsburg Confession, Article XIV, "Nobody should publicly teach or preach or administer the sacraments in the church without a regular call," that is without having been ordained and installed according to the order of the Church.

It would then be a gross misunderstanding to think that the reformers taught that now anyone who feels like it could preach and preside at the Lord's Supper. What they did teach was the adequate difference between the Old Testament priesthood with the purpose of offering sacrifices and the evangelical priesthood (the holy ministry) with the purpose of administering the means of grace. They also taught that through Christ's great sacrifice we all have free access to God's grace. All God's people are equals when it comes to approaching our gracious heavenly Father.

The general priesthood of all the baptized is called priesthood precisely because it is expressed in offering sacrifices: "You are . . . a holy priesthood, offering spiritual sacrifices acceptable to God through Jesus Christ" (1 Pet 2:5). The sacrifices of God's people have two directions, one of praise and thanksgiving to God and one in deeds of mercy toward fellow men: "Through Jesus, therefore, let us continually offer to God a sacrifice of praise, the fruit of lips that confess His name. And do not forget to do good and to share with others, for with such sacrifices God is pleased" (Heb 13:15–16).

This is what the general priesthood is all about in our everyday life. However, under certain circumstances any Christian may be called upon to do what normally belongs to the pastoral office. When a pastor is not available for someone who is dying or for someone in spiritual crisis, who needs to be assured that his sins are forgiven, a fellow Christian may pronounce that assurance in the Name of the Father and of the Son and of the Holy Spirit. In the same Name she may baptize a dying infant, when there is not enough time to call the pastor. In fact, you ought to ask yourself, "*If* God now, today, would call me to speak with His voice, baptize in His name, and forgive sins on His behalf, can I do that?" Yes, you may serve God in that way: in baptism you were consecrated to do it. You belong to the priesthood of all the baptized! You too are included in these words, "You are a royal priesthood, a holy nation, God's own people" (1 Pet 2:9).

* * *

Finally: How does the hotly debated issue concerning the *ordination of women* look in the light of the New Testament concept of the pastoral office?

After all that we so far have said here, it ought to be clear to everyone that it is not because of a supposed conservative attitude that the church so consistently opposes the ordination of women.

If the pastoral office were a commission from the congregation, a salaried position that people with good intentions had set up, then there would be no reasons founded on principle against opening the pastoral office for women. However, the offices of the Church are different. From the very beginning, their authority, their rights and their duties were based on the commission by which Christ sent His apostles out in the world. They have literally emerged from the consecrating hands of the apostles. Creating something completely new alongside the original offices of the early church is a perilous enterprise. The pastoral office is an apostolic commission, which you cannot take upon yourself. It must be totally clear that it was given to you as Christ designed it. Speaking in His name and with His authority is too serious a matter to do without full and established certainty that you really are commissioned by Him to serve in the pastoral office.

Of course, anyone with the certainty of a personal calling may appear and speak with the right of a prophet, and with the risk of being a false prophet! However, a prophet's appearance is not based on a commission from the Church. Handed down from the time of the apostles, the Church has three offices which she continues to commission to ever new generations of servants. She has no mandate from the Lord of the

Church to create a new office, which could never gain the same character of apostolic commission as the old offices inherently have.

It is also inconceivable that the Church would open to women the already existing pastoral office. The practice of the early church, based on the teaching of Christ's chosen apostles as documented in the New Testament, rises like a wall against such an idea. That men and women stand equally close to the heart of our heavenly Father is beyond discussion from the Christian point of view. In their mutual relationships, we acknowledge no degrading attitude or behavior whatsoever. The Church is the Body of Christ, where we are all members serving one another. The only difference is because of the distribution of work duties and the variety of gifts that God Himself has arranged (1 Cor 12:17–18). A Christian gladly and gratefully respects this order knowing well that one member is not less or more valuable than another, just because God gave them different tasks. Part of this order that God has determined is the clear testimony of the New Testament that women are not called to serve in the pastoral office.

Christianity knows right from the beginning no other office in which women may serve than the deaconess office. The meaning of the Bible is here so clearly expressed (1 Tim 2:11–15; 1 Cor 14:34–38) that it is impossible to introduce a pastoral office for women without consciously setting aside what both Scripture and the unanimous tradition of the Church in no uncertain terms teach and uphold. While agreeing that the plain teaching of Scripture is indeed clear, some proponents of a change argue that we must act according to "the spirit of the gospel." They seem to think that the apostles did not correctly understand Jesus and His intentions; He supposedly did not have any apprehensions about a pastoral office for women.

However, it is a striking and remarkable fact that Jesus Himself never called a woman to be an apostle. And yet, there are many women among the Jesus' followers, whom the gospels portray as good examples of discipleship. It shall never be forgotten that after the apostles fled there were some women who faithfully remained at the cross. Women, too, were the first witnesses of the resurrection. Even so, none of them was commissioned to be a witness of the resurrection as an apostle. The reason could not really have been a concession to Jewish custom. Jesus could be demonstratively free in acting contrary to Jewish customs which did not measure up to God's true law and mercy. He transformed the role of married women, who previously had no legal rights in marriage. But he did *not* call a woman to the apostolic office.

Christ's own apostles were obviously convinced that the commission they had received was for men only. Among the pagans there were, to be sure, plenty of priestesses. During the initial period of some congregations when not all things had been settled in an ordered way, it could occur that women, too, preached and taught at the services. The apostles could not approve of this. They were not impressed when their opponents tried to claim the authority of the Spirit. Paul had the answer ready, "If anybody thinks he is a prophet or spiritually gifted, let him acknowledge that *what I am writing to you is the Lord's command*" (1 Cor 14:37). The early church did not know any higher instance. The matter was settled. This became the accepted order for the whole Christian church, laid down both in the Bible and the church orders.

If the Swedish province of the Church decided to change this order, it would result in the most serious consequences. It would signify that we have surrendered the entire foundation on which we so far have been building: Holy Scripture, interpreted and expounded through the unanimous tradition of the Church catholic and through the Reformation's genuine experience of the Pauline message. We would abandon this old foundation and instead rely on a new idea supposedly as an expression of divine revelation. We must then realize that in so doing, we would be on a way which led the Roman church to its doctrines on Mary and on the papacy. We shall also make it clear to ourselves that we thereby make a reunion impossible with those churches which remain on the foundation established in the early church for all times. As long as our church continues in life and faith and doctrine to confess herself as being the Church in Sweden, the Swedish branch of Christ's one, holy and catholic Church, such a step is unthinkable.

Further: such a step remains unthinkable as long as our church desires to be faithful to her Lutheran legacy, expressed in that zeal and love for Holy Scripture, which has been her greatest asset ever since the Reformation era.

Nothing is more urgent in our discussing this issue than that we all would renounce heated feelings and arguments which are foreign to the gospel. That way of arguing concerning ordination of women is easily done not only by anyone who is fighting for the rights of women in all areas of society but also by anyone who wants to uphold the age-old stand of the Church without understanding her innermost motives. There is a lot of inveterate conservatism and male arrogance among some men, an attitude that should have no place neither in the Church nor in society in general.

The issue of women's ordination is for the Church never a matter of women's rights in the same way as in society in general. For the Church it is altogether a matter of being faithful toward the legacy and commission given to her by the Lord of the Church. The reason the Church cannot establish a pastoral office for women is because she has no right to do that and also because it could never be an office in a churchly sense, since it could not be based on an apostolic commission. Therefore it could not be administered in unreserved dedication to the apostolic message. On the contrary: through its very existence, it would in no uncertain way declare that we no longer are bound to the faith of the apostles but reserve for ourselves the right to revise them.

There is a great need in our day and time for more women to serve on behalf of the Church: among the youth, in various institutions, among groups of career women, and so forth. This need is now so extensive that it cannot adequately be met by volunteers. The natural way for the Church in this situation is to train women for different fields and specialties, and then bestow on them *the office of the deaconate* thereby commissioning them to serve the Church as *deaconesses,* in full harmony with and faithfulness to biblical and churchly order. Such faithfulness is the only guarantee that this office would be beneficial as well as giving the office holder security and joy in her work. There is no valuation or ranking, when God's Word assigns one particular office for men and another for women, but rather a guarantee for the gifts to be used in the best way. Christ's Church can never acknowledge any other right than the one to receive God's unmerited gifts of grace and then in gratitude serve the Lord and our fellow men.

2. SUCCESSORS OF THE APOSTLES

The congregation has elected a new pastor. Today he is presiding and preaching in his new parish for the first time. Attendance is much higher than usual. Some parishioners that seldom are seen in God's house are here today. There is expectancy in the air. Everyone follows the liturgy with the kind of attention that it deserves but not always gets.

Some attend the service today out of pure curiosity. Tomorrow at work, they will give a report about the new parish pastor. Others have mixed feelings of sympathy and anxiety. They voted for him, and now they are hoping that he shall meet their expectations, and even gain the approval of those who voted against him. Maybe he will be with us for twenty years: just think of the impact he then will have in the life of our congregation!

Then we have the faithful who are here every Sunday. They do not show much of any curiosity, they bow their heads in prayer before the service begins, praying also for their new pastor. They sense the magnitude of that life's work that he now is about to take on. Maybe they think of previous pastors, shepherds with great zeal who will be difficult to follow, or tragic figures whose enthusiasm burnt down and went out in the piercing chilly wind of indifference. He is indeed facing a tall order, our new pastor. Will he be able to manage his many demanding duties well enough?

Now he is in the pulpit, his eyes looking at hundreds of worshipers. He too senses the pressure of many questions in his heart and mind. The task he is facing is inhumanly vast. Is he the man to break through the wall of polite but hard as stone indifference that his predecessor had mentioned? By what right does he stand here as teacher and caretaker of souls in this parish? Many of the people right here at church today are older than he, with more experience of life. By what right can he expect them to give up a lot of their free time on Sundays in order to come here and listen to him week after week?

Such questions are not unknown to any pastor who is committed to his calling with his whole being. In fact, they can be pure torture if he began with that view of his office that has become more and more common nowadays and that more often than not has been regarded as the only really spiritual and humble view. It is often maintained, both in pious and secularized circles, that the authority of the pastoral office depends entirely on the personal qualities of the office holder. His position is not really different from that of others who are involved in the life of the congregation. If his words are valuable, it is because of his personal religious experiences, his endowments of character or his ability to present the message in a captivating and moving manner. His gown and collar mean nothing. What possibly means something is the religious person wearing them: the eloquent preacher, the skillful administrator, the dynamic youth leader, etc.

There actually may be some relevant truth embedded in those kinds of expectations concerning a good pastor. Yet, any pastor will soon realize that if that is the whole truth, he will collapse under the exorbitant weight of his charge. He will be asking himself if he as a person is so important that he on that basis can be an authority for all these very different people in his parish. Can he really with his eloquence and personal experiences year after year captivate them with his sermons? Can he expect to gain and keep their attention in the midst of the cacophony of propaganda, programs, and advertisements that continuously are demanding their time and commitment? The more conscientious he is, the more he will experience his personal insufficiency. If he has nothing else to fall back on than his own personal qualifications, he might as well give up.

However, he does have something more. He has *the office entrusted to him in the ordination.* This statement may be irritating to some, because there are so many misguided conceptions of the pastoral office. It is all too often the fault of the pastors themselves that these misconceptions are so deeply rooted. Abuse of the pastoral charge is something very offensive and damaging in the minds and hearts not only among church members but also among the outsiders. But the pastoral office, when carried out in faithfulness to the New Testament, is something deeply edifying. It is such a spiritual asset both for the pastor and his congregation. A church that is about to lose the appreciation of it really is in the process of giving up something that has always been essential to the Church from the very beginning. We need indeed to regain the original authentic understanding of the pastoral office, so that it once again would have its due place in the life of our church.

* * *

We have pointed out earlier in this chapter that in the early church the understanding of the pastoral office had two focuses: *the commission* and *devotion*. The commission is from Christ Himself, given to His authorized representatives, the apostles, and by them to the next generation and thereafter to all succeeding generations. Devotion is the officeholder's whole-hearted and uncompromising obedience to the message that he is charged to proclaim.

We have also seen how this sacred commission has been transferred from generation to generation, from nation to nation, so that our Swedish bishops today are the apostles' successors just as our pastors (priests) have received the same consecration as Paul and Titus once submitted to their presbyters. One does not need to be strictly Episcopal to appreciate this succession of the pastoral office from the apostles. At the same token, we should be careful not to exaggerate its importance. We cannot accord to it any decisive significance for a valid celebration of the Lord's Supper, as some Anglicans do. Further, we cannot regard the apostolic succession as broken even if it was not transferred by pre-Reformation bishops through the rite of consecration to a new generation of bishops. This was the case when the Reformation was introduced in Denmark and Norway. However, the true apostolic succession was actually restored in those countries as well as in Sweden during the 1500's in that the authentic biblical message from the apostles once again was proclaimed in the Church.

Nevertheless, we do maintain that the normal and natural state of the matter, based on the understanding of the pastoral office that we have received from the New Testament and the early church, is that there ought to be an unbroken succession from the apostles themselves, meaning that the commission emerged from them. It also underscores that this commission no one can usurp. It can only be given. Since such a succession has been preserved in the Church of Sweden, there can be no doubt that the New Testament understanding of the pastoral office not only may but should be applied in our church. This is of the greatest significance both for the pastor and for the congregation he serves. It means for the pastor that he will avoid both conceit based on his accomplishments and despair brought on by his failures. Instead he will experience renewed boldness and devotion knowing that he is a messenger in the Lord's service.

Boldness: because the commission is from the Lord Himself. The pastor is convinced of this not only because of an inner experience of his being called to become a pastor, but most of all is his confidence based on his consecration, when he became a pastor in Christ's Church. This consecration means for him as a pastor the same as his baptism means for him as a Christian. Christ has spoken here, audibly and irrevocably, making him His messenger. He never need to ask himself if he possibly misunderstood his feelings that time when he decided to become a pastor. The commission that through the centuries has been handed down from Christ Himself has as a matter of fact been given to him. He can never doubt that. This fact rests not only on his being a link in the unbroken chain of pastors in the apostolic ministry ever since Christ gave His commission to the apostles, but also on the biblical faith in the Church as the body of Christ, immersed by His Spirit.

Because the Church is an organism where the living Lord continues His work, we know that He is present at every ordination. The commission does not only come down through the ages, through the long line of His authorized servants. It is also given at the moment of the ordination by the living and present Lord himself. In that sense, our evangelical confession also acknowledge the consecration of a pastor as a *sacrament*. Anyone to whom the pastoral office has been given can administer it in the immeasurable certainty that *the Lord wants it*. The Lord himself has chosen him and will see to it that His servant will not fall short, as long as he is a faithful steward.

This sacramental view of the office means an immense relief for the pastor. He is released from his anxious introspection. He does not need any longer to ask himself how he shall be able to deliver captivating sermons Sunday after Sunday. There is no need for him to wonder if he would be quick at repartee in defending his faith against all hairsplitting critics. No longer does he need to exert himself to impress people in order to exact attention. As long as he has the idea that his "personal qualities" validate his being a pastor, he will be tormented by constant anxiety as he asks himself whether he really is catching on with his parish, whether the youth like him, whether he carries enough weight to gain respect for "his" faith, and a score of other issues which are gnawing at the pastor's heart as long as he is handling his charge by just drawing from his own resources. All these questions and concerns are now erased. Having received the commission from Christ Himself, according to His plan and not according to his own plan, by His power and not by his own power, the pastor knows that his work in the Lord shall not be without fruit, provided that he is faithful in the office that was given him by the Lord.

This view of the pastoral office means therefore a keener sense of *devotion*. Since it is not an office created by man, which I should try to manage according to my best judgment and personal qualifications, but a commission from the Risen Lord, I am called to acknowledge it as a commission to which I am devoting my life without any reservations. I actually become my Lord's serf and slave. I become nothing and He everything. Any thought of measuring, sifting, or disputing my commission from the

Lord, adapting it to "cultural trends, demands from contemporary society," modern psychology, or any other norm, must be altogether foreign to me. I *either* receive the message without any reductions in order to proclaim it without reductions, totally trusting in my Lord's authority and His divine truth, totally bound to His Word, *or* I do not have an office as designed by the Lord. My preaching should be "not with enticing words of man's wisdom, but in demonstration of the Spirit and of power" (1 Cor 2:4), which I can expect only from Him who gave me the commission. "I am compelled to preach. Woe to me if I do not preach the gospel!" (1 Cor 9:16).

Faithfulness to the commission becomes faithfulness to the Word. It is no longer a matter of sifting and sorting out. It is a matter of listening to catch the message that my Lord and Savior has commanded His herald to present. It is a matter of being permeated with that message, by living by it, by assimilating it in its whole organic context and its full richness, and thus presenting it without excuses, with accountability to the Lord and boldness before men.

Faithfulness to the commission also means that the pastor's own person with its natural demands for prestige and influence must withdraw. The selfish will that desires to hold its own, that desires to have the last word, that desires higher salary and a nicer home, must be crucified with Christ. The holy commission cannot tolerate at its side any private goals and interests. If the pastor attempts to apply the authority that rightly belongs to the pastoral office to his own person with its desires and endeavors, then he is abusing his office. Concerning his own person, he must be prepared to suffer injustice and scorn, to be misunderstood, slandered and belied. His consecration to the pastoral office is also a consecration to suffering. This he knows from the teaching of his Lord. But he also knows that this suffering is a privilege, a blessing, a creative force, a belonging to the unsearchable mystery of the salvation drama. It is a part of the apostolic commission given to him, to the glory of God and for the salvation of souls.

A German pastor writes with humor and pathos about devotion in the office and about all the human substitutes which are used to replace it. He thinks of pastors

> "as either work horses, race horses, merry-go-round horses, or oxen.

Work horses are those who are trying to do everything. They are consumed, torn apart and devoured by endless chores. They are administrators, social workers, youth leaders, board members, newspaper writers, scientists, astronomers etc., etc. But the main thing they cannot do: to operate upon the sick souls, to cut, dress, heal, and save: they cannot bear to see blood!

The race horses are running around, always and everywhere, in their parish and outside the parish. They are everywhere and nowhere. As speakers they are in demand for festivals and celebrations. But they do not stand on the courtyard as the twelve oxen with the molten sea of grace on their backs (see 1 Kings 7:23–25), ready to wash the unclean souls . . .

The merry-go-around horses are the amusement directors, who are so good at entertaining their congregation. They organize trips, participate in shows, do athletics, go hiking, arrange movie- and story-gatherings, and a whole lot more. But they do not go forward one inch with the congregation. In spite of all the activities, they remain as the merry-go-around on the same spot.

Repent and turn around, you pastors, and be shepherds, caretakers of souls, father confessors, healer of hearts . . .

Pray to God that He would give His poor church shepherds who are not so eager to reach high but rather be content to be simple and foolish oxen from the country, who know nothing but their Lord and their office, and who desire only *one* thing, to serve the Lord in His courtyard with the sea of forgiveness on their backs, until they have broken off their horns and their backs ache, until they have served their time, and then yet are ready to be slaughtered and sacrificed for their Lord.

My dear fellow pastor, have no other ambition than having these words engraved on your tombstone: Here rests an old simple and foolish ox from the country. Isaiah 1:3 refers to such a servant of the Lord, *The ox knows his master.*" (Quade, Gustav: *Vom Pastor zum Beichtvater! Eine Heilige Kirche*, 1935, pages 261–262.)

* * *

Maybe now we can better understand the new pastor in his pulpit. Standing there, he is not promoting himself. Least of all would he imagine himself to be so interesting and important that he week after week could lay claim to his parishioners' attention. One thing he does claim is that he has the commission to present a *message* which is so important and so necessary for all people that *this message* has the right to lay claim to their attention. That he of all people now has been put here to proclaim the message is not because he would be more important or remarkable than all these people in the pews. No, it is because he has by God's grace been consecrated and set apart for this task in life.

The influences and circumstances that led him to become a pastor would most likely lend material for a long story. He would certainly tell us about certain events which planted the first ideas of going into the Holy Ministry. And soon enough he knew in his heart and mind: you shall be a pastor! Or maybe he had to struggle for a long time before he dared to choose the way leading to ordination after many years of demanding theological studies. Impatiently longing for the time to come when he finally could serve his Lord in the pastoral office, maybe he grumbled about the many "useless" days spent with commentaries, dictionaries and Hebrew grammar at the seminary. Now afterwards, he knows that it all was necessary. He would never have been able to proclaim the message correctly, if he had not acquired the tools to dig deeper into the Word than a Bible translation allows. He got his seminary degree and could look forward to the decisive step: the ordination. No theological degree as such entitles anyone to be accepted for ordination. The bishop accepts or turns away the candidates according to his judgment. Knowledge in the various theological fields of learning is indeed one of the conditions precedent for the pastoral office, but it is not the most important one. The bishop has the same authority as Timothy and Titus in the early church. He too must therefore follow Paul's advice to them, "Do not be hasty in the laying on of hands" (1 Tim 5:22). The bishop must be convinced that the candidate has not only knowledge of the message but also faith in the message of our Crucified and Risen Lord and Savior Jesus Christ.

Now the bishop is ready to ordain this "Candidate for the Sacred Ministry" (Sacri Ministerii Candidatus) at the high altar in the cathedral. The ordinand first gives his vows, demanding vows that will be beneficial for him as guiding stars in his ministry. Kneeling, he then receives, through the laying-on-of-hands by the bishop and the assisting pastors, the holy commission which now is bestowed on him from the apostles, indeed from the Lord Himself. He is now a pastor, consecrated and set apart to proclaim the apostolic message and administer the holy sacraments.

With this consecration, God has laid the foundation for the pastor's whole ministry. It will carry him when he staggers under the weight of his duties. There will be times where he will have little desire to preach. If he would have become a pastor only based on his own inner calling, he would then end in unbearable pangs of conscience. It would have been dishonest of him to enter the pulpit. He knows now that he does not preach because he feels so or so, or thinks so or so. He knows that he has *the commission*! In virtue of this commission he returns faithfully to the preparation of his sermons, and again he will experience that the Lord does not abandon His servant, as long as he just remains faithful to what he has received.

This commission gives his words authority at the death beds: the Word is not his but the Lord's. It gives him boldness in preaching. It grants him perseverance in adversity. He knows where the help is: going back to the message, digging deeper in it, devoting more time for sermon preparation and confirmation instruction, giving more attention to the administration of the sacraments, and penetrating the Word with even more sincere study of it. External success is no measurer of his value as pastor, only the inner faithfulness to the message and the commission.

That is why, in spite of all, he is ready to take on all the demanding tasks that really are beyond human ability, and do this with joy and boldness. He would never have dared to do it, if he had followed his own reason, just as little as the apostles ever would have gone out into the world with their message. But just as their faithfulness to the message that time enabled them to accomplish the impossible, the message of the atonement and the resurrection does the same today as well, where it is presented in faithfulness. It is on that requirement that the pastor must examine himself every day. But if he knows that he is willing to be faithful, affirming with all his heart his *Yes* to the commission from his Lord, then he can with confidence put all the other concerns in His hand and save himself from all unnecessary worries about the results of his ministry. He can with boldness and in earnest exhort his parishioners faithfully to attend the services and to use the means of grace, not for his own sake, but for the sake of the message. He can lay claim to their attention, their time, and their interest, not for himself, but for the Lord. He has the right to go to see the sick, visit the mourners, warn the unforgiving, intervene in circumstances which he as a private person never would have concerned himself with, all this in virtue of his office. And this is so, "for we do not preach ourselves, but CHRIST JESUS as LORD, and ourselves as your servants for Jesus' sake" (2 Cor 4:5).

Maybe the congregation as well could have similar thoughts about the pastor? Where that happens, the impact of the Word is sure to accomplish more than elsewhere.

There are areas in our country, where the pastoral office is respected as Scripture admonishes us to do (1 Thess 5:12–13; 1 Tim 5:17; Heb 13:17). In those areas people tend to have a healthy view of the pastor as person. His personal opinions concerning practical matters in the parish are no law. They are respected but not necessarily followed. The parishioners feel free to voice their opinions even if they are absolutely contrary to the pastor's. But in God's house, the people attend the service with deep devotion, listening with sincere attention to the Word and accepting it "not as the word of men but as what it really is, the word of God" (1 Thess 2:13). They partake of the Lord's Supper and bring their babies to be baptized, in the sure knowledge that it is God who is at work here for their everlasting welfare. If something is lacking in the pastor's way of speaking or conducting the service, they are willing to accept that. They are not seeking a pleasant atmosphere, not a beautiful show, or a rhetorical achievement. They are in church to hear the precious Word of God.

If they have concerns about the contents of the pastor's sermons or about something in his lifestyle, they will pray faithfully for their pastor, interceding in his behalf before the All Merciful God. It could also happen that someone would invite him for dinner after church, eventually sharing with him a sermon from one of the old teachers, thereby indicating that the Church has a firmer and richer message for the souls than what was offered from the pulpit today.

In all this the people remain undisturbed in their trust in God, keeping their joy in worshiping Him in His temple. They know that even if the pastor does not manage his sacred commission as well as he should, even so the Lord is present. He continues to speak from the Bible, He listens all the while graciously to the prayers and the songs of praise from His people, and He still invites sinners to His table of Holy Communion.

If I would be told that I was baptized by an alcoholic and unworthy pastor, I would still thank God for my baptism, because I know that it was He Himself who baptized me. The shortcomings of His servants cannot invalidate the sacraments. "For the gifts and the call of God are irrevocable" (Rom 11:29).

The same holds true when I partake of the Lord's Supper. How awful it would be if I had to question whether the pastor is worthy enough to administer the sacrament! There is no way that I would know what is going on in his heart and mind. If the validity of the Lord's Supper would depend on the pastor's piety, then there would not be much comfort in the sacrament. But now I know that the Savior Himself has placed him here. Just as He has chosen this insignificant piece of bread to give me the gift that is beyond all human understanding, likewise He has chosen this human instrument to hand me His gift. What happens here does not depend on the bread or on the pastor, neither on any of us or our righteousness, but only and solely on Christ and His words by which He instituted this sacrament.

We can go on. When I in private confession have confessed my sin, I hear the words of absolution, the incomprehensibly bold pronouncement that my sins are forgiven. If I would measure that pronouncement according to my human reasoning, I must say as the Pharisees said about Jesus, "Who is this who even forgive sins?" (Luke 7:49). But now I know full well that my pastor speaks with apostolic authority having been ordained to say the words of absolution by Him who said, "If you forgive anyone his sins, they are forgiven" (John 20:23). So when my pastor says, *"In the stead and by the command of my Lord Jesus Christ I forgive you all your sins,"* then it is God's own voice I hear.

Thus it is justified that the parishioners have a certain degree of indifference with regard to the pastor as a person while at the same time having the highest appreciation for the pastoral office in which he is God's servant. This indifference does not exclude a great solicitude that the pastor as a person and as a Christian really lives in healthy relations with both God and fellow men. It is indeed in those parishes where the people know that not everything depends on how gifted the pastor is as a person, that they are more eager than elsewhere to have pastors who are sincere in their faith and upright in their living. Even if a baptism is valid and the Lord's Supper right, no matter how defective the human instrument may be, the proclamation of the gospel and the care of the souls cannot be the same when the pastor is lazy or not converted, as it would be when he himself walks the narrow road that leads to life.

The pastor in his turn has similar thoughts about his parish. He belongs to the people there and becomes their friend, precisely because God has tied him to them. He experiences a close bond with them, when he thinks of and prays for each one of those whom the Lord has given in his pastoral care. He will once give an account for how he served as their shepherd.

The pastor has often been close to succumbing under the responsibility. But then once again he sees the office, the great commission, in all its glory. God wants it! It is God who has put him here to be His servant in this congregation. Then he again enters the world of prayer and thus strengthened he takes on anew the manifold tasks waiting for him among his people. Once again he plunges deeper into the Word and into the inexhaustible legacy of the Church which constantly fills his hands with new treasures. The more he suffers and the more he rejoices in his service as a pastor, the better he understands the words in 2 Cor 5:18,20, that deeper than anything else express the essence of the pastoral office, its holy calling to be God's voice in the world and an instrument for His saving presence in the midst of this world of sin and decay:

> *All this is from God, who reconciled us to Himself through Christ*
> *and gave us the ministry of reconciliation . . .*
> *We are therefore Christ's ambassadors, God making His appeal*
> *through us. We implore you on Christ's behalf:*
>
> **Be reconciled to God!**

Author's Postscript

THIS BOOK ON THE Church does not give a complete picture of Christ's Church. It demands a sequel in order not to remain flagrantly one-sided. Here I have attempted to describe how the Church has her origin in another world, how she represents a new era that in her appearance is mysteriously present here on earth. I have again and again been aiming at bringing home the fact that the Church is being built from above, that she is not a human organization but the body of Christ, through which His heavenly kingdom is among us on earth as well. I have underscored that her holiness is God's holiness and that her back-bone and her inexhaustible wells of strength are the Word and the Sacraments where God is present and active, in spite of all human disbelief and human failures.

This is what is essential for the Church. This is what makes her the Church. This is what I have pointed out in chapter after chapter in this book. It needs to be said with relentless persistency that even to people who call themselves Christian, the Church becomes all too often nothing more than an association of people who have become believers. They think that her foundations are placed in the human heart, that her beginning is the conversion of her members, that her attributes are certain pious characteristics, and that she is made up of people who think, act, and believe in a certain way.

Such an understanding of the Church loses her most important features. It leaves out her head, which is Christ, and her living pulse, which are the means of grace. It deprives her of that which makes her the Church, that which is not of this world but exists beyond all time and independent of all people. It reduces her to something far more insignificant than she actually is.

Yet, if I conclude here, I would not have given a true picture of Christ's Church, because she lives also in her members. She also exists in the work that God does in the hearts of people. After all, it is for their sake that God built her on earth. What happens in a repentant and believing heart is thus part of the same divine work that occurred when the Word became flesh, and that still happens when the Word proceeds from God's mouth or when Christ comes to us in the Sacrament of His Body and Blood.

It is thus a flagrant misunderstanding of the essence of the Church, if we would allow all our love and all our concern to stop at the true knowledge of the Triune God and the right administration of the means of grace but would neglect the need for revival and conversion. Yes, Christ and the means of grace are indeed the Church's foundation; without them there is no true church. And yet, the whole Church is actually present only where people use the means of grace. What happens among the people is really of the greatest importance.

It is of utmost importance that people repent and trust in Jesus for forgiveness of their sins. It is so important that there is joy in heaven each time that a poor sinner thus repents. It is not unimportant whether a church member prays, and does it correctly and devoutly. On the contrary, it is so important that prayer in spirit and truth is pointed out by Jesus as the very key to the storehouse of heaven. Neither is it without importance how a person lives his everyday life. On the contrary, it is so decisive that on the great day of reckoning it will be asked who fed the hungry, who visited the sick, and who welcomed the stranger.

All that is included in the words *conversion, devotion,* and *Christian everyday life* actually demands its own book. I have therefore also been working on presenting in a separate volume certain aspects of the Christian life, as it appears toward the background of that view of the Church that has been presented here. This future work, which I will give the title *Church Piety,* shall thus be regarded as a sequel of this book. (The first edition of *Church Piety,* in Swedish *Kyrkofromhet,* was published later in the same year, 1939, as the first edition of *Christ's Church;* for more information, see the Introduction in this book.)

This coming book is also all about the Church, although the presentation in it will follow the flow of life from Christ out to its ramifications among the people. I hope then to make clearer what I only could give an idea of here: that the firm and objective and the institutional in the essence of the Church is not a shackle and an obstacle for the personal

Christian life with its experiences and individual piety but just the opposite. The strong church walls standing through millennia and the old orders with apostolic origin are the solid rock from which the water of life flows fresh and clear, in each new generation bringing forth a new spring of spiritual life, individually and distinctly experienced and yet altogether ruled by the same Spirit who from the beginning has been the creative force in the Body of Christ.

Thus we are to honor and love the sacramental life and the divine message, which remain independent of any human thought and action. At the same time, we love and nurture our personal Christian life in all its nuances, more and more experiencing its richness. In so doing we shall truly comprehend the essence of the Church, as we live her life in the indestructible and imperishable fellowship of the Body of Christ.

Appendix 1
Bible Reading Plan

THIS IS AN APPENDIX to *Christ's Church* by Bo Giertz, published in 2010 by Wipf and Stock Publishers, Eugene, Oregon. The Bible Reading Plan is composed by the Rev. Hans Andræ, who translated CHRIST'S CHURCH from the Swedish original, KRISTI KYRKA. The plan may be copied freely for private or public use, provided that both pages are distributed together. Jesus said, *"If you abide in My word, you are My disciples indeed."* John 8:31 NKJV

THE BIBLE IS ALL ABOUT OUR LORD AND SAVIOR JESUS CHRIST

Jesus said, *"All things must be fulfilled which were written in the Law of Moses and the Prophets and the Psalms concerning Me."* Luke 24:44 NKJV

THE OLD TESTAMENT →
Prophecy, Promise: **"He will come!"**

← THE NEW TESTAMENT
Fulfillment: **"He has come!"**

Unit #	O.T. Reading	N.T. Reading	Date(s) Read
1	Gen 1-20	Matt 1-5	
2	Gen 21-35	Matt 6-9	
3	Gen 36-50	Matt 10-13	
4	Exod 1-21	Matt 14-18	
5	Exod 22-40	Matt 19-22	
6	Isaiah 1-19	Matt 23-25	
7	Isaiah 20-37	Matt 26-28	
8	Isaiah 38-51	Rom 1-5	
9	Isaiah 52-66	Rom 6-10	
10	Psalms 1-33	Rom 11-16	
11	Lev 1-14	Mark 1-4	

Unit #	O.T. Reading	N.T. Reading	Date(s) Read
27	Ezek 20-33	Galatians	
28	Ezek 34-48	Ephesians	
29	Psalms 63-88	Phil, Col	
30	1 Sam 1-18	John 1-4	
31	1 Sam 19- 2 Sam 7	John 5-8	
32	2 Sam 8-24	John 9-11	
33	1 Kings 1-10	John 12-16	
34	1 Kings 11-22	John 17-21	
35	2 Kings 1-13	1 & 2 Thess	
36	2 Kings 14-25	1 & 2 Tim, Tit, Philem	
37	Daniel	Hebrews 1-8	

Appendix 1

Unit #	O.T. Reading	N.T. Reading	Date(s) Read
12	Lev 15-27	Mark 5-8	
13	Num 1-16	Mark 9-12	
14	Num 17-36	Mark 13-16	
15	Jer 1-15	1 Cor 1-6	
16	Jer 16-31	1 Cor 7-11	
17	Jer 32-48	1 Cor 12-16	
18	Jer 49-52, Lamentations	2 Cor 1-7	
19	Psalms 34-62	2 Cor 8-13	
20	Deut 1-17	Luke 1-3	
21	Deut 18-33	Luke 4-6	
22	Josh 1-12	Luke 7-9	
23	Josh 13-24	Luke 10-12	
24	Judges 1-11	Luke 13-17	
25	Judges 12-21, Ruth	Luke 18-21	
26	Ezek 1-19	Luke 22-24	

Unit #	O.T. Reading	N.T. Reading	Date(s) Read
38	Psalms 89-115	Hebrews 9-13	
39	1 Chron 1-17	Acts 1-5	
40	1 Chron 18-2 Chron 8	Acts 6-9	
41	2 Chron 9-28	Acts 10-13	
42	2 Chron 29-36 Ezra	Acts 14-18	
43	Nehemiah, Esther	Acts 19-23	
44	Job 1-21	Acts 24-28	
45	Job 22-42	James	
46	Prov 1-16	1 & 2 Peter	
47	Prov 17-31	1, 2 & 3 John, Jude	
48	Eccles, Song of Sol	Rev 1-4	
49	Psalms 116-150	Rev 5-9	
50	Hosea, Joel	Rev 10-14	
51	Amos, Nahum	Rev 15-18	
52	Hab, Malachi	Rev 19-22	

Flexibility is a special feature of this 52-unit reading plan. Reading an average of one unit per week would thus cover the whole Bible in just one year, which is impossible for most of us. Take your time: 2, 3, or even 4 years! And be **flexible!** Sometimes you may indeed have the time to read a unit in just a week. Other times a unit may require several weeks.

Appendix 2

The Front Cover Picture

THE PICTURE ON THE front cover of this book shows the altar triptych in the Linköping Cathedral in Sweden. It was painted by Norwegian artist Henrik Sörensen (1882–1962) and placed in the cathedral in 1934.

This painting is a striking and powerful presentation of *Christ and His Church* and is thus a most fitting illustration for this book: *Christ's Church*. Bo Giertz, the author of this book, and eight other men were the first candidates to be ordained before this altar painting, namely on Holy Innocents Day, 28 December 1934. (On a personal note, even your translator was ordained at this altar, together with his twin brother Göran on Holy Trinity Sunday, 24 May 1959.)

On each side panel of his triptych, Sörensen has included twelve figures, who with one exception are figures from the Holy Bible and church history. Most of them are mentioned in this book; see Index of Proper Names.

On the left panel we see standing from the right: *David, Ezekiel, Amos, Isaiah, Laurentius/Lawrence* (only partly visible), *Ambrose*, and *Augustine* (partly on the cover, partly on the spine). Lying down from the right: *Jeremiah* and *Paul*. On the spine from the left panel: *Olaus Petri* leaning to embrace a *young boy*, and *Luther*.

On the right panel we see standing from the left: *Moses, Peter, Luke, Mark, Matthew, Erik, Ansgar, Nikolaus Hermanni*, and *Birgitta* leaning to embrace a *young girl*. Kneeling from the left *John* (the apostle) and *Stephen*.

Henrik Sörensen was one of the most prominent artists in the 20th century. He was in great demand, especially as a painter of large motifs for monumental buildings. For *Oslo City Hall*, built 1931–1950, he completed one of the largest frescoes anywhere. That painting, known as "Work, Administration, and Feast," covers about 5,400 sq.feet! He also contributed in 1939 a painting of substantial size for the headquarters of *The League of Nations* in Geneva.

Hans Andræ
Translator

Bibliography

Arseniev, Nicholas. *Die urchristliche Realismus und die Gegenwart.* Kassel, 1933.
Aulén, Gustaf. *Evangeliskt och romerskt (Evangelical and Roman).* Uppsala, 1922.
Brilioth, Yngve. *Svensk Kyrkokunskap (Swedish Ecclesiology).* Stockholm, 1933.
Bring, Ebbe Gustaf. An essay in *Swensk Kyrkotidning (Swedish Church Times).* Uppsala, 1856.
Clement of Rome. *Epistle to the Corinthians.*
Cyril of Jerusalem. *Catecheses.*
Elert, Werner. *Morphologie des Luthertums.* Munich, 1931.
Fridrichsen, Anton. *Kyrka och sakrament i Nya Testamentet (Church and Sacrament in the New Testament),* an essay in Svensk Teologisk Kvartalskrift 1956.
Heiler, Friedrich Johann. *Vergebung der Sünden, Eine heilige Kirche.* 1935.
Holmquist, Hjalmar. *Svenska Kyrkans historia (The History of the Swedish Church).* Uppsala, 1933.
Ignatius. *Epistle to the Ephesians* and *Epistle to the Smyrneans.*
Irenaeus. *Adversus haereses.*
Justin Martyr. *Apology I.*
Luther, Martin. *The Large Catechism* (1529). *Commentary on St. Paul's Epistle to the Galatians* (1535). *The Smalcald Articles* (1537).
Melanchthon, Philipp. *The Augsburg Confession* (1530). *The Apology of the Augsburg Confession* (1531).
Quade, Gustav. *Vom "Pastor" zum Beichtvater! Eine Heilige Kirche.* 1935.
Schmid, Toni. *Sveriges kristnande (Christianity Comes to Sweden).* Uppsala, 1934.
Schütz, Paul. *Warum ich noch ein Christ sein.* Berlin, 1937.
Söderblom, Nathan. *Kyrkan i Sverige (The Church in Sweden).* Stockholm, 1923. *Svenska kyrkans kropp och själ (The Body and Soul of the Swedish Church).*
Wallerius, Ivar. *Kristendomens självständighetskrav (Christianity's Quest for Independence).* Göteborg, 1927.
Zernov, Nicolas. Essay in *The Church of God* (edited by E. L. Mascall). Oxford, 1934.

Index of Proper Names

Abraham	12, 13, 17, 30	Elert, Werner	47, 70
Ambrose	182	Emund	75
Amos	110, 182	Erik	75, 182
Andræ, Anders	VI, XIII	Ericsson, Lars Magnus	XII
Andræ, Tor	XIII, XIV, XV	Ezekiel	182
Andreae, Laurentius	77	Francis of Assisi	73
Ansgar of Hamburg	74, 76, 80, 182	Fresenius, Johann Philip	148
Apollos	152	Fridrichsen, Anton	67
Arseniev, Nicholas	102	Fry, Franklin Clark	XVII
Athanasius	118	Giertz, Knut Harald	XII
Attila	92	Gustav V	XVI
Augustine of Hippo	69, 182	Gustavus Vasa	77, 78
Aulén, Gustaf	70	Gustavus Adolphus	84, 85
Bergkvist, Olof	XV	Halsten	92
Bernard of Clairvaux	73	Hedegård, David	V
Birger Jarl	92	Heerbrand, Jacob	70
Bonhoeffer, Dietrich	XX	Hergeir	74
Birgitta of Vadstena	75, 93, 182	Hermanni, Nikolaus	93, 130, 182
Brask, Hans	93	Holmquist, Hjalmar	77, 78, 83, 85
Brilioth, Yngve	58	Ignatius	60, 68, 154, 155
Bring, Ebbe Gustaf	59	Inge the Elder	92
Calvin, John	48, 82	Ingegerd	75
Carl XVI Gustaf	XIX	Irenaeus	68, 127, 155
Chrysostom, John	69	Isaac	17
Clement of Alexandria	68	Isaiah	17, 182
Clement of Rome	68, 153	Jacob	12, 17
Constantine the Great	92	Jacobi, Sven	77
Cyril of Jerusalem	61, 66	James the Apostle	42, 182
Dacke, Nils	79	Jaroslav of Kiev	75
David	8, 182	Jeremiah	182
Diocletian	92	John the Evangelist	65, 155, 182
Eidem, Erling	XVI	John the Baptist	8

Judas Iscariot	157	Sigismund	83
Justin Martyr	127	Simeon	11
Karl VIII Knutsson	93	Sirach	17
Karl IX	83	Spegel, Haquin	84
Laurentius (Lawrence)	182	Stefan of Uppsala	84
Lewis, C. S.	XX	Stephen, First Martyr	182
Luke the Evangelist	182	Sverker	92
Luther, Martin	47, 48, 53–54, 62, 69, 73, 83, 87, 90, 120, 138, 142, 160, 182	Söderblom, Nathan	70, 83–84, 88
		Sörensen, Henrik	182
		Tertullian	68, 127
Mark the Evangelist	182	Timothy	152, 153, 155, 159, 172
Matthew the Evangelist	41, 182	Titus	153, 155, 172
Melanchthon, Philipp	70, 77, 138, 160	Titus, Emperor	92
		Ulfsson, Jakob	84
Melchizedek	30	Viktoria, Queen	XII
Moses	30, 182	Wallerius, Ivar	104
Nero	35	Wallin, Johan Olof	84
Nicholas I, Pope	44	Zacchaeus	144
Nicodemus	124	Zernov, Nicolas	50
Nygren, Anders	XVI	Zwingli, Huldreich	48, 82
Odovakar	92		
Olof Skötkonung	75		
Origen	127		
Osmund	74		
Paceanus of Barcelona	70		
Paul the Apostle	18, 21, 43, 50, 55, 57, 83, 150, 152, 153, 158, 164, 182		
Peter the Apostle	70, 42, 43, 153, 182		
Petri, Laurentius	78, 79, 81, 82, 84, 88		
Petri, Olavus	76, 77, 182		
Polycarp	68, 127, 155		
Pyhy, Konrad von	78		
Quade, Gustav	140, 171		
Ragvaldsson, Nils	84		
Rudbeckius, Johannes	85		
Saint Bridget (see Birgitta)			
Schartau, Henrik	54, 148		
Schmid, Toni	74		
Schütz, Paul	50		

www.ingramcontent.com/pod-product-compliance
Lightning Source LLC
Chambersburg PA
CBHW071442150426
43191CB00008B/1212